The Modern Arabic Short Story

Also by Mohammad Shaheen

GEORGE MEREDITH: A Reappraisal of the Novels

SELECTED LETTERS OF GEORGE MEREDITH

The Modern Arabic Short Story

Shahrazad Returns

Second Edition
Revised and Expanded

Mohammad Shaheen
Professor of English
University of Jordan

palgrave
macmillan

First edition 1989
Second edition 2002

Published 2002 by
PALGRAVE MACMILLAN
Houndmills, Basingstoke, Hampshire RG21 6XS and
175 Fifth Avenue, New York, N. Y. 10010
Companies and representatives throughout the world

PALGRAVE MACMILLAN is the global academic imprint of the Palgrave Macmillan division of St. Martin's Press, LLC and of Palgrave Macmillan Ltd. Macmillan® is a registered trademark in the United States, United Kingdom and other countries. Palgrave is a registered trademark in the European Union and other countries.

ISBN 0–333–64136–1 hardback
ISBN 0–333–64137–X paperback

This book is printed on paper suitable for recycling and made from fully managed and sustained forest sources.

A catalogue record for this book is available from the British Library.

A catalog record for this book is available from the Library of Congress.

10 9 8 7 6 5 4 3 2 1
11 10 09 08 07 06 05 04 03 02

Printed and bound in Great Britain by
Antony Rowe Ltd, Chippenham and Eastbourne

For Flavio and Judith

Contents

Preface to the First Edition

The translation of any material here from Arabic into English is, unless stated otherwise, my own. Most of the text of the stories, poems, and various extracts I have translated appear in English for the first time.

I am grateful to all individual authors for allowing me to translate and publish their poems and stories. Also I am indebted to E. J. Brill, who has given permission for reprinting 'The Blue Charm and the Return of Jubaynah' and a revised edition of the commentary on it which first appeared in the *Journal of Arabic Literature* in 1984.

I am most grateful to Michael Macdonald for his penetrating comments on earlier drafts of this book, particularly that of Part I. Moḥammad 'Asfūr kindly drew my attention to Jabra's contribution to the modern scene in Arabic writing, and his comments on Arabic poetry were invaluable. I would like to mention with great appreciation the stimulating conversations I have had over the years with Eid Dahiyāt. To 'Adnān Bakhīt go my sincere thanks for his unfailing enthusiasm and active support.

Preface to the Second Edition

One reviewer of the first edition pointed out that I should have acknowledged the translation of 'The Blue Charm [Bead] and the Return of Jubaynah' by Cēza Qāsem and Saneya Shā'rāwī (*Flights of Fantasy*, Cairo, 1985, pp. 219–24), assuming that the translation was already in print. Had this reviewer not overlooked the reference to the story in my preface or even in my Bibliography, and realized that my translation of the story appeared earlier (1984), she would have probably asked the two translators to acknowledge mine instead. Yet the whole matter is more interesting.

My first encounter with the translation of the story by CQ and SS was in July 1987, when I was visiting my friend, the publisher Donald Herdick of the Three Continents Press, who was the distributor of *Flights of Fantasy* in America. As soon as Dr Herdick was able to get hold of my translation, he compared it with the other translation and concluded that the translation made by CQ and SS was no more than an edited version of my own. He wrote to the publisher in Cairo, Elias Modern Publishing House & Co., who wrote an evasive but courteous reply to him and to myself, pointing out how superior my translation was in comparison to the edited one. However, Eva Elias, as Herdick said to me, failed to convince him that the whole practice of CQ and SS was not a copyright infringement.

In my pursuit of the matter I learned from the editor of the *Journal of Arabic Literature* (in Oxford at the time) that he had passed the script of my translation with my commentary (from which she derived the title in the table of contents) to Cēza Qāsem as early as March 1983 to read, presumably, as a referee. In any case the two versions are available to readers and reviewers alike to judge for themselves.

I would like to acknowledge the assistance of Rula Qawas and Tim Kapp in the preparation of the text of this edition.

My special thanks go to Sulayman Shaṭṭī for his insightful comments on the text of his own story 'An Oil Slick' whose narrative still depicts the politics of the time with a great deal of authenticity and effect.

Since the publication of the original version of the book in 1989 much work has been done (mainly in Arabic) and various aspects of the topic are somehow known in some detail. The additional material included in this new edition is intended to show that the main issues the original version initiated for discussion continue to provoke the same serious questions.

Introduction to the First Edition

This book offers a selection of short stories I have translated from Arabic and commented on, making particular emphasis on the literary scene of the 1960s and 1970s. The poems included here have a specific relevance to fiction and will be discussed later. The selection is by no means exclusive, nor is it representative of any particular trend of modern short story writing. It rather aspires to demonstrate that some authors have been able to survive the restrictions imposed on the Arab writer and follow their artistic bent without drifting into aimless experiments in technique.

It is not a usual practice to put the text of a study and its analysis side by side in one volume. Yet the attempt is prompted by more than sheer enthusiasm for practical criticism. For various reasons inherent in the present state of Arabic publishing and the inadequate provision of bibliographical information, it is often quite difficult for the Western reader, even the Arabist, to obtain published material in Arabic without considerable delays and detective work. In a review of a publication on Arabic fiction, Robin Ostle remarks that 'the wider Western reading public will devote more attention to Arabic literature only when we have more translations which reflect the power and intensity of the original creations.'[1] Assuming that the translation I have done has some of 'the power and intensity' of the originals, I feel it may be helpful to bring these stories to the attention of the reader who, for various reasons, may have no easy access to them.

The selection presented here is based neither on the easy availability of the texts nor on the popularity of the authors; for I have dug up some of the stories from back issues of journals (some of which are important) and local publications which are already obscure. Some of the stories I have selected here are written by authors who are not well known, even in literary circles, a fact that is mainly due to the state of publishing in the Arab world, and is no reflection on the quality of their fiction. Indeed the absence of responsible publishers and responsible critics, added to the oppressive effects of censorship, make popularity an extremely dubious criterion by which to judge an Arab author.

The critical analysis here is essentially intended to provide some elucidation of the text rather than to supplement it; for until there are sufficient translations of Arabic literary material, criticism on its own would appear rather superfluous. If a justification of any critical evaluation be required, I would seek it in a review of modern Arabic poetry which can equally apply to the short story; 'Much modern Arabic poetry is inexorably linked to a peculiar and painful search for cultural religious and national identity in a world marked by uncertainty, upheaval and change. Without some understanding of the background in terms of that search it is extremely difficult to appreciate the poetry.'[2]

* * *

Part I presents the dilemma (a word which has particular urgency to the Arab writer) of the short story and the unfortunate circumstances surrounding the genre at a time which was supposed to be the high season of its growth and development. Writers evaded the dilemma either by looking at it always in retrospect, as Sabrī Hāfiz did, for example, or engulfing it in generalisations and rhetoric as many other writers did. Perhaps Yūsuf Idrīs was the only writer who took the risk of exposing censorship, the origin of the dilemma, with courage and frankness. He also blamed critics and commentators for maintaining silence over the tyranny of the censor.

This part discusses as well the strange phenomenon of literacy as embodied in *al-Qiṣṣah* (the journal sponsored by the censor) which, instead of publishing short stories, published tales and anecdotes. One can presumably say that the level of its narratives dated three decades back in the century.

Another unfortunate example discussed in this part in terms of its negative effect on the development of the short story is Rashād Rushdī's criticism of the short story which won popularity in the late fifties and early sixties. Rushdī turns to the romance of Maupassant which established the reputation of the Taymūrs earlier in the century in the same way *al-Qiṣṣah* adopted the romance of Kāmil Ḥusayn (al-Muḥāmī) whose fantasies dominated the early part of the century. Being favoured by the censor throughout his literary career, Rushdī was in a position to promote what looked like a canon of the short story at the time.

Yet censorship was limited to its own region. Thanks are due to *al-Ādāb* of Beirut, which was the haven for free expression for writers from all over the Arab world. Yaḥyā Haqqī, for example, turned to it, as we see in Part I, to say what he could not say in *al-Majallah*, or elsewhere in his own country. When writers in Egypt were unable to say all that they could they looked to Beirut as we see in the case of Ṣabrī Ḥāfiẓ, who turned to *Ḥiwār* to publish a discussion of the dilemma of the short story. But *al-Ādāb*, more than any other literary journal in the Arab world, took the initiative of publishing Arab writers with serious concern for political and social issues of the time, and no study of modern fiction will be complete without heavily drawing upon the short stories it published.

In this study I have deliberately avoided the critical surveys and anthologies which usually begin with the Taymūrs and proceed to include Tawfīq al-Ḥakīm and probably Ṭāha Ḥusayn up to Yaḥyā Haqqī. A disruption of tone is certainly anticipated in a study or an anthology which brings together the early writers of the century who fantasised about fiction and the later writers who actually wrote short stories and developed the genre. For this reason I limited my discussion in Part I to the existing problems which the short-story writer had to face. Yet the rest of this study will demonstrate, I hope, how some writers were able to write outside the difficult condition of their time and achieve positive results.

* * *

The stories I have discussed here show that the modern Arabic short story is not altogether an imitation of the Western genre as some Arab writers would have us believe.[3] For example, all the stories included here have a local folktale motif which forms the basis of their structure. A most common motif is that of Sindbad which has been explored by some writers with great skill as we see in Part II. The Sindbad motif seems to provide writers with the inspiration needed. Evidently it provided them with the confidence to travel outside the boundaries of censorship, because in its original form it provided a timeless tale of imagination, freedom, adventure and hope. The most elaborate picture of this Sindbad motif appears in *Layālī Alf Laylah* ('The Nights of *The Arabian Nights*') by Najīb Maḥfūz published in 1979, as the crowning example of that motif. In this complicated novel Maḥfūz gives Sindbad a prominent role, and leaves him with the crucial function of weaving the plot and shifting the point of view. For example, Shahrayar eventually finds his salvation through what he hears from Sindbad, who appears at the beginning of the narrative and reappears before its ending with experience and wisdom. No other work in modern Arabic fiction tackles the conflict between ruling institutions and opposition as Maḥfūz's novel does. It is regrettable that a work of such magnitude has not been given the reception it deserves and that only after Maḥfūz won the Noble Prize that critics and commentators began to explore its crucial issues.

Maḥfūz's novel certainly deserves a separate study to emphasize the effect of Sindbad on modern Arabic fiction and to confirm the potential of that story to address serious modern issues. Evidently Maḥfūz found in Sindbad what his predecessors had done before him, but he expanded the motif to express his complex vision, and a comparative study of Maḥfūz's achievement in relation to those of others (which is not the subject of this study) needs further exploration.

* * *

It is worthwhile noticing, I think, that poets captured the story of Sindbad before Maḥfūz and his fellow short-story writers. Part II discusses the motif of Sindbad in poetry and fiction and points to a kind of continuity between poetry and short-story. In this Part Khalīl Ḥāwī's poem receives special attention because I believe it is particularly an important document in the literary history of modern Arabic writing in general.

Despite the importance of Ḥāwī's poem, it is surprising how little attention has been devoted to it even in Arabic; and in a publication of modern Arabic poetry translated into English Ḥāwī, for example, is represented by five lines, though he would fit into the design of the anthology better than the other poets who have been represented at much more length.[4]

I have demonstrated in the same part that Ḥāwī's poem influenced almost every writer who used the Sindbad motif. Though to a lesser extent, Surūr's poem and ʻAflaq's dramatic dialogue and his short story, (all of which preceded the short stories of the 1960s and 1970s) have exercised a similar influence. The stories under discussion show how authors of short stories maintained emphasis on the Sindbad motif as they continued to elaborate on its theme and form. They also demonstrate the shift of tone from the prophetic dream of poetry to the realistic nightmare of fiction. The nightmarish atmosphere dominates the last three short stories discussed in Part II. For example, Fahmī's ‘The Seven Voyages of Sindbad’ recalls Gothic fiction, and it can be most relevant to Najīb Maḥfūz's novel written fifteen years later. Being still uncertain that his story would escape the attention of the censor who might catch him in Beirut, Fahmī attaches an amusing note square-bracketed at the bottom of the first page:

> Appeal from Sindbad to all the "cultured" of the Earth; my tales are simple. I wrote them for the innocent who are simple. I wrote them for the innocent who are below sixteen, and the wise who are over forty. For the sake of my age and for the sake of those readers, I beg you, I beseech you, to spare my tales your judgments, interpretations and analyses. Try, if only for once, to read with innocence and wisdom. (p. 11)

This is obviously reminiscent of Twain's "Notice" at the beginning of the colloquial narrative of *Huckleberry Finn*:

> Persons attempting to find a motive in the narrative will be persecuted; persons attempting to find a moral in it will be banished; persons attempting to find a plot in it will be shot.

Of course Fahmī indirectly incites the reader to read neither with the innocence of a child nor with the experience of an old man but rather with the point of view of the artist concealed in what seems to be a rejection of the order of poetics in fiction. He also tends to promote the emphasis on the realism of the situation implied rather than rendered .

The short story ‘‘Abd Allah Sāmsa in Wāqwāq Island’ by Muṣṭafā al-Masnāwī, is another story with a horrifying atmosphere. The Sindbad motif (the old Sindbad, we know, comes back from the remote Wāqwāq Island with the wonders of the world) is twisted and transformed into a Kafkaesque horror. ‘Abd Allah Sāmsa is tortured to death. In the third story Mohammad al-Mansī Qandīl's Sindbad goes through an ordeal in which he watches his ship and property being sold in auction. It is obvious that the three Sindbads in the three narratives are presented in a state of defeat, the portrayal of which dominated the literary scene: a juxtaposition of the defeated Sindbad and the old Sindbad who always came back triumphant even from the wonders of Wāqwāq Island.

* * *

The motif used in Part III is that of Shahrazad which, as we know, comes from the same source as that of Sindbad. ‘The Blue Charm and the Return of Jubaynah,’ one of the three narratives discussed in this Part, is not directly associated with Shahrazad or with *The Arabian Nights*, but Jubaynah, the main character of a folktale, has enough qualities in common with Shahrazad to make her qualify for identification with her fellow woman. Both Jubaynah and Shahrazad have the great desire for survival and the eternal dream of return. Obviously the narrative tone of Shahrazad in this chapter has the quality of a dream rather than of a nightmare as we find in the previous Part, for the picture the traditional Shahrazad evokes in our minds is the beauty of narration and the fascination of suspense. Earlier in the century some major Arab writers had tried a Shahrazad narrative in one way or another. Examples of this are Ṭāha Husayn's *The Dreams of Shahrazad*, Tawfīq al-Ḥakīm's *Shahrazad*, and Ali Aḥmad Bākathīr's *The Mystery of Shahrazad*. But those Shahrazads were written mainly as a kind of homage to the grandeur of the old Shahrazad, and they are different in purpose and design from the Shahrazad under discussion. Yet the two Shahrazads being considered: of Zakariyya Tāmir's,and Emīle Ḥabībī's — both have the majestic dream of the old Shahrazad and the poetic effect of both Najīb Surūr's and Khalīl Hāwī's.

In this Part there are also three motifs which are comparatively less popular than that of Sindbad and Shahrazad. Abu Zayd is a folktale hero known for his infinite courage and endless travels between the various parts of the Arab world from Arabia to Morocco. In the old days the life of Abu-Zayd must have been a main source of entertainment for countryside *fallāḥs* who, at evening gatherings, would enact his adventures by telling, showing and singing the various accounts of his adventures. 'Shāṭir Ḥasan' is quite a well-known folktale and the first name is an adjective which stands for popular trickster, and it is originally more of a children's story. This third motif has some locality, but it is not difficult to work out its meaningful association once it is put into a new context.

In this Part the tone of narrative shifts from the political to the social, despite the fact that the two institutions are inseparable. In any case, characters in these narratives are *fallāḥs* who represent a large segment of the population and who always lead a wretched life with perhaps the lowest standard of living. They are on trial not because they stand against institutions as in the intellectual Sindbad of al-Masnāwī and others, but rather because they have been traditionally neglected over the centuries.

What makes the motifs here particularly an appropriate form of expression is that they belong in origin to the life of the *fallāḥ* who actually lived closer to the context of folktale life. The *fallāḥ* and even his narrative survive in society as aliens, and the assimilation of one into the other helps intensify the effect of alienation; in his relation to society the *fallāḥ* becomes as alienated as the intellectual despite the big gap between the two in real life.

With great skill the affinity or what may look like natural piety between the *fallāḥ* and the folktale is cultivated to present an effective picture of the *fallāḥ* as we see in the imaginary figure of Abu-Zayd and the *fallāḥ* or in the concrete symbol of the cow and the *fallāḥ* or in the *fallāḥīn* (plural this time) of the fantastic trickster by Shāṭir Ḥasan. 'Abu-Zayd Surrenders' ends in a state of defeat; 'The Orphans' Cow' carries almost the same tone except that a dream of hope emerges just before the closure of the narrative. 'Shāṭir Ḥasan' ends with a triumphant voice as the *fallāḥīn* find no alternative but to forget about the intermediary Shāṭir Ḥasan and depend on themselves to find water. This narrative and perhaps 'The Orphans' Cow' have the same tone as that of Surūr's Sindbad.

If a concluding statement is needed for the short story in the 1960s and 1970s, one can possibly say that its theme was mainly determined by an alternation of vision between nightmare and dream. Sometimes the two dimensions of vision alternate in one narrative, at others between different narratives. In all cases it is the dialectic alternation between real life and imaginative art.

Notes

1. Robin Ostle, rev. of *The Arabic Novel: An Historical and Critical Introduction* by Roger Allen, *The Times Literary Supplement*, 3rd September 1982, p. 978.
2. Walter G. Andrews, "Four Modern Poets", *World Literature Today 57* (1983), p. 165.
3. In his introduction to an anthology of short stories in Arabic, Maḥmūd Manzalāwī remarks that 'the experiments of twentieth-century western writers have impinged thick and fast upon the awareness of Arab readers, so that, in something like fifteen years, the different attitudes that have revealed themselves in Europse over the last sixty years or so, have demanded assimilation by the younger Arab writers and thinkers'. Earlier Manzalāwī says that 'an awareness of western explorations in technique, and of twentieth-century questioning around the human condition has modified the attitude of most writers.' (*Arabic Writing Today, The Short Story*, Cairo: American Research Centre

in Egypt, 1968, p. 21).

Also Ḥusām al-Khaṭīb adopts a similar attitude in his study of comparative literature when he says that 'both genres [short story and novel] developed in similar circumstances: direct imitation of western technique in fiction.' (*Comparative Literature*, Vol. II, Damascus: al-Insha' Press, 1982), p. 28.

4. See 'Abd Allah al-'Uḍharī, ed., *Modern Poetry of the Arab World* (Penguin: 1986, p. 119).

Introduction to the Second Edition

There may be little need to introduce this edition, simply because the censorial atmosphere of the 1960s and 1970s (the main span of this book) affecting, to a great extent, the literary scene of those decades still remains. Jābir 'Aṣfūr, once editor of *Fuṣūl* (an avant garde journal) and Secretary General of the Supreme Council of Culture in Egypt, sums up the situation whereby, whimsical local politics determines the life history of any book in the Arab world in general. His remarks on the occasion of Cairo's Annual International Book Fair (1995) were:

> The Sudanese reader, for example, is deprived of access to Egyptian literature as long as the two governments are at loggerheads. Iraqi literature is banned by many countries who seek to voice their opprobrium of the Iraqi regime by boycotting Iraqi cultural output. Literature, it would appear, will always be the victim of any chilliness in the political climate. Just try finding an Iraqi book-stand at any international book fair. The same applies to foreign, non-Arabic literature, which appears in bookstore windows overnight, and vanishes just as quickly, according to the political affiliations of ruling regimes.

Such speedy exits and entrances are intrinsically bound up with the activities of the national censorship bureaux. I use the plural advisedly, because these bureaux are many indeed. In Egypt there is the Postal Censor's Office which functions under the mandate of the Authority of Transport and Communications, the Information Censor's Office under the Ministry of information, the Security Censor's Office under the Ministry of Interior, the Religious Censor's Office, an arm of al-Azhar, and the Office for the Censorship of the Arts under the Ministry of Culture.[1]

Unfortunately the censors Jābir 'Aṣfūr complains of are still in business (see note 1 in Introduction to the First Edition). At Cairo's Annual International Book Fair (February 2000), a winner of the Arab Fiction Prize was 'Abd al-Raḥman Munīf, whose novels were banned. The incident (while surprising enough) was reported not only in the local but world press, as the novelist is well-known.[2] In Kuwait, Parliament took legal action against Layla al-'Uthmān, a celebrated writer of fiction. In the Sudan, Sayyid al-Ḥirdello was jailed for a poem he wrote and the publisher Kamāl Bakhīt was sent to jail as well. In Lebanon, Marcel Khalīfah was accused of blasphemy for singing a certain poem written by Maḥmūd Darwīsh, and he had to appear in court to defend himself. And the saga of censorship in the Arab world seems to have no end.

* * *

The new material in this book is only a demonstration of the fact that the institutions of the past have continued to exercise dominance with little or no interruption, and that the tension between author and authority has not eased. The two pieces which, presumably more than any others, should have been included in the first edition, are a poem by Badr al-Sayyāb, the most celebrated modern Arab poet, titled 'The Sindbad City', and a short story by Michael 'Aflaq titled 'Sindbad' and his Mistress'.

The poem is a typical, profound expression of the negation of reality, similar to that derived from *The Arabian Nights*, by writers already discussed in the first edition. One would like to add here that had al-Sayyā come back to life (he died in 1962), he could not have written a poem to better express the existing situation. As for the short story which I have dug up from a forgotten journal (and promoted its publication in book form), I would like to suggest that it is the first Arabic short story that also qualifies as a modern one in the aesthetic sense of the modern short story. In this story 'Aflaq sets out the main preoccupation of the modern Arab society as a Christ baptized (at the same time he presents his attitude as a Christ crucified in the dramatic monologue of the one-act-play narrative) while he then happens to fulfil the technical requirements of the modern short story. So this story (along with the narrative), I believe, initiates modernity in the genre, as the detailed discussion hopes to show.

Though the three stories added here were written after the 1970s, they express a sense of continuity with the same spirit characteristic of the two earlier decades. They even intensify the futility of the situation. Riyad al-Marzūqī's 'Night 1002' openly expresses negation, for it shows Shahrazad's failure and Shahrayar's despotic triumph under the impact of political and social disintegration. The narrative has enough authenticity to make it stand as an example in any Arab country and at any time from the 1950s onward.

As for Sulaymān al-Shaṭṭi's 'An Oil Slick', written during the Iraqi–Iranian war, which I consider is a distinguished narrative both in technique and vision. If it is read without one being aware of the time of its composition, one would immediately assume that it was written during or after the Gulf War, due to the prophecy perceptively worked out in the narrative. When I first read the story, anthologized in a collection of Arabic short stories published by the popular Arab journal *al-'Arabī* (1989), I found it disturbing, because of the sinister atmosphere controlling its action. In an attempt to find out something about the story, I asked Iḥsān 'Abbās, the eminent critic who wrote the introduction to the collection, and his answer was that the narrative is excellent surrealism. Read in retrospect after the Gulf War, the story can yield more, for the suspended vision is eased and its prophecy is consequently revealed without exhausting the generative effect of the continuity extending between the now and then. I have been recently illuminated by the writer's remarks, kindly sent at my request, and used later in the comment on the story.

The other story was published in *al-Tarīq* journal in 1990 with the year 1993 bracketed at the end of the story, presumably intending to remind the reader of the prophetic perspective the author has already emphasized. The title of the story ''Antar Ibn Zahībah' immediately shows the origin of the narrative, which is a popular folktale in Arabic heritage. In this story the author crafts many twisks in the beautiful romance of 'Antar and 'Ablah so as to create a new structure of parallelism in order to accommodate the most critical situation in the politics of the region. The present 'Antar is a romantic leader of a Don Quixote type who drags men into wanton wars to satisfy his selfish desires. Life for him is sport and demonstrating courage and gallantry. *'Antariyyāt* is the term coined in Arabic to describe such irresponsible behaviour where sheer whimsy determines the fate of the community. 'Antar is very reminiscent of Shahrayar (in 'Night 2000'): both are sadists, led by compulsive acts which satisfy their ego with tragic outcomes for their communities.

Interest in Arabic folktales has increased in recent years, while the quarterly literary journal *Fuṣūl* devoted the three issues of 1994 to the literature of *The Arabian Nights*, for the first time treating this heritage on equal terms with high-brow literature. More reprints of the *Nights* and folktales have been made available in various other editions. Najīb Maḥfūẓ's *Layālī Alf Laylah* (*The Nights of The Arabian Nights*) published in 1979 has come into focus, but only after Maḥfūz had won the Nobel Prize. Michael 'Aflaq's 'Sindbad' first appeared in 1936 and has been made available (along with other literary pieces by the same author) for the first time in book form in 1993.

This change of heart towards the folktale is presumable much indebted to the writers such as those included in this book who were able to find inspiration in the heritage once excluded from the great tradition of Arabic Literature.

Notes:

1. Jābir 'Aṣfūr, 'Thresholds of Fahrenheit 451' *al-Ahram Weekly*, February 1995, p. 5. Looking at Jābir 'Aṣfūr's observation here in the light of the vicious reac-

tion against Ḥayder Ḥaider's novel *A Feast for the Seaweeds*, we do realize how perceptive 'Aṣfūr was in sensing the dangers of censorship. It was the same censor (mentioned above) who raised the feverish battle against Ḥaider's novel (reprinted in Cairo, April 2000 under the auspices of the Supreme Council of Culture).

2. See Jamāl al-Ghīṭānī's editorial: 'Hideous Censorship,' *Akhbār al-Adab*, 20 February, 2000, p. 3. This journal has become a banner of freedom and defence against the censor.

Part One
A Critical Study

I
The Situation of the Short Story

This Part presents some aspects of the dilemma in which the Arab writer found himself in the 1960s and 70s (which unfortunately still goes on). It particularly shows how little support authors of short stories have from their fellow writers such as critics who are supposed to promote them.

In June 1964 the journal *Ḥiwār* published an article titled 'The Dilemma of Freedom in Modern Arabic Fiction' which, despite its obvious limitations, is relevant to the subject under discussion. Although the writer of the article Ṣabrī Ḥāfiẓ shows that he was not unaware of the dimensions of the dilemma facing the Arab writer, he was by no means equal to the task he had set himself, since he does little more than hint at conditions in the contemporary scene, especially those in Egypt. He confirms, however, that no Arab writer in tune with contemporary realities has failed to deal with the dilemma of freedom in one way or another.[1] He also remarks that the issue of freedom has suffered from its identification with that of independence, that is the self-deluding belief that independence from foreign intervention naturally brings with it freedom; and the failure to realise that after independence it is far more difficult to fight the national authorities which emerged as the new enemies of freedom.

Ḥāfiẓ believes that even 'Abd al-Raḥmān al-Sharqāwī, whose fiction *The Earth, Empty Hearts* and *The Narrow Streets* is particularly concerned with social and economic problems, gives no special prominence to the issue of freedom; instead, Ḥāfiẓ remarks, al-Sharqāwī offers us a metaphysical treatment. The same evaluation is applied to Najīb Maḥfūẓ, who is often preoccupied with society and politics. Similarly he considers that Iḥsān ʻAbd al-Quddūs' view of the crucial events which preceded and presumably prepared for the Egyptian Revolution of 1952 is inferior. Concluding his survey of the Egyptian scene, Ḥāfiẓ dismisses the works of other Egyptian authors such as Tawfīq al-Ḥakīm, Ḥasan Muḥasib, Laṭīfah al-Zayyāt and Fatḥī Ghānim as insignificant.

In discussing Arab writers outside Egypt, Ḥāfiẓ remarks that the fiction of such writers as Suhayl Idrīs, Muṭāʻ Ṣafadī, and to some extent, ʻAbd al-Salām al-ʻUjaylī, was dominated by existentialism. This also affected, Ḥāfiẓ believes, the work of leading Arab women authors such as Emily Naṣrallah, Layla Baʻalbakī and Collette Suhayl, whose efforts were further vitiated by sentimentality and emotionalism.

It is not my intention here to show whether Ḥāfiẓ is actually justified in giving such critical evaluation of those authors, but rather to point to the way he digresses from the origin of the dilemma. Ḥāfiẓ evidently was not unaware that the dilemma lay neither with the milieu of al-Sharqāwī and Maḥfūẓ (the 1930s and 1940s) nor with that of Yūsuf Idrīs and Iḥsān ʻAbd al-Quddūs (the 1950s). It lay rather with the oppressive conditions created by the political establishment in the 1960s, and this evidently has been overlooked by him.

Writing in the 1970s Ḥāfiẓ looked back in time and we can now see that he disguised his comments on the contemporary scene by appearing to consider the decades before the 1960s.[2] His own reticence on the subject of the dilemma which he is supposed to be discussing is hardly innocent. Indeed one wonders whether the distortion of reality in the fiction he discusses is entirely the fault of the authors he castigates. We know that such distortion was an inevitable result of the oppression of the regime under which those writers lived. But Ḥāfiẓ had himself experienced this, and yet felt unable even to touch on it, until it had become past history.[3] He should have realised that he was as much caught in the dilemma as the writers he discusses, and so was led to keep silent on the critical issues of the time, which seems to dominate the writing scene altogether.

The discussions of this dilemma by authors in the 1960s and 1970s revolved in a vicious circle, and writers diverge only to conceal the common ground they have. In a special issue on the short story (August 1969), the journal *al-Hilāl* published a discussion by some outstanding writers titled 'The Dilemma of the Short Story.'[4] Tawfīq al-Ḥakīm, for example, remarks that the writer has to overcome the discomfort caused by his time in order to have the time for his own dilemma. It cannot be denied, Najīb Maḥfūẓ confirms, that there is a dilemma in the short story, but it is circumstantial; that is, he believes that the dilemma is related to certain social circumstances which tend to blur the writer's vision. He also believes that the popularity of the form means that publishers find it impossible to cope with the vast number of stories submitted to them. Coming closer to the central problem than his fellow writers, Yūsuf Idrīs traces the crisis to the lack of communication between the writer and his reading public. He points to the fact that society deliberately refuses to see itself portrayed by writers because the portrait shows the face and not the mask. He particularly refers to the hypocrisy of those critics and reviewers who claim that writers before and after the June 1967 setback were passive, remarking that a close examination of the writings of those writers proves the fallacy of this claim. In attacking those hypocrites, Yūsuf Idrīs says he wishes he could demonstrate his point from the dozen examples he could give, but then declines to do so for unstated reasons, concluding that the matter is at all times the responsibility of courageous critics and commentators, who, by implication, were absent from the scene.

Yūsuf al-Shārūnī feels that the short story in the 1960s has recovered from its recession in the early years of the decade, and he applauds the revolution in the genre against the realism which had rendered it for twenty years. He notices how the innovators in the art of the short story deal with local problems in a cultural context which had characterised the fiction of the previous two decades, and he thus finds the new writings gratifying because they are reminiscent of his own essays on the genre in the 1930s and 1940s.

A common feature of the description of the dilemma is the evasive terminology which, as Yūsuf Idrīs remarks, serves as a veil protecting the writer. For example, whatever would be expressed in social, local, cultural, individual, historical or human terms, that might be taken as relevant to politics and government, particularly in their demagogic, despotic, or tyrannical aspects, were omitted, and especially anything which might point to the oppression practised by the regime in power. Writers tackled the situation with great caution simply because they knew the consequences in advance. This can be further demonstrated from an article published in the same issue of *al-Hilāl* in which the writer comments on the emergence of a new realism among the younger generation:

> It is noticeable that Mohammad al-Busṭāmī, Mohammad Rūmīsh, and Yaḥyā al-Ṭāhir [short-story writers] focus their narrative on a complex network of social relationships in the Egyptian countryside. The resulting picture shows in grim detail the fates which befell their human models and in the midst of this the following issues are discussed from various

> points of view: the relative meanings of death and fall, the savage clash of conflicting interests, or the conflict between social structure and tradition which crush the simple individual and strip him of his social existence then cast him aside.[5]

In his article 'The Quest for a New Course in the Egyptian Short Story,' 'Abd al-Raḥmān Abu-'Auf describes the dilemma as a spontaneous response by a young generation of writers to the Arab defeat of 5 June 1967 for which he metaphorically uses 'the setback'. But he makes no specific references to illustrate what he sees as the emergence of a new sensibility. He gives, instead, a brief description of each writer's technique which is far too general to be of any use in evaluating the label of 'modernism' which he accords these writers. His article consists mainly of stock rhetoric which does not explore the implications of the title or come to any purposeful conclusion. This is how he ends his comment:

> In conclusion we would like all our judgments to be considered with reservation despite the fact that the new birth of our short story stands as evidence of the emergence of a new literary perspective which is in itself a new attitude towards reality ... For the first time a new comprehensive vision is born. It is a vision of nature and man, of the external world as well as the world of man, of need and freedom, and this is the judgment of the future which would extend to the present.[6]

Obviously the young generation of writers at the time needed what Yūsuf Idrīs described: a courageous critic whose close reading of their stories would give them an altogether different perspective. They certainly needed a criticism (not flattery) which would show in concrete terms how the new sensibility shaped itself in their stories.

The dilemma then was one of communication and was mainly

the responsibility of the commentators and critics who hid from the central issue either behind empty rhetoric or, as Yūsuf Idrīs said, hypocrisy. I would like to illustrate this matter by quoting from a special issue devoted to the short story of *al-Majallah*. First, the reproduction of a painting depicting a *fallāḥ* on the cover of the journal and in miniature on the second page with the following comment '*al-saqqa* who is the *fallāḥ* water carrier to the village houses ... in the old days!' The commentator adds: 'This is a picture from the past whose features are almost lost in the dominant glories of the Revolution.' Obviously the commentator was not unaware of the fact that the picture as well as the commentary were merely a mask!

In the editorial of the same issue of the journal, the chief editor, Yaḥyā Ḥaqqī, a respected literary figure, makes a similar comment in support of the mask. He blames the young generation of short-story writers for being out of harmony with society (of course, the new society of the Revolution). He urges them to respond to the new patterns of life (brought about by the Revolution) with new modes of realism instead of those of surrealism and the absurd which they were actually employing.[7] As an example of those many new 'admirable patterns', he glorifies the dramatic change the life of the *fallāh* has undergone. The once deprived *fallāh* has become a 'land-owner'.

This comment and the previous one were not arbitrary; they were intended to protect the journal from the powerful censor who might see through the mask of the drawing and in the moving story of the *fallāh*, 'Abu-Zayd Surrenders', which is discussed in this study, two grim but revealing pictures of contemporary life. Yaḥyā Ḥaqqī had to be careful to publish only material which would not stir up trouble with the censor. To protect the journal, he sent the stories in their typescript form to commentators and critics, and then published the stories and the resulting critiques side by side.

'Abu-Zayd Surrenders' received a critical note (to be discussed later in the text) similar to that of the picture on the cover.

The concluding remark of the editorial suggests that Yaḥyā Ḥaqqī, like his fellow writers, was not unaware of the dilemma, but rather unable to expose it in explicit terms:

> The gloomy atmosphere we find in most of the stories published nowadays is related to the confusing gap between literature and society. These stories express a sense of loss, annihilation, despair and despondency. This kind of atmosphere is nerve-wracking. We wish it would disappear or recede. What remains to be found is a means of re-establishing realism in a modern form in which Egypt would feature largely in a new picture.[8]

The question remains whether the reality of Egypt was presented any better in the writing of the late 1960s and 1970s, or whether the newly born vision which Abu-'Auf envisaged for the future was in fact no different from the one preceding the defeat of the fifth of June. An answer can be found in another special short-story issue, this time of an avant-garde journal outside Egypt, *al-Ādāb*, and the answer came from Yaḥyā Haqqi himself, who contributed a short story to the journal. Fatḥiyya, the main character of his story 'A Poor Woman', says in the course of the narrative, 'Today is like yesterday and tomorrow is like today.'[9] The story presents a picture of what has come to be known as the 'petit bourgeoisie' which was well fed and carefully bred by the Revolution. The managers of the hospital and of the civil airline in this story are examples of the corruption which was typical in the institutions of the regime in power at the time. The corruption extends to Fatḥiyya, who, instead of helping her beloved husband who is ill, and his pathetic disintegrated family, climbs the ladder of corruption following the manager of the airline who travels with her to Europe on the same plane. The narrator comments towards the end, 'The trip to Europe was the first step of the climb to the top'.[10]

Contributions to the same issue of *al-Ādāb* by other Egyptian writers were probably more nerve-wracking for Yaḥyā Ḥaqqī because of their despondent tone, and some of them would induce nausea in the reader. They are 'Innocence' (al-Barā'ah) by Yūsuf Idrīs; 'The Alter Ego' (al-Qarīn) by Sulaymān Fayyāḍ; 'The Last Fishing (al-Ṣayd al-Akhīr) by Ma*ḥ*mūd Diāb; 'Voices in the Night' (Aṣwātun fī al-Layl) by Abu-al-Ma'āṭī Abu al-Naja; 'An Egyptian Dry Day' (Yawm Miṣri Jāff) by Mohammad al-Mansī Qandīl.

Equally gloomy are those stories by other Arab writers such as 'The Enemies' (al-A'dā') by Zakariyya Tāmir; 'The Smell of the Houses' (Rā'iḥat al-Buyūt) by 'Abd as-Sattār Nāṣir; 'Silence' (al-Sukūn) by Ghānim al-Dabbāgh.

A close examination of all the stories published in that issue of *al-Ādāb* reveals a very gloomy atmosphere. An important reason for this was the common reality of life all over the Arab world which must have created a unified consciousness among the writers of different Arab countries, to recall the main point made by Ḥqqī's editorial in *al-Majallah.*

The dilemma was completely ignored in the romantic stories which the journal *al-Qiṣṣah* published for over two years. This journal was launched in 1964 with the intention of promoting the short story as a genre to be patronised by some literary elites then in favour. Its editorial policies were unfortunate, for it opened its pages to the kind of fiction which would have no positive effect on the development of the art; and the sort of narrative encouraged by the journal was typical of a group of writers who had begun their careers earlier in the century with stories dominated by romance, and who continued to write in the same vein. Examples of such writers are Yūsuf Ghurāb, Maḥmūd Taymūr and Yūsuf 'Izz al-Dīn

'Īsa, summaries of some of whose stories are given here merely to show the quality of fiction written almost out of any serious context in the journal which was supposed, more than any other journal, to promote the art of the short story.

In Ghurāb's 'Crying' (Bukā'), Kamāl, the narrator, meets a stranger at Aswān Railway Station while on his way to Cairo. They board the train, and during the journey the stranger confides his unhappiness to Kamāl, who finds himself immediately involved in the story. Though already married, the stranger is in love with another woman; tears are the only relief. When they arrive in Cairo they confide their sorrow to each other. They go to the hospital together in order to visit the woman who is the object of the man's passion. The stranger is delighted to learn from his beloved that Kamāl is a friend of the family. The story concludes with Kamāl asking his friend's permission to weep. A similar story by Ghurāb is 'Two Glasses' (Ka'sān) in which the narrator befriends a destitute woman, and she is overwhelmed with happiness when she discovers that her benefactor has smuggled into her handbag a five pound note. A third story by Ghurāb is 'The Woman and the Lion' (al-Mar'ah wal-'Asad). On one of his visits to the Sudan, the narrator is told this story by his aunt. It is about a woman whose husband deserts her. When she asks a Shaykh to make her an amulet for a remedy, he recommends, on the suggestion of the jinn, that she must remove three hairs from the mane of a lion which lives in a nearby valley. The woman goes and does what she is told; but when she returns, the Shaykh disappoints her by commenting, 'I am really puzzled by you, woman. You are able to tame lions, and yet you come here asking me to tame your man for you. You are just like all women.'

Another writer whose work is full of sentimentality and melodrama is Maḥmūd Taymūr. His 'The Ghost of Zahīrah' (Ṭayf Zahīrah) is typical. The narrator is writing the last chapter of a narrative in which the protagonist is a coquette. As he writes he is interrupted by her frequent apparition which tries to dissuade him from killing her off. Night after night she visits him, eats and drinks with him, and keeps him up till dawn. For him it is an experience out of *The Arabian Nights* in which he is Shahrayār and she, Shahrazad, trying with her charm to win time.

A particularly sentimental story is 'The Jasmine Tree' (Shajarat al-Yāsamīn) by Yūsuf 'Izz al-Dīn 'Īsa. The story begins as follows: 'Jasmine flowers were once my favourite, but whenever I smell them now I am overwhelmed with painful memories which take me back to where we lived some years ago at Ḥadā'iq al-Qubbah in Cairo.' One day the narrator opened his window and saw a boy standing by the tree crying, for he had lost his mother; his step-mother was cruel to him and his only consolation was the jasmine tree, to which he resorted in times of trouble. The sympathy between the two soon became apparent and before long the tree was withering as the boy himself was dying.

* * *

All these writers seem to have viewed the short story as a sequence of events determined by what is known in the jargon of fiction as 'the external time.' With their emphasis on story-telling as the basis for narration, they seem to be unaware of developments of technique in modern fiction. At the same time it is surprising that these writers make little or no distinction between tales and short stories. To make the stories credible they use a naive device in which the narrator is the author; and this results in losing any aesthetic distance between character and author. The narrators further assert that they were involved, directly or indirectly, in the events of the narrative, that is, that the story is true. Thus, some writers resort to their own past to assure us that the story actually happened to them. For example, Mahmūd Taymūr in his 'The Hat' (al-Ṭaqiyyah) records his own nostalgia, and Najīb al-Kīlānī, who wrote in a similar vein, sets forth his memories of a ruthless arithmetic teacher in his story 'The Aliens' (al-Ghurabā').

While some writers used 'personal experience' to bring an air of authenticity to their narratives, others turned to traditional motifs. Maḥmūd Aḥmad Khalaf published a series of stories of mixed origins under the title 'From the Legacy of the Past' (Min Aqāṣīṣ al-Awwalīn). Some of these are taken from traditional narratives of courtship such as that of Kuthayyir 'Azzah; others have their origin in the courts of the Caliphs; while a third source is the social history of the Arabs in general. One wonders, however, how these authors limited themselves to retelling tales and anecdotes while ignoring or failing to realise modern trends of fiction which were continuously discussed in the current literary journals and newspapers.

Whatever the reasons are, it is clear that *al-Qiṣṣah* set a bad example for short-story writers, and that this was particularly unfortunate since Egyptian writers were, at that time, looked upon by their fellow Arab writers as pioneers in the genre. On this subject *al-Ādāb* makes the following remark:

> Despite the fact that there were prominent writers of fiction in different parts of the Arab world such as Yusūf 'Awwād, Fu'ād al-Shāyib, Shakīb al-Jābirī, Ḍhonnūn Ayyūb and others whose writing was advanced compared to that appearing in Egypt, the stories written by these writers circulated only in their own countries. Meanwhile the fiction published in Egypt, which enjoyed a wide circulation, had a negative effect on the development of the Arab story.[11]

* * *

Another negative impact was Rashād Rushdī's attempt to theorise about the techniques of the short story, which, though it appeared in the late 1950s, continued to exert great influence in the 1960s, presumably because Rushdī was made by authority one of the most popular literary figures of the time and was consistently favoured by the regime.

Before it appeared in book form in 1959, *Fann al-Qiṣṣah al-Qaṣirah* (the art of the short story) was published and discussed on a variety of occasions. The main part of Rushdī's thesis is an analysis of the structure of the short stories he translated into Arabic. On this basis he states that the work must have a beginning, a middle and an end, and that the action should progress in parallel lines which, towards the end, should become entangled to complicate the plot. After some interplay of those lines of action, a moment of illumination should introduce the denouement.[12]

The story which Rushdī frequently quoted to demonstrate these rules was 'In the Moonlight' by Maupassant. It would be no exaggeration to say that Maupassant earned his reputation in the Arab world through this story which Rushdī seems to have promoted as an archetype of the genre. The romantic aspect of the story, as well as the oversimplified approach to it, gave the art of the short story a strong appeal, particularly among university students. I vividly remember science students from Cairo University attempting the genre under the banner of Rushdī's 'trinity' of technical divisions. Some of them would suspend the narrative towards the end for days in quest of the moment of illumination! I equally remember students of various specialities discussing their short stories in the light of what they had memorised of Rushdī's magic divisions of technique.

Influenced by Rushdī's 'golden rules' some writers went as far as applying them to their criticisms of the short stories written earlier in the century. Here, for instance, is a passage from a review article in 1968 dealing with the work of Mohammad Shawkat Attonī, a short story writer of the 1930s. 'The story 'Shaykh Ḥasan' proceeds consistently in one line without being interrupted by details which would be irrelevant to incident, character or plot.' Further, the influence is more explicit: 'For Mohammad Shawkat Attonī, the short story yields to the triple division well known in the field of narration where the story has a beginning, a middle, and an end.'[13]

However, one may well ask whether Rushdī was not misled by the deceptively simple technique of the short story in general, and that of Maupassant in particular. For example, Rushdī's treatment of 'In the Moonlight' is, to a great extent, a misrepresentation both of the author's tone, and of the character of the Abbe Marignan. Rushdī remarks that the story's action is divided into three lines: the first showing the spiritual side of Marignan's character, and his belief in the workings of cause and effect within God's creation; the second his dislike of women because of their seductive nature; and the third telling of Marignan's niece and her secular rather than religious interests. Rushdī further comments that these lines of action do not run parallel to each other, but are entangled in preparation for the resolution. Fascinated by the moonlight and awed by the mysteries of Nature, Marignan suppresses the anger he felt in observing his niece and her lover–an anger which anyway could never have been real–and leaves the couple alone.[14]

Rushdī views the conclusion of the story as an example of character revealed through action, and of how event and character can be unified, if not in the beginning and middle, at least, at the end. We are thus led to believe that Marignan's character underwent some crucial change brought about by the fascination he had always had for Nature.

Rushdī evidently fails to realise that the tone of the story is not as serious as he took it to be. He also overlooks the humour inherent in the fact that, unconsciously perhaps, Marignan is withdrawing in order to avoid provoking his own suppressed feelings. He is a religious man who is sceptical about God, and who, as a result, lives in Limbo. We cannot believe that Marignan would punish his niece when he learns that she has a lover; early in the story he shows much tolerance towards her, at least subconsciously:

> Often he talked to her of God, of his God, walking beside her along the footpaths through the fields. She hardly listened, but looked at the sky, the grass, the flowers, with a joy of living which could be seen in her eyes. Sometimes she rushed forward to catch some flying creature, and bringing it back would cry: 'Look, my uncle, how pretty it is; I should like to kiss it.' And this necessity to 'kiss flies' or 'sweet flowers' worried, irritated, and revolted the priest, who saw, even in that, the ineradicable tenderness which ever springs in the hearts of women.[15]

This 'ineradicable tenderness,' it can be suggested, is the clue to the story. The priest must have suffered from something of this sort, and this is perhaps what originally led him to enter the order. The story may be read as that of a priest who at one time has failed in love, and always remembers the experience with a spontaneous violence. Life for him was still a process of recovery rather than discovery. The humour in the story is generated by the irony of the situation. His niece was for him what is known as an alter-ego. The priest misses a world he violently abandoned in the past but still remembers. We can only laugh at the priest's longing for the world which he tries to conceal from us.

Rushdī's special emphasis on Maupassant was not, however, quite innocent. His performance was probably an attempt to recapture Maupassant's popularity in Egyptian fiction early this century. In a study on the impact of Maupassant on the Egyptian short story, Nādia Kāmil shows that Maupassant was introduced into Egyptian fiction by Mohammad Taymūr, who Arabized the same story 'In the Moonlight' by giving it the following title: 'O God, for whom did you create this happiness?'. This is how he introduces his version of the story: 'This story, by Maupassant, the famous French writer, has been Arabized by the translator who transformed its figures, time, place and even subject matter, nothing remains of the original except the atmosphere of the narrative.'[16] Taymūr goes on to say that he follows the influence of Tolstoy, who similarly translated Maupassant into Russian.

Nadia Kāmil further shows that the effect of Maupassant on Mohammad Taymūr goes beyond the atmosphere of this narrative as it can be clearly seen in his collection of stories *What the Eyes See*. Moreover the influence extends to Maḥmūd Taymūr, who inherited from his brother the spell of Maupassant, and whose pictures of Shaykh Jum'ah and 'Am Mitwallī are very reminiscent of Maupassant's portrait of the Abbe of '*In the Moonlight*'.

Rushdī's glorification of Maupassant was presumably promoted by the reputation Maupassant already enjoyed in Egypt. He seems to have believed that he would gain a popularity similar to that which the two Taymūrs (not to mention others) had achieved by bringing to the banks of the Nile a Maupassant in Egyptian garb. Rushdī's obsession with popularity perhaps blinded him to the fact that the short story requires more than a local garb to achieve a real success.

Yet the turn to romance whether we find it in the tendency to romanticise Maupassant or in the desire to tell tales of traditional sentiments (as we see in the stories published by *al-Qiṣṣah*) was not totally unjustified. Romance must have provided these writers with a protective cover. Since it could have been troublesome to tackle the contemporary situation objectively, a dissociation from it was the easy and safe way out of the dilemma. For example, Yūsuf Ghurāb was writing under the influence of Kāmil Ḥusayn (al-Muhāmī) who was the main pillar of romance in the 1930s and 1940s, and whose influence, surprisingly enough, extended to a whole generation of writers in the 1950s and 1960s. In his study 'Romance in the Egyptian Short Story', Sayyid Ḥamīd al-Nassāj records that al-Muhāmī announced in the journal *al-Jāmi'ah* a competition for the best love story and shortly afterwards, on 4 July 1947, he wrote an article in the journal *Ākhir Sā'ah* on the rules for writing love stories.[17]

Work similar to al-Muhāmī's was produced by Maḥmūd al-Badawī, whose romantic characters travel as far as China, where the main events of his narrative take place. It is indicative of the mutual interest between him and the literary establishment of the time that his romances continued to be published, broadcast and televised until 5 June 1967. As his contribution to the newly emerging realism after the defeat of the June War, al-Badawī wrote 'The Horse and the Horseman' (al-Jawād wal-Fāris) in which the protagonist, Shaykh 'Abd al-Raḥmān (a participant in the 1919 Revolution), takes part in the war of attrition and is seen chasing an Israeli plane with his old gun from the back of his horse.[18]

Critics and commentators have begun to realise how wide the gap was between the real situation in the 1960s and 1970s on the one hand, and its literary expression on the other; yet their realisation seems to be of little or no practical value to produce any real change. An example of this can be seen in *Fuṣūl*, a publication intended to express current literary activities in Egypt and to some extent in the Arab world as a whole. In the editorial of the special issue devoted to the short story, we find this comment on Najīb Maḥfūẓ *Layāli Alf Laylah* (The Nights of *The Arabian Nights*):

> Nabīlah Ibrāhīm's study of the subject draws our attention to the possible identification between the world of *The Arabian Nights* and ours ... . Like *The Arabian Nights*, Maḥfūẓ's work moves in a vicious circle, for each begins and ends with Shahrayar. Yet the difference between the old and the new Shahrayār is what makes Maḥfūẓ's work particularly significant. With the new Shahrayar there is the picture of a modern reality which insists on change for the sake of the ideal.[19]

The reference to the reality which demands change is too general to mean any specific situation. Moreover, the effect anticipated by the reference to change is dispelled by the counter reference to the ideal which makes the whole statement empty rhetoric.

Commenting on Edward al-Kharrāṭ's short story 'Fī al-Shawāri'' (In the Streets), which won the State prize in 1973, Āmāl Farīd says: 'The story is one of the most expressive pictures in our literature presenting an image of death as preying on life like a beast.' She goes on to say that 'The protagonist heard of a beast or an unidentified murderer roaming the streets and attacking pedestrians. Though the protagonist worried about the situation, he would not surrender, and he hopes to fight the enemy without himself or his children being harmed.'[20]

Edward al-Kharrāṭ himself, commenting on the work of his fellow writers in the 1970s, finds a sense of loss, disintegration, alienation, futility and the like, but only in general terms. For instance, he remarks that 'Barking' (al-Nubaḥ), a short story by Jār al-Nabī al-Ḥilū published in 1976, is a good example of rebellion against tyranny and shame, but makes no allusion to the agents of tyranny or the source of shame.[21] Similarly he remarks that 'Awaḍ

'Abd al-'Āl's collection *The One who Crossed the City* (Allaḍī Marra 'Ala al-Madīna) is moulded by traditional surrealism which, he maintains, is characterised by chaos in form and content.[22]

A similar comment on 'Abd al'Āl's work is made by Na'īm 'Aṭiyyah, who points to the obscurity of his fiction which inevitably produces a feeling of alienation in the reader. He goes on to suggest that obscurity and alienation are merely aspects of the objective reality which the stories depict. But although he refers to the stories as being a rebellion against the existing reality, he makes no specific reference to the reality in question. In his discussion of the stories of Yūsuf al-Shārūnī, published in the 1960s, he says that characters in those stories criticise society but without offering 'an ideal substitute' society for the one they denounce.[23]

Like their predecessors in the 1960s and 1970s, critics and commentators in the 1980s have moved in the same vicious circle. They have survived the 'dilemma of freedom' mentioned earlier by use of rhetoric just as those short story writers survived it by employing romance. For both it is survival by evasion and, as such, can leave no real impact on the development of the art.

Thus the short-story writer has to face the battle alone and to survive in the middle of censorship with all its curbs on creative activity and the limitations it places on topicality rendered in the art of the short story. He has an additional problem in that the comparative brevity of the form itself makes it a difficult medium for the presentation of serious issues. However, some writers (including those whose work appears in this selection) have taken advantage of this brevity, and have handled the form with such artistic flexibility as to turn it at the end to their advantage.

* * *

It is the intention of this study to demonstrate that the Arabic short story has not been altogether crushed by censorship, local romance, foreign imitation or compromising criticism. There are writers, I believe, who like Sindbad in Najīb Maḥfūẓ's *Layalī Alf Laylah*, opted to leave this world for a different one, which though close in reality is far away in imagination when skilfully transformed by them. The tone of their rejection of the existing reality can be identified with that of Sindbad, as portrayed by Maḥfūẓ. This is what Sindbad defiantly says on the occasion of his departure from 'The Cafe of the Emīrs', as he appears to receive with suspicion Shahrayar's new good intentions of forgiveness, and even declines to believe them altogether.

> To which Sindbad said defiantly, 'I am fed up with lanes and alleys. I am also fed up with carrying furniture around, with no hope of seeing anything new. Over there is another life: the river joins up with the sea and the sea penetrates deeply into the unknown, and the unknown brings forth islands and mountains, living creatures and angels and devils. It is a magical call that cannot be resisted. I said to myself, 'Try your luck, Sindbad, and throw yourself into the arms of the invisible.'[24]

The Physician 'Abd al-Qādir al-Mahīnī turns to Sindbad and says: 'May God protect you on your journeys, but be sure to sharpen your wits, and record whatever great things you come across, for it is God's order to do that!'[25]

No doubt, these writers sharpened their wits enough to survive the dilemma without sacrificing their artistic integrity; but they had also to survive it without much help from critics and commentators. Some of the stories included here seem to have inspired Najīb Maḥfūẓ's novel which apparently incorporates the various similar attempts in the 1960s and 1970s. Indeed close examination of *Layālī Alf Laylah* in relation to those stories whose motifs are directly or indirectly derived from *The Arabian Nights* reveals his affinity with his fellow writers. Perhaps Najīb Maḥfūẓ established the pattern earlier in his fiction when he probably taught younger writers to survive with art rather than to escape from it.

Notes

1. "The Dilemma of Freedom in Modern Arabic Fiction", *Ḥiwār* 10 (1964) pp. 52-62.
2. In his study published in 1975, Ṣabrī Ḥāfiẓ says: 'By the 1960s most writers had declined artistically, fallen silent or become repetitious, although, at the same time, they were the pillars of the formal literary establishment, dominating most of the country's cultural activities.'

   Later in his study, Ḥāfiẓ offers a more detailed picture of the situation:

   By the time the 1960s arrived, it was clear that the years of fear had had a very severe effect and the Egyptian short story was involved in another crisis. Y. Idrīs, after having produced annual collections, ceased writing short stories for a period of six years, during which he concentrated on drama and the novel. Moreover, Y. al-Shārūnī had for many years refrained from publishing short stories, even in periodicals, turning his energies to criticism. Sh. 'Ayyād similarly stopped writing in this genre; A. al-Sharqāwī turned to the novel, then to poetic drama; F. Ghānim turned to the novel, while B. al-Dīb and 'Abbās Aḥmad stopped writing altogether. It was apparent that the short story had come to a halt and that a new phase in the history of the Egyptian personality had been reached.

   (In R. C. Ostle, ed., *Studies in Modern Arabic Literature*, Warminster: Tedding House, 1975, p. 108.)
3. After writing this Part, I met Ṣabrī Ḥāfiẓ at a seminar and asked him why he had not written in the 1960s what he wrote in the 1970s. I

mentioned, in particular, an article he had published in *al-Majallah* in 1966 in which he ignored the dilemma. He replied that editors, being afraid of censorship, had refused to publish anything of a controversial nature. He even mentioned that the chief editor of *al-Majallah*, Yaḥyā Haqqī, had suppressed parts of his article and had told him personally that he could not afford to publish any material that could be construed as critical of the establishment. (Middle East Centre Siminar, Oxford, May 1983).

4. "The Dilemma of the Short Story: A Symposium", *al-Hilāl*, 77 (1969) pp. 122-37.
5. 'Abd al-Raḥmān Abu-'Auf, "The Quest for a New Course in the Egyptian Short Story", *al-Hilāl*, p. 89.
6. *Ibid.*, p. 91.
7. Yaḥyā Ḥaqqī, 'Editorial', *al-Majallah*, 10 (1966) p. 5. In a study on Ḥaqqī, Miriam Cooke remarks that although Ḥaqqī 'Was claimed not to be concerned with politics', his novel *Good Morning*, (Ṣabāḥ al-Khayr) which he published at his own expense, was voicing, only three years after the Revolution, a dissatisfaction with the dictatorial aspects of a regime others were praising'. (*The Anatomy of an Egyptian Intellectual: Yaḥyā Ḥaqqī*, Washington, D.C.: The Three Continents Press, 1984, p. 7).
8. *Ibid.*, p. 5.
9. 'A Poor Woman' (Imra'a Miskīna), *al-Ādāb*, 19 (1972) p. 155.
10. *Ibid.*, p. 157.
11. Salma al-Jayyūsī, "Commitment in the Last Quarter of the Century", *al-Ādāb*, 25 (December 1977) p. 142. A similar picture of the time occurs in Ṣabrī Ḥāfiẓ's "The Egyptian Novel in the 1950s", *Journal of Arabic Literature* 7 (1976) pp. 84-88.
12. Rashād Rushdī, *Fann al-Qiṣṣah al-Qaṣīrah* (Beirut: Dār al-'Awdah, 1959) pp. 17, 106. The book was reprinted several times in Cairo and Beirut in the 1960s and 1970s.

13. Sayyid Ḥāmid al-Nassāj, *The Development of the Short Story in Egypt* (Cairo: Dār al-Kitāb al-'Arabī, 1968), p. 239.
14. Rushdī, p. 47.
15. G. de Maupassant, *Short Comedies and Tragedies of Life* (Ohio, 1903, p. 12.
16. Quoted by Nādia Kāmil "Maupassantism and the Egyptian Short Story", *Fuṣūl* 2 (1982) p. 191. Nādia Kāmil quotes Rushdī, whom she considers a great critic, as stating in his book that '"the short story is Maupassant and Maupassant is the short story"'.
17. Ḥāmid al-Nassāj, 'Romance in the Egyptian Short Story' *al-Hilāl* 85 (1977) p. 14. One has only to remember what a critical year 1947 was for the Arab World, to be struck by the degree of insensitivity of a writer like al-Muhāmī.
18. Aḥmad Kamāl Zakī, "The Narrative Vision in Maḥmūd al-Badawī's Fiction", *Fusūl* 2 (1982) pp. 76-79.
19. "Editorial", *Fuṣūl* 2 (1982), p. 6.
20. Āmāl Farid, "Edward al-Kharrāṭ and the State Prize", *Fuṣūl*, p. 203.
21. Edward al-Kharrāṭ, "Panoramic Scenes from the Short Story in the 1970s", *Fusūl'* 2 (1982), p. 137.
22. *Ibid.*, p. 144.
23. Na'īm 'Aṭiyyā, "European Influences on the Egyptian Short Story in the 1970s", *Fuṣūl* 2 (1982), pp. 211-12.
24. Najīb Maḥfūẓ, *Layalī Alf Laylah* (1979) trans. Denys Johnson-Davies, as *Arabian Nights and Days*, The American University in Cairo: Cairo, 1996, p. 9. (I don't believe that the translation of the title is accurate).
25. *Ibid.*, p. 13.

II
Sindbad: The Other Voyage

1. THE OLD SINDBAD: AN IMAGE OF FELLOWSHIP AND SETTLEMENT

Like all narratives of great magnitude, the tale of Sindbad embodies the fascinating power of narration, which often curbs the desire of the reader to go further beyond the captivating story. We know, for example, that *The Ancient Mariner* can be read for its own plot as well as for the implications underlying the mere fascination of the narrative itself. But while the covert meaning of *The Ancient Mariner* has been given due consideration by literary critics, that of Sindbad has been overlooked, and this may be explained in terms of the generic nature of the tale of Sindbad. It is when the distinctions between genres have become less of boundaries than of signposts that Sindbad has been assessed as a work of literary value.

A close reading of 'Sindbad' will show that behind the adventures and wonders unfolded by the narration lies a picture of a stable community with permanent social values. This picture may be identified with what Raymond Williams calls 'the balance ... in which both the general way of life and the individual persons are seen as there and absolute.'[1] By this balance, Williams means that the claims of the individual have their own substance along with those of society, which, in turn, have their own as well.

In his travels, Sindbad enjoys a harmonious relationship not only with society, but also with nature. No human force restricts his free movement from Baghdad to Baṣra, then to the rest of the world. Also, he returns home freely and happily. The instinctive desire for travelling is not suppressed even by his own repentance, which is brought about by the memory of the dangerous experiences he faced on his first voyage. No sooner does he decide to renounce travel than he finds himself restless enough to start seafaring again, and the constant alternation between the impulse to travel and the intention to put an end to it becomes the framework for the successive voyages. It may be worthwhile to note here that this framework forms a main attribute of Sindbad's character, for it shows that he is a highly imaginative person and more than an ordinary seaman who is after fortune overseas. The original motive of trade which initiated his travel is never the only impulse which leads him to go on from one voyage to another; trade is only a vehicle for Sindbad, to carry him into the world of wonder, which he never abandons except to settle in old age and recreate his experience of that world, thus conveying it to posterity.

This is how the second voyage begins: 'I was living a life of unexampled pleasure when, one day, the old desire entered my head to visit far countries and strange people, to voyage among the isles and curiously regard things hitherto unknown to me; also, the trading habit rose in me again.'[2]

The successive voyages are all prompted by 'the old desire' to travel, which is intensified because it is enacted despite Sindbad's inward repentance of travelling and facing dangers during new voyages. The fact that this 'old desire' has not been suppressed by repentance or renunciation suggests how deeply rooted it is in Sindbad. The same 'old desire' must have prompted many famous narratives such as Johnson's *Rasselas;* Coleridge's *The Ancient Mariner*, and Conrad's *Heart of Darkness*.

Another main trait in Sindbad's character beside his distinctive imagination is the sympathy he extends to his fellow-men, and this leads us to the other important framework in the narrative. It is obvious that the story of Sindbad the Porter (or Sindbad the Landman) forms the direct motivation for the whole narration. The technical function of this framework is too well known for any elaboration here, but the underlying effect of this framework story is overlooked and consequently the substantial personality of Sindbad remains engulfed in the mystery of narration.

I would like to suggest here that the framework story of Sindbad the Porter is not a coincidence, in the sense that Sindbad the Porter happened to pass the door of a house which turned out to be that of Sindbad the Sailor, who welcomed him. What attracts the Sailor to the Porter is the latter's singing which must have aroused the Sailor's imagination. In his response, Sindbad the Sailor says, 'O Porter, your name is the same as mine; for I am called Sindbad the Sailor ... I requested you to come because I wished you to sing again those delightful stanzas which I heard when you were sitting outside my door.'[3] Taken aback by what he hears, the Porter says: 'In the name of Allah, do not blame me too much for my inconsiderate singing, for grief, weariness and misery may give birth to rudeness, foolishness and insolence in the best of us.'[4]

Evidently, Sindbad the Sailor does not interpret the singing as personal or look at the Porter as envious. With his imagination, he transcends the temporary private association which the Porter presumably intended to imply in his singing. Instead he sees in the singing the permanent vision of beauty and consequently replies; 'Do not be at all ashamed to have sung in such a manner ... be perfectly at ease here, for you are my brother. I pray you to sing your verses again, for they surprised me by their beauty.'[5] Sindbad the Sailor further sees in the Porter's singing a universal theme which embraces the two Sindbads, and by implication, humanity at large: 'My Destiny also makes a strange tale, which I will tell you,' he says.[6] Thus Sindbad the Sailor is inspired and the narrative flows, and narration itself becomes a kind of destiny where the Sailor is destined to tell and the Porter to listen, like the Ancient Mariner and the Wedding Guest, or like Marlow and his fellow men on boardship in *Heart of Darkness.*

This is how Sindbad is first motivated by travel, then inspired by narration, where one framework is integrated into another through the labyrinths of his imagination.

Yet Sindbad is not only imaginative, but also sympathetic. Beside extending his imagination to the wondrous world and to the narration of its marvels, Sindbad has sympathy to extend to the world around him. He is both at once imaginative and sympathetic. Thus Sindbad's character is particularly defined by the interplay of this multidimensional power.

What makes Sindbad's character attractive and memorable as well is his sympathetic imagination (or his imaginative sympathy). Sindbad's hospitality and generosity–two qualities made quite explicit in the narrative–seem to have overshadowed the deeper dimension in his character, which, in modern idiom, can be described as the sense of fellowship or the communal spirit. 'For you are my brother' the Sailor says to the Porter, who is assured by his fellow Sindbad of the identical name they both share. The First Voyage begins with a reference to the 'honourable porter who bears the same name as myself'.[7]

The intimacy which develops between the two Sindbads is not utilitarian in nature. It is not the kind of relationship which makes the poor and the rich meet to satisfy the desire of giving and taking. Nowhere in the narrative do we find that the Sailor resents the Porter or patronises him. The link between the two Sindbads is a kind of natural piety which flows spontaneously as soon as the Sailor hears the Porter, whose singing must have initiated the human bond between the two. Sindbad the Sailor must have imagined that a person who could appreciate poetry could respond with equal appreciation to story-telling, and this, I believe, is what makes the Sailor instantly perceive in the Porter a sense of fellowship, which forms a framework and a basis for the whole narration. Dozens of underprivileged people must have passed the door of Sindbad the Sailor before, but without succeeding in attracting his attention in the way that the Porter does. So the choice of the Porter as a framework by the Sailor is an exceptional privilege which may not have come about by chance. Again, to use the modern idiom, the Porter is a kind of co-author, and the fellowship here (the sympathy) can be described as aesthetic.

In practical terms, fellowship in Sindbad expresses itself in the way he willingly shares what he gains with others. For example, when he comes across that wretched merchant who fails to get any diamonds from the Diamond Valley, Sindbad gives him some excellent stones from his belt saying, 'Here is such profit as you have never dared to hope for in all your life', to which the merchant replies, 'A blessing be upon you, O my master. A single one of these diamonds would be enough to make me rich until extreme old age, for never in my life have I seen the like even at the courts of kings'.[8] It is true that Sindbad risks his life to gain property and wealth, but once he is prosperous, he never allows material interests to gain control over him. We know that he always gives away money to people in need and his generosity extends to friends and acquaintances. Of course, Sindbad's gains are never unearned. On the contrary, those gains are earned through great pains which do not allow him to forget the experience of suffering that yielded them. And this, I think, is what keeps and fosters the human bond between him and the underprivileged, and even people at large.

Sindbad starts his career as a simple ordinary merchant with a very small capital and it is never his intention to make profit. He is like a skilled labourer. When he is shipwrecked, Sindbad builds himself a raft in a sea full of monsters. During the Fourth Voyage he introduces the craft of making saddles and spurs, and consequently makes life in the city more comfortable. He makes saddles and spurs, not only for the King, his vizier and the dignitaries of the city, but also for its citizens. He wins the respect and esteem of the King as well as of his subjects, and for his contribution, Sindbad receives a big financial reward and is accepted by the city and its King, who extends his generosity to him. On various occasions, he earns his living by trading and on all occasions his money is clean. What determines the course of material interests in Sindbad's life (whether they involve earning or giving away) is sympathy. For example, Sindbad was sympathetic with the people of the city when he noticed that they were riding horses without saddles and he opted to make them saddles with no ulterior motive. Perhaps it was on his mind to make the life of the horses comfortable as well, for he is in harmony with nature as well.

However, sympathy in Sindbad is further demonstrated by his yearning to go home while he is away from it. Once 'the old desire' to travel is realised, a counter 'old desire' to return is aroused in him, and it drives him back home in the same way that 'the old desire' drives him away from Baghdad and Baṣra. Sindbad's yearning to go home is a characteristic pattern in his behaviour after he survives dangerous adventures, and the total framework of his whole story begins with one desire and concludes with another.

The Fourth Voyage concludes as follows: 'We sailed on and on until, by the permission of Allah, we came to Baṣra and, staying there only a few days, hastened up-stream to Baghdad. I went to my own house in my own street and, greeting my old companions and the folk of my family, gave alms to the widow and the orphan, because I had returned richer from my last adventure than ever before'.[9]

The Fourth Voyage begins with Sindbad telling us how 'my traitor soul only showed me the advantageous side of travelling in far countries, so that at last I could resist her whisperings no longer'.[10] Yet on the Fifth Voyage, Sindbad reconsiders 'the advantageous side of travelling' when all his companions perish (as in *Ulysses*) and he survives only to believe death imminent. He curses himself bitterly for his 'foolishness in voyaging again after having learned five times that death lies in wait for the wonderer. 'How many times did you repent and begin again?' I said to myself. 'Had you not enough riches laid by in Baghdad to suffice for the most reckless expenditure throughout two lifetimes?'[11]

Being a man of action, Sindbad builds himself a raft and escapes into a river, following its end, hoping for safety, putting his trust in Allah and remembering the words of the poet:

> Out of the country of oppression
> Depart and save your spirit whole;
> There are a thousand lands and but one soul,
> So leave the land and keep the soul's possession.
> Nothing unwritten shall surprise you,
> Nothing which has not been for ages,
> So hurry not for counsel to the sages,
> But stay at him and let your soul advise you.[12]

The blend of self-censure at critical moments and content in the aftermath is uniquely Sindbad's story. It is the eternal story of belonging which must have been the archetype of many fictitious accounts throughout the centuries.

This leads us to the other aspect of the balance to which Raymond Williams refers. Sindbad does not only extend sympathy but also receives it from the world around him. He is not simply a courageous, virtuous man who struggles against 'a vile society' but rather an individual who is harmoniously contained in a home country in the human world he deals with inside and outside the boundaries of Baghdad and Baṣra. Mia Gerhardt perceptively comments that 'Sindbad travels in a world where goodwill, mutual help and strict honesty reign supreme'.[13] Three times (rather than twice as Gerhardt remarks) Sindbad regains his wares, which he thought were lost forever at shipwreck. His fellow-men always keep his property with the intention of selling it on his behalf (believing Sindbad to be dead) and delivering its price to his heirs; and this pattern of behaviour recurs in three voyages: the first, the fifth and the seventh.

The *Ambassadorial mission* carried out by Sindbad may further demonstrate his sense of belonging to what Raymond Williams calls 'a genuine community: a community of persons linked not merely by one kind of relationship–work or friendship or family–but many, interlocking kinds'.[14] Thus, for example, begins one night during the Sixth Voyage.

> One day the King of Sarandib questioned me concerning the internal affairs of Baghdad and the government of the Khalīfah Hārūn ar-Rashīd. I told him how just and benevolent our ruler was, and laid considerable stress upon his virtues and excellent qualities. The King of Sarandib marvelled at what I told him and said, 'I see that the Khalīfah is versed in wisdom and the true art of government. I have conceived an affection for him through the account which you have given me; therefore I am very anxious to send him some present worthy of himself and I appoint you the bearer of it.[15]

The Khalīfah receives the present with great appreciation and sends the King of Sarandib a gift which Sindbad delivers with pleasure. What is particularly noteworthy about this enterprise is the nature of Sindbad's mission, which is undertaken freely and without any utilitarian purpose, for Sindbad undertakes it not as a subject ordered and forced by an authority, but rather as a free citizen who, to use Forster's phrase, has 'learned how to connect'. Sindbad needs neither money nor prestige from either the King or the Khalīfah. He does not look at them as authority either. When in Baghdad, Sindbad delivers the King's present to the Khalīfah by presenting himself to deliver the gift. And on no occasion do we record any fear on the part of Sindbad or of intimidation by either the King or the Khalīfah. We may be tempted to agree with Mia Gerhardt in her concluding remark that 'Sindbad the Sailor appears as a glorification of the mariner's calling, at a privileged time of history.'[16] Yet it is more than a glorification limited by a privileged time and place. Sindbad is a phenomenon that stands outside time and place. He embodies the claims of the individual, and it is the realisation of those claims that becomes an extension or expansion of society without either being obstructed or reduced by the other.

Conflict in Sindbad between the individual desire and the communal sense of belonging ends with the triumph of the latter. 'I told all those who gathered round me the story of my adventures and vowed that I would never leave Baghdad again.'[17] He announces to his dear guests that the Seventh Voyage 'definitely cured me of any further desire for travel.'[18]

Thus end the adventures of Sindbad in happy settlement, a conclusion often found in Victorian fiction (this presumably accounts for the popularity of *The Arabian Nights* in Victorian England).

To go beyond the sensational nature of the adventures is to explore 'the structure of feeling' (the phrase is Williams's) which lies at the core of the narrative. To further explore its structure is to identify the components of such structure, such as the rhythm which is seen in the recurrent frameworks, the balance where the potential in Sindbad prompts and is prompted by that of the world around him through free interplay, and finally the sympathy which defines the relationship between Sindbad and his community. The settlement which concludes the adventurous life of Sindbad is no expression of any conquering force, but a free choice on the part of Sindbad, who enjoys his individual freedom, and a communal sense of life, as well.

* * *

2. THE MODERN SINDBAD: A PORTRAIT OF A BLEAK HOUSE

Sindbad is in many ways the Arabic Odysseus. His wanderings, adventures, yearning for knowledge and experience, his quest for the unknown and his happy homecomings, all these qualities and more make Sindbad comparable with Odysseus, whose life is nevertheless more eventful and sophisticated. One wonders whether the narrative of the *Odyssey* forms the framework of the story of Sindbad, whose portrait, as we know, occupies a main part of the whole narrative of *The Arabian Nights*.

But who is this Sindbad who has been such a popular narrative figure in the minds of readers throughout the centuries? The story of Sindbad is not merely a fairy tale despite all the fantastic elements it provides. He is not as remote as the unknown islands and seas to which he travels, nor is he as terrifying as the objects and monsters he meets. The inhuman objective world of fear and terror which Sindbad inspires is counterbalanced by the subjective human qualities which he dsiplays – courage, patience, modesty, honesty and belief in survival. The desire to settle and the inclination for adventure are, as we have already seen, two opposite impulses happily reconciled in Sindbad, who has no scepticism about life. By Sindbad's seventh voyage, the reader wishes he could meet the old but wise, pleasant, cheerful, happy and optimistic Sindbad.

How is this Sindbad of old but all time presented in modern times? The modern Sindbad is often rooted in and affected by the present grim reality in which he finds himself inevitably caught. He is a sort of double, identified at once with the old Sindbad, but utterly different from him; and the identification is one fragment or the other of the old picture of Sindbad.

In general terms, the present-day Sindbad is a man who is seriously engaged in the contemporary political and social situation. He is no longer the free voyager who used to leave home out of his own free will and come back with the gain of experience and knowledge shared by people who impatiently awaited his return. Unlike the old Sindbad, the present-day Sindbad is heavily burdened with the various involvement of daily life which actually has its bearing on 'the common way of life' marked by Williams. Unlike the old Sindbad, the present-day one may not be considered 'the son of the people' (to use the Italian phrase of Conrad's *Nostromo*) who would gather around their son-voyager in suspense to hear the news of the world beyond their reach. In brief, the human bond between Sindbad and his community is lost in this modern world.

The modern Sindbad is, then, a man of sorrows who suffers from alienation. He is victimised by authority, which sees in him a threat to the stable institutions of society, and consequently deprives him of the dignity and reverence he used to enjoy amongst his people. He is ostracized and left helpless so that no communication between him and the world around him may be promoted. He is an alien whose suffering is intensified as a result of his awareness of the impoverished life he is forced to lead in isolation. His solitary being, we are made to realise, is not brought about by natural circumstances which are overcome by goodwill and fortitude as we comparatively find in the case of the old Sindbad. While the old Sindbad stands for a celebration of individual freedom, communal spirit, sympathy, courage, goodwill and the like, the modern one is the lamentation of the absence of these things. The discrepancy between the two Sindbads is, then, expressed by a kind of juxtaposition which enacts the dilemma in the modern consciousness of the Arab writer.

We may say that the modern Sindbad is everything the old Sindbad is not; or that he is the negation of the old Sindbad in the same way that the present consciousness of reality is negated by its past one. All this can be demonstrated from the poetry and short story of the period where the story of Sindbad seems to have provided those writers with the appropriate form or motif for the dilemma they felt they were undergoing.

In those writings which appeared in the journals of the time two main approaches can be distinguished. One is essentially characterised by nostalgic feeling for the old Sindbad as we find, for example, in the following titles: 'The Seaport of Sindbad', 'The Arab Sindbad' and 'When Does Sindbad Return?'[1] These poems are typical in using Sindbad as a motif of romance reminiscent of the happy old days, and Sindbad here may be a simple glorification of Shahrazad, the creator of the great voyager, Sindbad, as we find in the first poem. Sindbad may also be identified with a historical figure as we find in the second poem which is a long narrative about Usāmah Ibn Munqiḍ, a man of letters and a fighter against the Crusaders. Or Sindbad may be a yearning for the happy return of Sindbad which, like a rain cloud will, if ever it comes back, bring with it fertility and prosperity. In any case the approach to the old Sindbad here is characterised by being rhetorical rather than an extended metaphor or motif.

The other approach is different in the sense that it is a

dramatised consciousness, and the old memory of Sindbad is developed and integrated into a new sensibility which makes the total picture of Sindbad subtle enough to be effectively expressive of the present situation of the writer. This I would like to demonstrate from some narrative poems and short stories – all, I believe, deserve some detailed discussion. Yet before I proceed it may be worthwhile to give a brief account of a dramatic narrative and a short story written earlier in the century at a critical time of Arab history.

* * *

An early reference to Sindbad in modern Arabic literature is an account by Michael ʻAflaq titled ʻThe Death of Sindbad: A One Act Play' which is a dramatic interaction between Sindbad and society at large, where Sindbad is invited in a cynical manner to illuminate the situation with a verbal expression derived from his wisdom and experience.[2] Different people urge Sindbad to speak in the hope that he might expose himself to public humiliation, and when he finally opens his mouth to speak, a snake comes out of it, and the encounter ends with the conclusion that Sindbad's death makes us survive.

The encounter is quite revealing, especially when it is viewed in retrospect. It seems as if ʻAflaq was foreshadowing his own political future when he wrote that dramatic piece in 1935. In 1962, ʻAflaq ʻwent down to the ship' (to use Pound's words for the opening of Canto I) and left the Phoenician coast of Lebanon forever, saying little or nothing after he had been disappointed in his party.[3] We may remember that Odysseus prophesied his future as a man of no fortune and with no friends surviving the hardships of the journey.

The account is particularly interesting because it is evidently prophetic, for it seems to have summed up the situation of the Arab writer as a Sindbad about two decades earlier than the appearance of the first elaborate account published in the mid-fifties, an account which was followed by other serious works– some of which will receive detailed discussion here. In this prophetic vision we find the major features of the modern Sindbad, whether in the form of the distance between the Arab writer and his world or in the theme of oppression inflicted on him by his society in one form or another. ‘Aflaq's Sindbad is a Prometheus Unbound, a martyr, a Christ whose death, as the account concludes, brings about life for people. Not only does he defy the accusations and fabrications launched against him, but he also bears the sins of his people alone, like a prophet.

Yet in a further practice and at about the same time, ‘Aflaq advances his pioneering attempts with a secular rather than a divine or a moralistic view. ‘Sindbad and his Mistress’ is perhaps the earliest short narrative in modern Arabic derived from the tale of Sindbad to demonstrate a successful attempt in recreating the tradition of *The Arabian Nights* and using it as a motif. The editorial note which introduces the story shows that the anonymous editor (quite obvious ‘Aflaq himself) is very appreciative of the aesthetic element of the story. Firstly the note indirectly draws our attention to the fact that the story is not a sequential order of events, but rather a psychological, social, philosophical, symbolic, pragmatic and historical, and this simply means that the story is valued for its intrinsic rather than extrinsic quality. Secondly the note points out to the merit of the story where, it is remarked, the writer succeeds despite its brevity. More important, however, is the editor's awareness of the writer's imaginative power which lies behind the figurative language of the story.

The editor sounds apologetic for the brevity of the story but his remark on the subject is superfluous and in any case, he can not be serious because this brevity brings with it a high effect of articulation. Sindbad encounters his mistress with a vision made clear by means of dramatisation and figurative language extremely economical. Even the moral in the story is dominated by the aesthetic picture which prevents the situation from becoming rhetorical. 'Aflaq succeeds in fusing the poetic (lyrical) with the dramatic to produce a narrative of total effect, like a mosaic.

Right from the first sentence we sense the organic unity of the narrative where all the agents of action are presented in a state of interplay and its perspective is effectively presented. The night, Baghdad: the great city (and the mistress, as well) and Sindbad, the traveller–are all put together and activated by the perspective of a city in slumber like a traveller in extreme exhaustion, i.e., lacking the will to travel.

It is very significant that the story initiated at night as a motif. The night is a kind of primordial which has its own mythical sanctity by which Sindbad is helped to have his vision and restore the will for quest. When later in the narrative the reference is made to the long daylight in the north the narrator makes it a point that the pale daylight is befriended by the night so as to make a curtain promoting the night's mystery.

It is equally significant that the story ends at dawn where Sindbad is helped to hold to his vision and take his decision during the mythical night which can help him see more than he can during the daylight. At night Sindbad surrenders gradually to the primordial leaving behind the ephemeral reality of comfort and easy life to reach a higher level of consciousness. Sindbad, then, captures the quest dream and he is liberated from the comfortable material world which binds him to the static reality of the great city. The quest he is embarking on is the way to generate life (or regenerate it) in this great city. He and Baghdad are one. I would like also to suggest that his mistress is an extended metaphor of the great city caught by him asleep during the night, and that the arms of the mistress he dismantles himself from stand for the comfortable abode he is leaving behind in the great city.

However, the kernal motif of the story is presented just before the conclusion when Sindbad tells his mistress that he is called in his travel by the echoing voice of narration once delivered by the Indian sage, when Sindbad at the time was not attentive, being bored by travels already. The motif consists of polarities out of its interaction is generated the effect in perspective. Such polarities are past and present, event and memory, happening and narrating, here and there and now and then.

In the modern idiom of criticism this reference to the Indian sage forms a basic element in the poetics of fiction where the polarities mentioned are structured to bridge the gap between fiction and reality. Sindbad here is a person who enjoys making fiction out of reality by moving easily from one world into the other as if the two worlds are identical. The presence of one recalls the absence of the other and urges its presence; hence is the quest for travel which makes life generative for Sindbad and his great city.

Sindbad, then, is not an ordinary traveller. He is a storyteller as well. More than that he is a traveller and listener at one time (to the Indian sage) and a story teller to another listener (to his mistress) at another. He survives with the two strong impulses of travel and story telling. Sindbad tells his mistress that his legs insist on moving. ‘“My arms never rest without struggling against waves and rocks.”[1] So is his memory which urges him to recapture the glamour of narration. This immediately recalls what Sindbad the Sailor says to Sindbad the Porter in *The Arabian Nights*: ‘My Destiny also makes a strange tale, which I will tell you’ he says. Like Sindbad the Sailor, ‘Aflaq's Sindbad is inspired and the narrative flows, and narration becomes a kind of destiny where one tells and another listens, like the Ancient Mariner and the Wedding

Guest or like Marlow and his fellow men on boardship in *Heart of Darkness*.

3. THE SINDBAD POETRY OF THE SHORT STORY

The literary scene of the 1950s was particularly dominated by poetry, and the attempts to modernise poetry were undertaken by people whose names have become landmarks in the literary history of the time. Nowadays we remember Adonīs, Ḥāwī, Jabra, al-Khāl, to mention but a few of a long list, as pioneers who established the foundation of a modern movement in the contemporary history of Arabic poetry. Meanwhile figures like Rushdī, who presumably thought of himself as an innovator at the time, are remembered as amateurs nowadays. Also literary journals like *Shi'r* (founded by al-Khāl in 1957) were certainly superior to *al-Qiṣṣah* which was evidently intended to develop the short story.

However I have no intention here to go into the reasons which might have led to the dominance of poetry over the short story in this particular decade. But I would like to suggest that the spirit of the time demanded the medium of poetry, and that the poets themselves expressed in the form of poetry what the short story writers would have done in the form of fiction. One can probably articulate the relationship between the poet and the short story writer in terms of the identification which has already been noticed between Sindbad the Porter and Sindbad the Sailor, where one serves as an inspiration for the other.

As for the spirit of the time, we know that the 1950s represent a period of transition in the modern history of the Arabs, at least as far as their historical events are concerned, from overthrowing monarchy in more than one Arab country to the defeat of great foreign powers in the Suez Canal invasion. It was natural that such events made writers feel that their nation was on the verge of a new era and that old institutions were falling. Poetry rather than prose fiction seems to have been the most appropriate form of expression to produce immediacy of response. In a sense writers found themselves celebrating a jubilee for the first time in their modern history, and it seemed to them as if the long-awaited dream was becoming reality. Poets must have felt that they were witnessing the twilight of a long day of liberation and freedom, and that a poetic vision was needed to capture the situation.

It was not, then, the subject matter which determined the course of expression; rather it was the 'winds of change' which made the poet see that the dream was not fiction any longer, and that he should come to the fore to express it.In ordinary circumstances one would presumably say that the topicality of the subject matter (being public rather than private) could have been accommodated by fiction rather than poetry. Evidently the subject matter of contemporary reality was the concern of all writers, poets and otherwise.

Also poets became the main spokesmen of the decade due to the fact that their battle for modernising poetry and freeing it from its long-inherited conventions coincided with the public battle for freedom. New reality obviously demanded new form, and this issue was discussed by Jabra, who saw in the poetry of the fifties an expression of a new sensibility which characterises the literary atmosphere of the decade (as will be seen later in this study).

We may probably say that the poets of the fifties wrote the short story in poetry not only because they prepared for the development of the genre later in the 1960s and 1970s but also because they used a motif which basically belongs to the realm of fiction. How can we then explain the frequent resort of poets to Sindbad?

The Sindbad poems which I have included here for study and analysis express a public issue rather than subjective feeling which poetry often tends to choose for expression. In terms of form they have the general characteristics of narrative while they tell the story of the new Sindbad. For example, they have the preliminary description of narrative, dialogue, monologue, suspense and the narrative voice which dramatises the tension between the person and persona. Also these poems close with the revelation of a vision which comes as a result of the dream being in the process of realisation.

Yet the interrelatedness between the later fiction and the earlier poetry can be further demonstrated from examining the impact of one on the other. It is obvious that the poets of the period inspired confidence in the narrative tradition of Sindbad, as the mere choice of the narrative itself may show.

Looking in retrospect from the fiction of the 1960s and 1970s at the poetry of the earlier period we find that Sindbad survived in the later period but with a different voice altogether. The dream which emerged in the poetry of the 1950s from the old romance had been transformed into a nightmare in the fiction of the two later decades. The spirit of the time had undoubtedly changed. The 1960s witnessed many setbacks, from the separation between Egypt and Syria to the Arab-Israeli war in 1967, and the 1950s looked like an 'Indian Summer'. Unlike the Sindbad of the 1950s who arrives at the dawn of the day and with a vision of the dream, the Sindbad of the 1960s arrives at dusk and with no anticipation other than darkness to follow; and the 1970s, of course, clearly shows that his anticipations were not unfounded. A comparison between Surūr's and Hāwī's Sindbads, on the one hand, and Qandīl's and al-Masnāwī's Sindbads on the other, will suggest the distinction between the young Sindbad who was celebrating his time and the grey Sindbad who was undergoing different kinds of oppression by his time. Such comparison can also demonstrate the way the dream of the 1950s was transformed into a nightmare in the sixties and the attempts by writers to recapture the lost dream.

Interplay between the poetry and fiction of the time can be further demonstrated by a comparative reading of Hāwī's 'Sindbad on his Eighth Voyage' and 'Abd al-Raḥmān Fahmī's story 'The Seven Voyages of Sindbad and the Strange Incidents and Coincidences which he Met'. The story may be summed up as follows. He invites his friends and companions to join him in a celebration of eating and drinking. He also offers to tell them everything that happened to him with maximum authenticity. In this connection he criticises Shahrazad, who forges truth, and Shahrayar for escaping it. Yet Sindbad is seduced by Shahrazad, who is described as being seductive as a soft serpent. He gives in as she pleads to him for her life, for the potential of the narrative she manages to extract from Sindbad helps her to survive the death sentence by Shahrayar. Shahrazad makes Sindbad realise that the powerful word has in it saving grace and that the world would come to an end if it so happened that the word were to vanish. Also Sindbad is tempted by Shahrazad's offer to make him (and herself) immortal by telling the story of his seven voyages whose account she begs him to hand over to her. But the result is disappointing, for Sindbad knows from other people that Shahrazad distorted his life story by presenting him merely as a fortunate adventurer. Sindbad also knows from other people that there is a superior adventurer to himself named Hasīb Karīm al-Dīn (a fictitious name) who was able to drink the elixir of life and see the seven heavens as well as what was hidden beneath the earth. So Sindbad decides to tell his own story to correct his image in the eyes of people and to put things in order, so that he might recover his own and other people's confidence in himself. He asks his audience to warn their descendants against Shahrazad's abuse of him and to rely on his rather than her version.

The narrative begins and ends with the First Voyage which

closes with a promise to tell his audience what happened to him after he survived the danger of those evil creatures to whom he was exposed.

The first Voyage tells us that Sindbad is in debt and he seeks various means to pay off his debt so that his palace will not be auctioned. After he fails to get what he needs, he turns for help to Hārūn al-Rashīd as a last resort. It is there that he is thrown into a deep underground pit to be buried alive with the dead. Sindbad is, of course, horrified when he finds himself in what is like a chamber of horrors.

The most obvious resemblance between Ḥāwī's and Fahmī's Sindbads is related to the narrative voice. Both narrators adopt the strategy of handling the narrative themselves rather than through the intermediary narrator, Shahrzad. Each tends to emphasise the fact that truth has been overshadowed. Hāwī's narrator tells us that he relates what people usually know about him such as the sensational incidents of *al-ghūl*, his burial alive and the like; this obliquely suggests that the truth about him is not known to people through the traditional narrative. Fahmī, on the other hand, dramatises the situation and tells us openly that what people know about him is far from being true, and it is deliberately distorted. Yet neither tells us what the truth is, and they vary in the way they present its picture. Ḥāwī's narrator tells us that truth is suppressed and he has to create it as he transforms the fantasy of old romance into a dream relevant to present reality. Fahmī's narrator, on the other hand, twists both fantasy and dream and sees truth as a nightmare. Fahmī's picture can be identified with naturalism which tends to see things as they naturally happen (the narrator insists on rendering things as they happened to him). However, unlike Ḥāwī's vision, which enjoys perspective, Fahmī's vision has no perspective to show or even to suggest beyond what he actually tells us.

Another resemblance is thematic; it is the connection between the psychological isolation of the individual and the social disintegration of the community. In Ḥāwī's poem this theme is expressed through the metaphor of the house (home, dwelling) being emptied so that the new setting would be available for a new life; 'I stripped that pavilion / I turned it into an old shelter for old friends / I exorcised my home from the echo of their ghosts'. The other metaphor which the narrator uses to express social hypocrisy is 'the Caliph's honey and al-Bashīr's coffee'* which replaced his first version of the poem when it first appeared in *al-Ādāb*.

The picture of disintegration is also articulated by the corrupted old relationship between man and woman, presumably a reference to Shahrazad and Shahrayar.

> and the element of abuse that is in her blood
> and the blind tiger and the fever of his hand
> in his male jealousy:
> 'Lourka' and *The Wedding of Blood in Spain*
> and the sword of the Cock of the Jinn in Ḥamāh,
> the ivory neck is a red river
> what horrors has death frozen upon the lips?

In his short story, Fahmī develops the images Ḥāwī uses in his poem to express the horrors 'frozen upon the lips'. The narrative voice in Fahmī's 'Sindbad' presents us with an elaboration of the precise poetic metaphors. When a reading of Ḥāwī's poem is needed, Fahmī's short story can provide the closest reading possible which will obviously illuminate the images and metaphors of the serpent, the tiger, the Caliph's honey and the horrifying pictures of the pavilion.

However, Ḥāwī's main but indirect contribution to the short story through his poetry lies in his emphasis of vision rather than tale 'invented by tellers'. It is the emphasis of the linguistic potential in language which creates and recreates a new effect. In his confrontation with Shahrazad, Fahmī reiterates his conviction in the power of the word and its contribution to the creation of the world. He tells Shahrazad that 'his stories are the word of man'. The framework of Ḥāwī's poem is the single (eighth) voyage which stands in opposition to the previous seven voyages. Unlike the old Sindbad who comes back on every voyage with capital profit and adventurous tales to tell, Ḥāwī's emerges from his eighth voyage a visionary Sindbad who has already lost all the material gains of the previous seven voyages. In a similar way Fahmī revolts against Shahrazad for portraying Sindbad as only a fortunate adventurer. Like Ḥāwī he follows the same framework of the single voyage for his story, although it takes a different course, for it is the first, and he obviously meant it to be the only one. Perhaps this course helped him to be so evasive about the ending of his narrative, which is left open, calling on his audience to imagine what comes next after the horrifying voyage, and this is where the poem and the short story diverge, perhaps to suggest the changing spirit of the time rather than to articulate a major generic distinction.

It is worth remembering here that Ḥāwī's poetry is not limited in its impact to Fahmī's story. Later in this study I shall show that Ḥāwī's poem forms a basis for a famous short story written by a well-known short-story writer, Zakariyya Tāmir. Also many other writers have been influenced by Ḥāwī.

4. TOWARDS A MODERN SENSIBILITY

The situation of Arab writers in the middle of twentieth century recalls, in a way, that of the English writers towards the end of the nineteenth century, a period in English literary history sometimes known as the *fin-de-siecle*.[1] From the mid 1950s onwards, Arab writers became preoccupied with the theme of decadence that characterised the literary atmosphere of English writers in the 1890s. They underwent the feeling that the present, which was an extension of the past, was in a state of stagnation that was bound to end up in decadence. Also, they wanted to see the established forms of life and art vanishing, or at least moving into a new phase. One can imagine them in agreement with Dorian's outcry in Wilde's *The Picture of Dorian Gray*:

> '*Fin de siecle*', murmured Lord Henry.
> '*Fin du globe*', answered his hostess.
> 'I wish it were *fin du globe*', said Dorian with a sigh.
> 'Life is a great disappointment'. (Chapter XV)

In Arabic there is an equivalent saying for the *fin-de-siecle which* is *ākhir zaman*, and it is reiterated at times of great disappointment. However, this situation can be well demonstrated from a review article by Jabra Ibrahīm Jabra and Khalīl Ḥāwī's poem: 'Sindbad on his Eighth Voyage'.

In his review titled 'Shaking the Colossal Gate' which appears in a collection of essays and articles under the title *The Eighth Voyage*, Jabra gives an analytical account of initiation into what he calls 'new' Arabic poetry. Jabra refers to a limited number of unknown and unrecognised people who undertook the responsibility of shaking the foundation of a colossal gate which thousands of people insisted on keeping locked in their faces. The limited group includes Najīb al-Rayyes, whose collection of poetry *The Death of Others* is what prompts the review, Tawfīq Ṣāyigh and obviously himself. One other name which should have also been part of the group, although it is not mentioned, is that of Khalīl Ḥāwī.

Interestingly enough, the four poets share the common ground of exile, which is the milieu of their poetry. The four of them wrote their poetry from the River Cam, or on the London-Cambridge train, or in Oxford Street or in Soho Cafes. From those places, they overlooked their homeland thousands of miles behind, and reviewed their past and tradition hundreds of years back in history. Their initiation, then, has a Joycean touch of exile.

Jabra tells us about his own experience when he was a student at Cambridge in the mid-forties and says that he opted to write in English because he could not find in Arabic the forms that were adequate enough to articulate what he wanted to say. Also, he recalls how bitterly disappointed he was when his brother sent him a collection of poetry by Maḥmūd Ali Tāhā, considered in those days a miracle of creativity and creation. Jabra's brother assumed that Jabra would identify himself with the poet of *The Lost Seafarer*, the title of Tāhā's collection. Instead, Jabra found Tāhā's poetry to be 'nonsense, childish music composition and prosaic expressions which had all come together in those poems.'[2] Jabra's disappointment was similarly bitter when he returned to Aḥmad Shawqī's poems 'those Ottoman miniatures, which could no longer be sustained by the experience of a devastating war.'[3] Jabra continues to analyse the situation in a way that is reminiscent of English writers towards the end of the nineteenth century who were referred to by Yeats as the 'tragic generation'. What Jabra says merits quoting at length:

> We had become in those days, although we were a peculiar minority that had not yet been recognized by anyone, part of an era in which superficial 'beauty' was something to be criticized, something closer to the 'beauty' of artificial wax flowers which are not acceptable to a taste that does not find enjoyment except in tense experience and the intensity of feeling, violence and tragedy. We were no longer demanding 'beauty' of art; rather we were demanding vigour, intensity and strength. The tender

> phrase was no longer an objective of creativity, but rather the charged phrase agitated by its symbols. We were no longer lost sailors in a gondola that carried a blond Venetian. We were seas, infinities, mountains, making love, death and imaginary heroes passing through a world of nightmares. We had come to a point where we wanted poetry to provide movement, surprise and the collapse of the castles of illusion over people's heads. That is what I said then, and that is what I am still saying. Therefore, I wrote my poetry in English, because in its ever generative forms, I found space to build effervescent symbols in a few lines in which words would become fiery missiles, exploding and scattering their brightness and sparkling light in the form of meanings that would fall onto one's consciousness like rain. Thus did I want Arabic poetry to be; and it was necessary to wait for a few years, to try to confront deafness and blindness and those who would freeze the imagination until the characteristics of the new style would become apparent in Arabic poetry.[4]

Jabra's tone here echoes that of the literary scene of those English poets whose art was obviously characterised by intensity of feeling and the revolt against the established foundation of the past. Jabra then quotes Najīb al-Rayyes's poem 'Tawfīq Sayegh and the Blind Light' to demonstrate further the vigour of the poetry of initiation attempted by his fellow poet; and a close reading of the poem will bring back to memory the poetry of English poets such as Ernest Dowson, John Davidson, Lionel Johnson and others. Yet the Arabic poetry concerned exhibits more than decadence, intensity, aestheticism and mere reaction against the past. For example, the English poets were satisfied with concluding the revolt against the burden of convention through self-martyrdom because they saw the battle in terms of society versus the individual; i.e., man and artist became one in the battle for freedom from society. In that battle, the poets of 'the tragic generation' took vengeance on society by exhausting themselves emotionally and even physically, a privilege that was not easily available to the individual writer earlier in the century when the social self was obviously dominant.

The Arab writers, on the other hand, were not only dissatisfied with a long era of stagnation in the century to which they belonged, but also with a long history which stretched far beyond the history of the century itself. It was the heavy burden of a past which the Arab writer of the time felt he was carrying on his shoulders, and it was a complex history of politics and society. Perhaps this was the reason why the Arab writer could not afford to find salvation in the individual identity of the artist, or in a kind of autonomy, which, in fact, has been the general goal of the English writer since the latter part of the nineteenth century. This may explain the reason behind the tendency of serious Arab writers to be inevitably committed to a public cause, and their feeling that a non-committal attitude in art would seem to be unrealistic.

Jabra perceptively remarks that the voice of those poets he refers to earlier is more than a cry in the wilderness. It certainly goes beyond despair. It is a voice with a perspective. In the course of his comment on al-Rayyes's poetry, which he quotes, Jabra says:

> Verses that the eye picks out from these poems. Suddenly, they become connected, accumulate and materialize. They are the journey to the end of the earth from the end of the earth; the sharpness of desire in a world that the poet adores and at the same time hates. It takes the form of the desire to sail or ride 'white mares' or a train through plains or seas of sadness, the ship is in the folds of every dream here, going away to an island that resembles the South Sea Islands, where there are palm beaches, sands, burning lips and the last trance. However, this

very act of sailing on the part of the poet is an act of going around the self, the object, the beloved, the hated. He moves away from them all so that he may draw closer to them. He escapes them so that he may carry them on his palm and between his eyelashes. Travel here is not the travel of escape and disintegration in an opium-like illusion. It is the travel of searching and questioning. It takes a generalized form that weaves in all the wonder, fear and desire that a young man has when he, a university student, sees the world as a vision of a bare-breasted mistress. At other times, it takes on a form that is more peculiar to the poet himself, when we learn that he actually does return from London to Cambridge on the night train every Monday, as in the poem 'Tawfīk Ṣayegh and the Blind Light'.[5]

Jabra here sees in the poetry of al-Rayyes and his fellow poets more than Dowson's 'desolate and sick old passion' and Wilde's 'yellow fog creeping down the bridges'. He further notices the deep concern of those poets for man-in-society, which is characteristic of another decade of English poetry: the 1930s, often referred to as Auden's generation. One may say that the poetry discussed by Jabra is a mingling of the personal passion of the yellow 1890s and the public affection of the socially-committed English poets of the 1930s. Jabra would perhaps like to reiterate Auden's words in relation to the artist's social commitment, 'we are the conscripts of our age' and 'no policy of isolation is possible'.[6] Or, he might like to express the situation in Bernard Spencer's lines, which are frequently quoted as the representative voice of the thirties:

> The minimum wish
> For the permanence of the basic things of a life,
> For children and friends and having enough to eat

And the great key of a skill;
The life the generals and the bankers cheat.[7]

However, the voice of Jabra and his fellow poets is not as explicit as that of the 1930s because it is deepened by the intensity of their individual passion. Jabra sees it in the image which gives the poetry and fiction of the time its urgency and vitality. As he says above, 'the ship is in the folds of every dream'. In his quest, the Sindbad poet, Jabra imagines, knows no specific destination, and when he despairs, a counter power emerges to contain such despair or transform it into a positive power. The quest, Jabra further notices, carries with it infinite questioning, which, however, does not end with the traditional echoing reply of Khayyām and Abu Maḍi, 'I don't know', yielding nothing but pessimism and despair.

Part of the answer to the questioning, Jabra comments, is a rejection by the poet of the total reality around him, which he finds too demoralising to accommodate his yearning for a new life.

Out of this grim picture of reality, Jabra remarks, emerges the other part of the answer, i.e., the poet's outcry from a distant horizon coming through the same colossal gate which he carried all the way through. 'Through this very gate I shall return', the poet says, and the ship apparently has not sunk, but has arrived loaded with 'dimaqs*, scents and dew' after a diaspora 'at all gates'. Jabra then says that the poet may not necessarily return with the Golden Fleece. He may return like Ulysses 'to find his home in a state of ruin with its blocking doors falling down; he would return to the old clock which has stopped 'as if time has come to an end / and the last one of us / has perished / along with others.'[8]

Jabra concludes his review article by saying that the poet returns after voyaging and almost perishing with others, struggling with scepticism for the sake of faith and coming back from the underworld to the reality he once turned his back on, but now eager to see afresh, and with a new vision.

5. 'SINDBAD THE PORTER': A HOUSE WITH A VIEW

In its overt pattern Surūr's poem follows a traditional form of narrative: a narrator telling the story of Shahrazad, who, in turn, tells the story of Sindbad. The story-within-a-story pattern is what obliquely produces the subtlety of the whole narrative and creates the relational distance which determines the meaningful interrelatedness between narrator, Shahrazad and Sindbad. For example, the narrator hides himself behind Shahrazad in the same way that Shahrazad hides herself behind the story of Sindbad, and the result is that the story of one becomes inevitably that of the other. Like a symphony, the narrative in 'Sindbad the Porter' is divided into four parts. The first is a melody in which Shahrazad offers a celebration of life, despite its inevitable mortality, as she sings for the ephemeral but joyful part of life which precedes death. It is like a hymn or prologue where a generalisation becomes specific only later on in the other parts of the narrative.

The second part is a description of the reality in which Sindbad finds himself imprisoned. It is hell, and this is what drives Sindbad to consider leaving his home, wife, children and people. 'It is said he approached the sea one morn,' and it is here that his journey is suddenly discontinued, but only to bring about a review of his whole situation through deep contemplation. In quest of truth, he questions the various aspects of the objective world around him: 'And where the journeys of the birds did end!' (One really wonders whether this verse is the source of Muḥmūd Darwīsh's famous poem 'After the Last Sky', which Edward Sa'īd takes as the title for his book). The main part of his questioning, however, occurs when he says: 'For in this world is food / and within the seas and hills is wealth / enough to satisfy humanity / so why starve we?' This brings back to his mind the image of his home country, the City of Agony, where people are condemned to starvation and death. He also remembers his family and buries his tears in the sand, which he, in an earlier part of the poem, consults for the truth. But Sindbad soon notices a call coming from the dark like a ray of light, and this makes the grieving Sindbad smile.

The third part reiterates the conclusion of the previous one, but only to promote the call: 'A ship there along the horizon / like the shining wing of a bird.' The sight of the ship captures Sindbad's imagination, and he almost signals it. His imagination is further activated by the visionary Wāqwāq, the land of prosperity (it is also the land of terror). Again Sindbad is about to signal the ship. But the picture of his home country floods back into his thoughts, alive and more intense than before. Consequently, he becomes reluctant to go any further away from home. The conclusion of this part has a similar but finer tone than the previous one. It is the apparition of a true call pointing to salvation in the form of 'A flock of birds after a winter's journey / returns home.' In the previous part, we remember, Sindbad asks where the journeys of the birds end, but in this part, he sees them returning, and further asks what the reason behind their return may be. Then he himself decides to return.

In the fourth part, Sindbad himself returns to hell to create paradise. This is the familiar mythical return: *paradiso terrestra.* When the question about the way out is asked (whether by Sindbad himself to himself or by other people, it is not specified) the answer comes in the form of a tale which tells the story of the vulnerable chicks and the vicious raven. Only when a wise bird suggests that the raven should be killed are the birds confident that their little ones will be safe. Immediately afterwards 'all became Sindbad'. With this economical phrase, the sense of solidarity is made concrete. It is natural that a celebration follows, thus ending the tale with a crowning experience.

Between the beginning celebration and the closing one lies the covert structure of Sindbad's journey, which is told not through the traditional narrative sequence of events, but through a novel organic scheme of imagery and symbolism. The effect is gradually intensified as the narrative progresses from one part to another. A main part of the imagery takes the form of a flying motif in which the bird, as a symbol, plays an important part throughout the narrative. After all, Sindbad's journey is an act of flying which often suggests free movement and a yearning to reach the free remote world.[1] Like birds who migrate to a more congenial environment, Sindbad has the desire to move away from oppressive reality. This recalls Joyce's Stephen Dedalus in *A Portrait of the Artist as a Young Man*, where Dedalus makes frequent imaginative flights to overcome the sense of imprisonment which he finds himself undergoing. The motif of flying in Joyce's novel is familiar enough to preclude the need for further elaboration.[2]

However, Surūr's poem breaks fresh ground in presenting the total picture of Sindbad, particularly that of Sindbad the Porter, which has been overshadowed by its counter, Sindbad the Sailor. As a matter of fact, the narrative of Sindbad the Porter here is made to form the original framework for the narrative of Sindbad the Sailor, which probably accounts for the fact that the latter has overwhelmed the former.

Instead of basking in the romantic adventures of Sindbad the Sailor, Surūr probes and sifts rigourously for a serious perspective in the original framework of the story, which is usually overlooked and considered as being merely functional.

Surūr first makes Sindbad the Porter independent of his counterpart by making him lay down his heavy burden (sack) on a rock, whereas in the original narrative of *The Arabian Nights*, Sindbad the Porter lays down his load opposite the house of Sindbad the Sailor, and contact is thus eventually established between the two of them.[3]

Surūr then digs up two allusions from the original story and expands them to become the basis of the whole vigorous narrative voice. The first allusion in the original narrative evokes a sense of injustice, which Sindbad the Porter obliquely expresses when he sarcastically describes himself as being 'hot and tired and poor and miserable'[4] in contrast to Sindbad the Sailor and others 'like him', whose lives are full of comfort and delight. The other allusion comes in the verses which Sindbad the Porter sings just before he is invited (as a result of his voice being heard) to meet the master of the house: Sindbad the Sailor. These are the verses as they occur in the original:

> I have heard of poor men waking
> in the shadow of a palace
> but the solace
> of such waking
> is not for me.
> I have seen the rich man's burden,
> heavy gold on gold increasing;
> but the blessing
> of that burden
> is not for me.
> Though more heavy than those others
> is the load which makes me weary,
> what I carry
> is for others
> not for me.

Out of this embryo, Sindbad the Porter emerges and grows to become in Surūr's narrative a man of all people and not simply a poor man who realises his wretchedness in comparison to the rich people around him. He is no longer a man who roams around in self-pity.

However, Sindbad the Porter has something essential in common with Sindbad the Sailor. Both Sindbads are imaginative, and their wanderings are mainly related to their imaginative quest for truth. Such a quest can be identified with what Claude Levi-Strauss calls 'shared motivation', which relates the different parties of the narrative to one another.

It is imagination, then, that makes Sindbad the Porter strong enough to carry out a narrative independent of Sindbad the Sailor. Yet Sindbad the Porter distinguishes himself from Sindbad the Sailor by the way he allows this very power of imagination to affect him. Surūr puts his Sindbad in control of imagination instead of allowing him to be controlled by it as is the case with Sindbad the Sailor. This distinction takes place at what I consider the climax of the poem, where Sindbad the Porter resists the temptation of boarding the ship to the land of Wāqwāq, which would eventually take him away to see the wonders of the world. With Sindbad the Porter, imagination is not transformed into romance. The distinction between the two becomes clear, when one Sindbad curbs his imagination, which would enable him to see through the present situation, while the other Sindbad gives in to wild imagination which carries him to the land of romance, the Wāqwāq, for example.

In Levi-Strauss's terms, Sindbad the Porter can again be identified with the modern thinker whose intellectual powers help him to join 'at one extreme the history of the world and at the other the history of myself, and it unveils the shared motivation of one and the other at the same moment.'[6]

This is enacted throughout the recurrent duplication and expansion of Sindbad's consciousness. However, Sindbad's dramatic progression is not merely a state of flux presenting thinking as a thinking process, but rather a transforming power which brings about the realisation of his awareness of the situation.

Thus he abandons the waiting ship as the state of feeling becomes concrete specific thought that determines his course of action.

Sindbad's decision to return home can also be viewed in the light of the mythical thought in the *Odyssey*, where Odysseus's 'great shrewdness' guides him towards 'the return to life and light'. Although the narrative of Sindbad here is obviously much compressed, and is comparatively far less in magnitude, identification of the folktale Sindbad with the mythical Odysseus is, I think, illuminating. The invocation with which the narrative begins has the bearing of the mythical prologue and ritual. More obvious is the City of Agony, which can be read as the underworld, Hades, where the spirits of the dead reside. Furthermore, what Sindbad sees in the City of Agony recalls the picture of the dead in Hades:

> The thousands within the City of Agony
> are captives-like women-behind a wall
> are chewed by eagles and hawks
> ....
> In the City of Agony the women are eaten
> the men are crucified behind its impenetrable gate
> the young are buried alive
> blood is drunk
> ....
> heads are strung into necklaces
> and skins are ripped off.

The picture of 'lions crouching at the great gate' of the City of Agony brings back to memory the gate of Circe, whose residence in the *Odyssey* is midway between the two worlds where she stands to usher the hero into the underworld and to receive him back again from it. The ship which Sindbad resists the temptation of boarding is like Circe's own. Both Odysseus and Sindbad guard themselves against the temptation of being carried away to the world of oblivion.[7]

However, the most striking correspondence between Sindbad and Odysseus is summed up in the following two lines: 'Sindbad was fleeing from all / he returns not who enters hell.' Whether it is Dante's hell or Homer's Hades, it is the same mythical place which stands at the centre of mythology. Like Odysseus, Sindbad survives it all and alone.

More corresponding details can be seen in the thousands (including Sindbad's wife and children) left in the City of Agony to suffer. This recalls Odysseus's companions who perished during the journey. Another detail is the solar mythology, which is activated throughout the narrative. The sun's positive as well as its negative aspects play an important role first in the destruction of life and then in its resurrection. Thus the rotary cycle of nature then enacts the human cycle, and this, we know, is most characteristic of the mythical cycle. A third detail is the country of Wāqwāq, which inspires the picture of the Lotus-eaters, or the place of oblivion in the lower world (and this recalls al-Masnāwī's Sindbad).

Thus the folktale of 'Sindbad' is seen in a new perspective which promotes its effect to the level of myth. Surūr, here, gives the familiar narrative of Sindbad an intellectual dimension which curbs the formless flow of traditional romance and restores it from the world of wonder and darkness to the world of 'life and light', which writers in the 1950s seemed to have envisaged as imminent.

6. 'THE FACES OF SINDBAD': A HOUSE IN EXILE

More than any modern writer Khalīl Ḥāwī was seriously preoccupied with the story of Sindbad, and this can be well demonstrated by his Sindbad poems which were published in *al-Ādāb* between 1958 and 1960. 'The Faces of Sindbad' was the first poem in what looks like trilogy, and it was published in the first number of *al-Ādāb* in 1958. Later in the same year 'Sindbad on his Eighth Voyage' was published, and about two years later the same poem with some revisions and a shifting of emphasis was published in the same journal, and this last poem has become the main poem in any collection of poetry by Ḥāwī. This demonstrates Ḥāwī's deep concern with the story of Sindbad as a motif for his poetry.[1]

'The Faces of Sindbad' has no direct bearing on the original story of Sindbad and the allusion Ḥāwī makes in his modern poem to the old Sindbad is quite oblique. Except for the title there is no explicit reference to the old story of Sindbad upon which Ḥāwī draws. It seems that Ḥāwī drew upon the general framework of the tale of Sindbad, making the voyager in life undergo different circumstances, and consequently becoming a different Sindbad each time. What attracts us most to the story of Sindbad is not the amazingly sensational effect which its adventures conjure up, but the vigour and vitality which Sindbad displays in those adventures and the way he adapts to new circumstances, out of which emerges a new personality. Ḥāwī develops this framework of changing situation which results from the interplay between Sindbad and circumstances by internalising the external effect of the old story. His Sindbad looks into himself to explore the changing states of mind which express themselves as changing phases. It is a journey within rather than a journey without.

Also Ḥāwī exploits the thematic pattern of Sindbad sailing after the unknown, but while the old Sindbad sails in the wide world for this purpose, Ḥāwī's Sindbad sails through his complex psyche in a similar quest. The shift of emphasis is obviously from the objective world to the subjective self. Ḥāwī introduces his poem with a discussion presumably designed to serve as a kind of prologue in which he remarks on how Dante, Rossetti and Hopkins believe in the ideal beauty as the origin of that which is real yet ephemeral to this world. Meanwhile he criticises Yeats for shifting the emphasis of the tension that moves between the mortal real and the immortal ideal, to the realm of art as the permanent ideal of beauty. Imagination, Ḥāwī remarks, is a haven where escapists find a shelter. Ḥāwī concludes his preface by asserting his belief in what D.H. Lawrence terms 'the life of the blood' as the only immortal force which survives from one generation to another. This force, Ḥāwī believes, is what defeats the conquering power of time.

Ḥāwī's conviction is embodied in the last part of the poem, which he titles 'The Eternal Face'. In this part the speaker invites the beloved to collect the ruins of both herself and himself (metaphorically) in order to build a new life after the exhausting journey which has left them both lost, as their faces evidently show. Out of the ruins, he envisages, resurrection will take place. The last stanza is an invocation to that effect.

The poem is divided into nine parts with the following titles: 'Two faces'; 'A Prisoner in a Train'; 'With the Gypsies'; 'After Fever'; 'The Paradise of Boredom'; 'Forged Cards and Masks'; 'In the Darkness of the Womb'; 'The Two Faces'; 'The Eternal Face'.

The divisions are obviously made after the traditional numerals of Sindbad's voyages, and the fact that Ḥāwī makes the number of divisions here (and in the other poem) exceed seven, simply suggests his intention of going beyond the traditional tale of Sindbad without following its wide canvas of narrative but while preserving its wide perspective.

In all its parts the poem presents the speaker's face left behind with the beloved in the cedars of Lebanon and the other faces encountered in his migration to the north, to Cambridge. The poem can be read as an alternation of the face he has at home and the mask he travels with away from home in England.[2] This is again the story of the old Sindbad who survives with two conflicting impulses; one for peaceful life at home and settlement and the other for an adventurous life in the remote regions of the world. The temporary dominance of one at any given time does not efface the other, and this is what keeps the alternation of effect in a state of flux.

The first part tells us about the face as seen in the beloved's eyes, a tender brown face whose image has not been affected by what the other face has actually experienced and suffered over the years. The other face, the speaker tells us, is composed of many faces; it is the face of the one who went astray.

The second part describes the experience of the first day which the speaker underwent in a foreign land. 'Bitter were his monotonous nights' as he often slept with frustrating desire and gnawing memory. 'A prisoner in a train / deprived of the elixir of the sun / and the salty shower of the sea-wind'. The experience of the Cambridge train at night (which has been the attraction of many English writers like Virginia Woolf and E.M. Forster) is juxtaposed with that of the sunny sea-shore of Beirut. The two faces are put in juxtaposition. But soon the speaker's face is eaten up by dust (metaphorically referring to time) and a new face emerges with no past or memory.

The third part is about the speaker's participation in a gypsy dance which may not be more than a wild party. He acquires the face of a gypsy. To use Eliot's term he is caught between desire and memory, and runs from the fever of one to the fire of the other as his face shows.

The fourth part briefly alludes to the face which recovers from fever and settles in a vacuum with a winter fire ablaze.

The speaker's face is neutralised in the fifth part with no impression to reveal. It is the face of that student who sits in a corner of a museum or a library, a face sweating and crucified on an old journey, on silent old pictures and on stone faces. Eternal silence inspires him with comfort. Boredom is in his blood and in his eyes. 'His face is made of stone / among stone faces.'

The sixth part shows how the speaker wears masks whenever he is invited to socialise with others, and although he prefers a woman's company to that of a man he is not himself with either. As he walks in the dark street, some light steals through to disperse the emptiness of masks. However one mask stays with him and he gazes at it, but decides not to go along with that mask even if he were invited to do so. Here is a turning point in the poem similar in pattern to that in the story of 'Sindbad the Porter', who almost gives in to the appeal of the waiting ship and almost signals it as we see above. Like Sindbad the Porter, the speaker resists the temptation of following a dream from which he may not be able to come back to reality.

Only in this sixth part the mask acquires specific reference. In the previous parts the mask is only hinted at by responding to a passive desire in the attempt to search for an alternative to a restless situation which results from leaving the speaker's face (always home in Sindbad's case) behind. The close contact between face and mask seems to bring about a new awareness which leads the speaker to a decisive attitude, and the following three parts demonstrate this attitude in a state of gradation.

The seventh part, as its title 'In the Darkness of the Womb' shows, is a kind of rebirth. The speaker pleads with passers-by to tread gently on 'our nerves'. 'We are rather tired, not dead / of a dirty fog with a dodging worn-out face / winding like a snake, an acrobat / with riddles / Ours is the womb of the earth not the nasty weather.[3] The same pleading is continued. 'We are in the darkness of a comfortable arch / removing fever from our faces, making up, singing / concealing ourselves / and hiding what we have suffered over the years.'

All this leads to the act of separating the face from the mask in the eighth part, 'The Two Faces', and the revelation of the face which he left behind comes suddenly:

> While I was removing the dust of the arch
> from above my face [its memory],
> I looked around and bowed
> over her eyes, I saw
> the face of a child
> choked with tears, in the airport cafe
> when she said to me what she did often and again
> as if time makes no difference to defying maids
> like fairytales to children.

The last part begins with a confession on the part of the speaker who admits that neither his beloved's face nor his own can escape the tyranny of time, and this, he says, is evidently seen on both faces. 'Some life in us has died, let it be buried, but why / should we weave illusion and close our mind?' The call for a union with the beloved then follows. The poem concludes with a tone of prophetic morality similar to that of Lawrence and many other modern writers.

7 'SINDBAD ON HIS EIGHTH VOYAGE': A HOUSE RESTORED

In the early poem Ḥāwī concerns himself with the question of immortality which takes the shape of a polar tension between the two impulses of settlement and travel as we find in the old Sindbad. Yet the resolution of polarity is not the same; while the old Sindbad opts for settlement, Ḥāwī's modern one searches for continuity as seen in the universal motif of the child and the archetype of resurrection. Ḥāwī's Sindbad has the same traditional romantic tone of the old Sindbad, but romance is presented only to defy its structure and transform it into a solid perspective of reality. It seems that Ḥāwī starts his poem from where Shahrazad finishes the story of Sindbad:

> Sindbad the Sailor gave a feast to his guests, which lasted thirty nights, and then appointed Sindbad the Porter to be his major-domo. The two lived together in perfect friendship and joy until they were visited by that which breathes upon delight, which snaps the links of friendship, which destroys palaces and raises tombs where once they stood: by bitter death. Glory be to the Living who dies not![1]

Ḥāwī evidently tends here to defy domineering time with all its mortality. He similarly tries to go beyond the traditional nostalgia for the past, the face he had left behind.

Also in 'Sindbad on his Eighth Voyage' Ḥāwī begins from where all Sindbad's travels end, as the title itself obviously suggests. In a similar way, Ḥāwī prefaces the poem with a statement in prose from which we know that Sindbad's journey is a rejection of the material world for the spiritual one. It is a journey within which he explores the trying experience of sailing inwards. The preface points to 'Sindbad's suffering over the period of his ascension from the labyrinths of his self until he experienced the dawn of resurrection and the certitude of his knowledge was complete'.

This poem is undoubtedly a remarkable expansion of the previous one. It intensifies the effect of 'The Faces of Sindbad' and extends its new dimension. The face becomes Sindbad's home which he carries in exile and tries to rebuild by first emptying it of its past in the hope of tempting that passer-by (a vision, an inspiration or an apparition) to stop and be claimed by the speaker who feels it within him but cannot make it concrete for himself. In order to have communion with this vision he has to dissociate himself from all the restrictions of his home as embodied in the heavy burden of the past which ranges from Moses's fiery chisel to al-Ma'arri's deep cavern.

The house, then, is an extended metaphor of the face; and the attempt to empty it of all that it contains (including the material gains of Sindbad gained over the years) is an attempt to remove the mask from the face. Yet the tension between face and mask in this poem acquires a deeper but clearer dimension. The mask is the decaying history which the speaker makes his journey through and the face can be identified with Jung's 'primordial experience'.

Unlike the early poem, this one is not a simple, straightforward narrative structure of metaphors. It is rather an elaborate image of self-exploration. Sindbad here is not concerned with telling the story of the adventures he has already experienced.

> My seven voyages and my treasure amassed
> through the bounty of the Almighty and trade,
> the day I slew the monster
> and the devil, ... my burial,
> then that crack in the cave,
> I have told the tales they usually tell about me.

All these incidents occur in the tale of the original Sindbad and the speaker here lays emphasis on his intention to break away from that Sindbad by adding: 'I suppressed what cannot be rendered in words, / yet continue to go in pursuit of him.'

Ḥāwī's Sindbad makes it clear that his purpose goes beyond the sensation of story-telling and adventure. His reference to the fact that he related what people usually relate about him obliquely refers to the deeper level of reality which narration cannot probe and convey to people. Even the narrator himself may stand helpless as he tries to communicate in narrative the sensation he feels, and the gap between narrator and audience remains forever without a bridge, as demonstrated by Conrad's Marlow, who is the classical example of this literary phenomenon.

The speaker is concerned with creating a reality which he does not know rather than telling of a familiar reality. The poem can be described as 'a portrait of the artist as Sindbad'. It is here that the tension between face and mask is intensified, as Ḥāwī sees it in the eternal tension between life and art, history and fiction or between romance and reality. Ḥāwī's Sindbad, who is much more than a figure of romance, stands for the artist who is seriously preoccupied with seeing through the facade of reality often created by story-telling.

The tension of creativity is expressed in the line which is reiterated throughout the poem: 'I sense him within me yet I do not grasp him.' This can be read in the light of what Jung says about the creative process in art:

> Any reaction to stimulus may be causally explained; but the creative act, which is the absolute antithesis of mere reaction, will forever elude the human understanding. It can only be described in its manifestations; it can be obscurely sensed, but never wholly grasped.[2]

In his reiteration of his state of feeling the speaker in Ḥāwī's poem implies that the poem is a process of creation rather than a mode of narration. For this reason he expresses himself in terms of ideogrammic thought which shows rather than tells. The poem recalls 'The Waste Land', for it has the manifestations of Eliot's 'The Burial of the Dead' and 'What The Thunder Said' which prepares for rebirth at the end. Its imagery is elaborate enough to deserve a separate discussion. Yet Ḥāwī's Sindbad is more than Eliot's portraits because he survives 'life in death' and is eventually saved with the gracious vision.

The tension in the poem develops in the polarity between the creative mind and the suffering person (to use Eliot's description). On one occasion the speaker describes this tension as follows:

> and a vision that could find no word,
> choked, tears shone and trembled.
> Is it an invitation to love this voice
> the phantom that shone in the sun
> took on flesh and scooped from my body
> bread and salt,
> wine and fire?
> Alone I wait.

Yet the tension is released when the vision is captured:

> Today, as the vision sings in my blood
> with the tremble of lightning and the brightness of morning,
> ....
> The vision overflows, and what then!
> There shall come an hour,
> when I say what I have to say.

Before the vision is realised the speaker experiences 'the vision that occasionally overpowers [him]' and he cries.

Suffering and creating are obviously interrelated. 'I spat out the poison and the curses, / words flowed from my mouth.' In Eliot's phrase the process of creation is known as the depersonalisation which demands that the personality of the artist be separated from the creative mind, and this is what presumably causes suffering. Before the resolution of the tension the speaker struggles quite hard to empty his house from all that makes it, and in specific terms, to dissociate himself from all that makes up his present self as it stands in its state of consciousness, which is the accumulation of the past.

To bridge the gap between mask and face, between vision and reality, between what he senses and what be cannot grasp, some kind of metamorphosis between him and nature takes place:

> Perhaps it was the sea and the chafing of the waves and wind
> perhaps it was the white trance and the ice
> that sealed my veins to the veins of the earth,
> the white shroud was a shield
> under which the spring fermented,
> my heart grew verdant,
> throbbed with the tender-winged sails of the lilies.

Union between speaker and nature which further promote the sense of metamorphosis is given detailed description in part seven of the poem, and Ḥāwī here seems to find in Fry's archetype of cyclical nature an appropriate form for his expression.[3] Earlier in the poem the speaker makes it a point that the process of transformation which led to capturing the vision is not abrupt or incidental, and it is, by no means, a kind of 'deus ex machina': 'I shall not claim that the angel of the lord / poured holy wine and live embers / into my body imprisoned by ice, / drained my veins of the blood / congested with gas and poisons.' Also there is particular emphasis in the poem on the fact that the speaker's vision is more than individual and that he unites with nature as a collective consciousness seriously concerned with society: 'I would not have been able to celebrate / the sun had I not seen you all bathing / at morning in the Nile, the Jordan and the Euphrates / freed from the stain of sin.' This is, I think , a crucial point in the poem where the personal is fused with the public.

The visionary perspective of the poem is made clear towards the end, in the conclusion of the ninth part: 'There will come a time when I shall embrace / the land and purify her heart / wipe away the borders.' Earlier in the poem the distinction between the speaker Sindbad and the old Sindbad is made clear: 'A certain vision realised by the eye and the touch / not a tale invented by tellers.'

However this is not a parody in which the speaker Sindbad ridicules the old one. Ḥāwī here touches on a fundamental generic issue in art which has been a serious concern for modern writers. Lukacs, for example, wrote *The Historical Novel* (1920) with the intention of making the novel substitute the form of epic literature, and when Pound began his *Cantos* in the second decade of the century he was not comfortable with verse as an epic form, and this obviously justifies the continuous revisions of the early *Cantos*.

Commenting on Pound's performance in epic form Michael Bernstein quotes Eric Havelock saying '"The narrative is ... to be regarded not as an end in itself but as a vehicle for transmitting the material of the tribal encyclopaedia which is ... dispersed into a thousand narrative contexts."'[4] With this notion of the narrative, Ḥāwī writes his Sindbad. Ḥāwī transmits (and transforms as well) the material of the old Sindbad in a way that renders the original narrative not more than a motif. We know, for example, that *al-ghūl* in the old Sindbad is a legendary monster with infinite power, and that Sindbad not only encounters but also subdues that monster. Ḥāwī's *al-ghūl* is an extended metaphor which stands for human monstrosity and corruption in present society, its conquest means a triumph over evil, and this is demonstrated by the poet from his reference to those historical incidents which took place in the 1950s, the two revolutions in Egypt and Iraq, the Suez Canal Crisis and the liberation of the army in Jordan. This is how the speaker celebrates this triumph: 'Long have I rebelled, lashed the monster / and his toadies in my land. / I spat out the poison and the curses, / words flowed from my mouth / a torrent of packs of wolves.' Immediately follows the speaker's vision which crowns the celebration.

In reading the poem it is essential, I believe, to see how or when the speaker captures his vision! The speaker is evidently inspired by the bright spot of his national history and this is what helps him empty his house, and further sees life coming out of decadence, as the vision finds a concrete expression in cyclical nature. The personal element in the speaker and the public one in his history are fused together in such a way as to make one transformed by or into the other to realise what is known as the totality of vision.

The poem concludes with a final celebration when the speaker, Sindbad, returns home, not though like the old Sindbad with capital and profit. He lost both and came back with a vision which is his tale to his tribe:

> I have lost the capital and the profit,
> I return to you a poet with a gospel in his mouth
> saying what he says
> with an instinct that feels what is in the womb of the season
> sees it before it is born into the seasons.

Ḥāwī's Sindbad loses the capital and the profit in a way similar to that of Surūr who misses altogether the ship of capital and profit, and although the two poets use different symbols the perspective of their vision is the same, in the sense that both see a restored unity with nature and fellowship with society.

8. 'THE SINDBAD CITY': OUT OF PLACE

The city is Baghdad, the capital of the glorious Caliph, Hārūn al-Rashīd. Sindbad lived and prospered during what is known as a legendary history of the great sovereign, who ushered Arab Islamic civilization into the golden age.

With the title of the poem Badr al-Sayyāb, a most celebrated poet of Modern Arabic poetry conceals himself behind the tale of Sindbad in the same way Sindbad concealed himself behind the egg of the rukh, the monstrous bird, and made his plans during the night to get out of the island where he found himself strangled (see note 1. Sindbad the Porter). Jabra, the well-known novelist, said to me that his fellow poet called on him one night just after he had been released from jail and talked to him about escaping the city of Sindbad to Kuwait or Beirut, and that he could not bear more torture and humiliation morally and physically (he was quite fragile). Surūr's imaginative 'City of Agony' has become here a real one as its agonizing experience the poet has been actually exposed to at the hands of the party regime (1959-60).

With the exception of the title the poem makes no explicit reference to Sindbad, and the effect of the motif is made through what is referred to in social discourse as the absence of the 'Other'. By suppressing the traditional picture of Sindbad, the poet depends on the convention of the tale whose details readers are quite familiar with. Raymond Williams once observed that Conrad was able to say so much about imperialism in *Heart of Darkness* without having to mention imperialism itself by name.

Without any instruction from the poem the reader is aware of the fact that Baghdad, which is the subject of the poet's experience, is not the city of the most happy traveller who used to come back to it with great longing. The contrast between that Baghdad of the Sindbad and the present Baghdad is marked by the speaker's rhetorical question which articulates the irony in view:

> Is this my city?
> With 'LONG LIVE LIFE'
> Traced on those ruins
> ....
> Is this my city, the daggers of Tartars

Are embedded over its gate
....
Is this my city with wounded domes
....

The poem can be titled or subtitled with such question which obviously leads to a similar rhetorical question: What happened to my city? Yet the present title remains safer for the poet as it can conceal the straightforward shift of time which forms some protection against the offensive authority he has already known.

The articulate effect generated in the poem depends mainly on the old pattern of the tale whose reality is structured around the communal sense of life. For example, there is no reference to any personal loss on the part of the speaker. It is 'the whole way of life' in Raymond Williams' terms which is affected and reaches such lamentable state. The portrait of Sindbad city can be also viewed in the light of Eliot's 'objective correlative' where the evocation made by the various images ends up in objectifying (equating) the feelings of the individual poet. Thus the significance of the poem lies in the disruption of rhythm in Sindbad's communal life.

As mentioned above, the disruption of rhythm in Sindbad's life has become the inspiring motif for the portrait of this different Sindbad in modern Arabic poetry and fiction. Yet writers vary in handling this motif after they take the disrupting rhythm as a starting point. Some portraits of Sindbad discussed above end with a perspective which the usual Sindbad tale normally generates at the end implying a hopeful tone. 'Aflaq's Sindbad, for example, leaves this world as a Christ crucified for the welfare of humanity afterwards; Surūr's 'City of Agony' is destroyed at the end and replaced by a steadfast one where youths are wedded and singing goes on until morning; Ḥāwī's Sindbad returns a poet with a gospel in his mouth ushering the productive prophecy of seasons.

Al-Sayyāb, on the other hand, ends as he begins with the palm trees wailing upon the short-line.

It may be interesting to remember that Ḥāwī and al-Sayyāb wrote their Sindbad poetry at about the same time, but from different places with different experiences. For Ḥāwī, Sindbad was a home in exile which inspired him on Cambridge train, in the great libraries and museums of the City of Cambridge, and no doubt such milieu is expected to yield a positive inspiring effect to balance or, at least, to alleviate the sense of loss already encountered by the poet. Al-Sayyāb was actually witnessing death 'in a handful of dust', Evelyn Waugh's phrase which was used by Eliot in 'The Waste Land'. It was natural that the scene would be rendered in a naturalistic manner, with the pressing sense of death which leaves little or no room for accommodating an alternative with a way out of the dilemma.

In Auden's words quoted above with reference to the socially-committed poets of the 1930s, al-Sayyāb is one of the great 'conscriptors of our age' who was able to capture with great vigour the reality of a 'whole way of life' breaking down shortly after the Revolution. To realise how prophetic al-Sayyāb was, we have only to read or reread what he wrote in the 1960s. One of his poems, and a very popular one, is titled 'The Blind Prostitute', another evasive title for 'The Sindbad City'. Yet the poem which was written in this context and celebrated as one of the greatest poem in modern Arabic poetry, often considered the Arabic Waste Land, is 'The Song of Rain'. In this poem al-Sayyāb presents the 'Sindbad City' or to be more comprehensive the Sindbad Country from Baṣra to Baghdad as a dry arid place waiting for salvation to restore life to it. Its beginning reminds us of the ending of the 'Sindbad City' where the image of the palm tree is crucial. Here are the two verses, memorised by various Arab readers, which the poems begins with 'Your eyes are two palm-groves at dawn / or two battlements that the moon begins to leave'.

The 'Sindbad City' serves, I think, a good link, if needed, from the Sindbad poetry to the Sindbad fiction, at least for its controlled sentiment of poetry which probably lends it the special privilege of objectivity fiction (more than poetry, perhaps) enjoys.

9. 'THE SEVEN VOYAGES OF SINDBAD': A NIGHTMARE VOYAGE

Fahmī's narrator distorts every romantic element of Sindbad's tale and the atmosphere of *The Arabian Nights* to make them functional enough to express modern reality. He makes the distortion almost complete and, with the exception of Maḥfūẓ's novel *Layālī Alf Laylah*, Fahmī's Seven Voyages of Sindbad remains the most extended work of fiction which expresses traditional romance with such obvious but expressive inversion.

The dignified Shahrazad becomes in The Seven Voyages a narrator whose mission is to forge truth even when she is warned against doing so by Sindbad, who hands over his own life story to her (at her urgent request) and finds out later that she makes no effort to tell the truth about him. She and Sindbad believe in the power the word can generate in human beings, but they have different attitudes towards its function. Although she knows the truth, Shahrazad tells Shahrayar what he wants to hear. Here it seems that Fahmī makes a perceptive portrait of the existing authority which insists on a certain type of truth for its institution, establishment or regime, so that people will not see it as it actually is. Another portrait is made of Shahrazad, who contrives certain stories for Shahrayar's benefit, and the official voice of authority, which has no choice about what it conveys through the mass media to the public. This, Fahmī must have thought, applied to a number of qualified people who put their skills and intelligence at the service of authority.

Sindbad, then, finds it crucial to take over narration and he justifies the matter to his friends (an imaginary audience addressed as friends in the oral tradition) saying:

> I would like to refute Shahrazad's practice of forgery and tell you myself my own life story. I am the earth. I will tell you of my own panting along the way; I will let you hear my hoarse cough behind the damp wall. But that will not scratch your ears, for you are all like me, panting on a far-stretching path. Some of you pant after a glowing pearl; some of you pant after a rusty coin; and some of you pant towards a stagnant pond. But we, all of us, pant, sweat and cough, and all of us at the end of the path die and to the earth we return. (p. 11.)

The last phrase does not suggest the traditional reconciliation to eternity as we find in the original conclusion of Sindbad's Seventh Voyage, but rather the continuity of life which results from the organic unity between man and nature, an emphasis made earlier by Ḥāwī in his two poems. Sindbad had lived close to the earth long enough to be able to see reality in various modes relevant to the earth. (reference to 'earth' is very frequent in the early part of the narrative). A less frequent reference is made to 'the damp wall' which may suggest the atmosphere of a cell, perhaps an evocation made by the original Sindbad's cave.

Thus begins the First Voyage, and the entire narrative flows in a series of parallel incidents which are obviously an inversion of the original Sindbad's account. The narrative opens with the chief merchant trying to calm down his fellow merchants, who are furious when they hear that Sindbad is broke, because they fear that he will not be able to pay off his debt to them. He acts as a mediator who tries to prevent an attack on Sindbad. In the end

Sindbad's palace is auctioned under the supervision of the chief merchant, but Sindbad withdraws before the auction is finalised, promising the chief merchants to find ways and means of paying the merchants their money. He thinks his friends will lend him the money needed, but none of his ten friends shows up although they are supposed to have met at Sindbad's palace for entertainment that same evening. His mistress advises him to go to Hārūn al-Rashīd for help. When he is ushered into the palace, Sindbad is questioned by the Caliph to see whether he is a poet to praise him; a biographer to narrate the life of his grandfather al-ʻAbbas; a debaucher bringing Circassian girls, a comedian with jokes or a singer to entertain! As he finds that Sindbad is none of these he asks his guards to dump him into the deep pit under the palace, and there he lies to experience hell itself.

In comparison we find that the original Sindbad's fellow men always extended help to him and even protected his property when he was thought to have drowned; and as pointed out in Section II.1 (The Old Sindbad: an Image of Fellowship and Settlement) Sindbad's goods were auctioned on his behalf with the intention of sending the money to his heirs. The old code of mutual trust between Sindbad and his fellow men is countered here by a world of total mistrust.

The other parallel incident that is inverted involves Sindbad and Hārūn al-Rashīd. The *Ambassadorial Mission* of Sindbad is a most memorable incident in *The Arabian Nights*, and it reveals the total confidence between citizen and state. In contrast we find in Fahmī's story a hostile and corrupt Hārūn al-Rashīd who does not mind torturing his subjects to death.

Also the pit has a parallel in the old Sindbad, and Faḥmī certainly patterned it on the incident in which Sindbad is buried with the dead. But the old Sindbad's burial was not a punishment; it was the custom of the community to bury the surviving partner with his dead one as a sign of fidelity to partnership. Sindbad knew about this and anticipated his burial ahead of time. Also there was a beast which the original Sindbad saw frequenting the cave. The difference, however, was that one beast was sent by the sovereign with a definite motive, and the other was only part of wild nature which had nothing to do with evil designs by man against man. No where in *The Arabian Nights* does Sindbad encounter a ruthless man; on the contrary people whom he meets, no matter how strange they are, have sympathy and hospitality to extend. Despite the dangers the old Sindbad experiences, none is brought about by the malice of man or a vile society, and this, I think, accentuates the contrast between the cases of the two Sindbads.

Yet the contrast between the scene of the cave and that of the pit is further emphasised by the different effect each scene leaves on us. In the old scene of the cave we are under the spell of romance and the wonders of the world, for Sindbad always fights the same battle against wild nature which he always has the courage, patience and skill to tame and subdue. The pit scene, on the other hand, stirs horror in us because this Sindbad is first horrified by the wickedness of man and then terrorised by the beast which man uses to inflict on his fellow men the penalty of death.

This is part of the pit scene, which I am quoting here at length for its significant climactic effect:

> I suddenly realised that I could no longer hear the lion's steps or feel his breath, and I remembered that I had not heard them since my eyes had glimpsed the opening. Where had he gone? Undoubtedly, he had not left through the opening, so I was separated from him only by a few steps. Where had he actually

gone? Or had he never really been there at all? I had heard him roar, felt the walls of the pit shake to his roaring and seen his fiery eyes, but where was he now? Would the people in Baghdad believe me when I told them that I had seen the roaring lion beneath Hārūn's palace? Would I believe myself when I went outside into the light and regained my strength and freedom? Or would I return to my old way of thinking of him as a myth? A myth! But here I was, thanks to him, getting out of Hārūn's pit, which no one before me had escaped. Yes, here I was getting to the opening, whose light was almost blinding my eyes following the night of black darkness in the pit. Here I was wriggling my head out through it, then my shoulders, then my body came out of it part by part until I felt my swollen feet touching the ground outside the pit. But where was the lion?

The pains of the previous night accumulated in my body, and I was unable to continue wondering about the lion and looking for him. I stretched myself out on the ground, which was covered with soft green grass, and gave in to deep sleep.

I do not know how much time passed while I was asleep, but I woke to the feeling of a hot liquid pouring over my face and wetting my body, and I felt something softer than Indian silk, although it was heavy and sticky, wiping my face. For a moment I thought that the lion was tasting me to see if my flesh was tasty, and I was paralysed by a fear that surprised me ... It was I who had followed the lion all the way from the pit to this place without fearing that he would see me and devour me. But after I had left the pit I felt that life was sweet and deserved to be lived out to the full. I would not have cared if the lion had devoured me in the pit, I might even have been pleased to have been spared by him from dying slowly of hunger, thirst and fear. But for him to have waited for me to get out into the light and feel secure of my release, and then to come and devour me, that was a sick joke which I could not accept. I felt an angry strength springing into my arms, and I raised them to push away that heavy sticky thing. No sooner had I done so than I heard a soft, beautiful voice resembling that of my beautiful concubine saying, 'God be praised, he has really awakened, God be praised.'

The King said:

'God be praised, why did you not say that you were hungry, God be praised.'

'God be praised, this is my son and you will enjoy his tender flesh. God be praised.'

Then he twisted his son's neck, separated it from his body and began to dismember him whilst I screamed in terror, 'What are you doing, O King, for God's sake, what are you doing?'

He said merrily as he put before me a piece of his son's thigh, 'God be praised, I am sure you will enjoy his flesh, God be praised.'

He tore the remaining parts of his son's body and threw strips of his flesh to those sitting around, who ate it with enjoyment and assurance.

I could not believe my eyes, O honourable gentlemen, and I imagined that I was in a heavy nightmare ... that all that I had experienced since being thrown into the pit was a terrifying nightmare. I closed my eyes and prayed to God to wake me from the nightmare, even if that meant returning to the terrible pit. I would have preferred to awaken and find myself still in the pit with the remains and the corpses, the darkness and the fear, than to find that my escape to the Dinosaur People was a reality. But I did not wake up because I was not asleep, nor was I dreaming, and those eating the flesh of their King's son were an actual reality taking place before me.

The King and those present noticed that I was not eating and stared at me in surprise. The King said, 'God be praised, why aren't you eating? God be praised.'

Disgust and terror prevented me from speech, so I kept quiet. One of those present, an elderly man, misunderstood my silence and said as he went forward towards the King, 'God be praised, perhaps Sindbad does not like the flesh of the young, so let him taste me ... perhaps he will like me, God be praised.'

He put his head between the King's hands, and the King twisted his neck and began to dismember him. Then, I could not help screaming. Everyone stared at me in great surprise, and the King said, 'God be praised, what would you have us eat? God be praised.'

I don't know what they did with me after that, for I lost consciousness out of fear. When I awoke I found myself alone on a bed of stone and darkness covered everything in the city, which was calm. I realised that the giants had gone to sleep, so I slipped out of bed and out of the house that had no doors and I ran through the streets of the city, returning to the entrance of the dungeon.

Had I really escaped the Dinosaur People? What happened to me after I left their city? That is what I will tell you on my next voyage.

Thus ends the story.

The image is not an experiment in the art of the grotesque, nor is it a casual description which occurs here to conform with the total horrifying tone of the narrative. It may not be presumptuous to conclude that writers extracted such scenes from the massacres they witnessed in the 1960s and 1970s, and the ironic reference in the narrative to the language of Adnān (Arabic dialect) and the frequent reiteration of God's name may support this assumption.

Yet no matter how grotesque the image may seem to be (and Arab critics and commentators would probably ignore such a narrative altogether because of its grotesque elements) it is not without an illuminating background. In Arabic culture cannibalism is an image which used to describe complete disintegration among members of society. A harmful piece of gossip is like eating one's own brother's flesh. In the Koran cannibalism is strictly prohibited and is considered one of the deadly sins, and the verse, which is widely quoted by people, rhetorically asks whether anyone would ever contemplate eating the flesh of his dead brother!

When the original Sindbad tells us about his encounter with cannibalism we feel that he was an observer who was detached enough from the cannibals to be able to view them as nothing more than odd people who provided fit material to tell wonders about. He was (and continues to remain) as far from them as we are. In Faḥmī's the narrator and character are one, and consequently the experience is very intense because it lacks the distance which usually brings with it the humour of romance. We always laugh with and at the old Sindbad even when we see him in critical situations. Not here!

The old romance of dream becomes the new realism of nightmare. For this reason Faḥmī (like his Arab fellow writers who used the Sindbad motif) reduces the quantity of narrative with its infinite time and space and intensifies its quality with the two images of the beast and cannibalism, which enhance the effect. The lion and the cannibals in the end become one: agents of a nightmare. That is why one voyage is sufficient to tell us what happened to our Sindbad on seven voyages.

Faḥmī's nightmare is very reminiscent of Kafka's famous one in *Metamorphosis*, which al-Masnāwī handles with particular attention in his story of Sindbad.

10. ''ABD ALLAH SAMSA in WĀQWĀQ ISLAND': SINDBAD PERSECUTED

This story is particularly interesting as it incorporates two different motifs and integrates them together to produce a unified total effect. The first motif is from Kafka, and the author makes this quite obvious. Like Gregor (servant's name in *Venus in Furs*) 'Abd Allah Samsa, God's servant (Von Sacher-Mosach), is presented as waking up from a dream. This is how Kafka's *Metamorphosis* begins: 'As Gregor Samsa awoke one morning from uneasy dreams he found himself transformed in his bed into a gigantic insect.'[1] When interrogated, 'Abd Allah, like Gregor, remains silent about his condition and shows no inclination to communicate with people who persistently but in vain try to extract information from him. Gregor would not even answer when he was called by his sister 'the old dung beetle'.[2]

However, al-Masnāwī draws upon the general theme of *Metamorphosis*, as he finds the archetypal nightmare in Kafka appropriate enough for the specific details of his own 'metamorphosis'. This is made clear right from the outset of the narrative: 'When 'Abd Allah Samsa woke from sleep one morning, after a disturbing dream, he found that he had not been transformed into an amazing insect, but that a thought had been imported into his head.' It is here that the story of al-Masnāwī diverges from that of Kafka. Gregor's 'uneasy dreams' are basically individualistic in that they are his own creation. He is possessed by guilt feelings which he is unsure whether to reveal or conceal, and consequently he lives in a paradoxical state of mind. The metamorphosis apparently suggests Gregor's dream of escape as being realised as a result of his indignant feeling about exploiting and being exploited by the job of a commercial traveller.

'Abd Allah Samsa is condemned for a different reason and by a different force altogether. His condemnation as well as his accusation are caused by an external brutal force. ''Abd Allah Samsa in Wāqwāq Island' moves in an opposite direction from that of *Metamorphosis*. While Kafka shows how the unreal can become real, al-Masnāwī presents the real as unreal. The common ground is, of course, the horrible reality in both. The different situation al-Masnāwī treats obviously determines the different direction of action, for the Ungeziefer which is seen as something imaginary but made real by man in *Metamorphosis* is actual in ''Abd Allah Samsa in Wāqwāq Island'. While the horror in Kafka is externalised, in al-Masnāwī it is internalised, and this further determines the difference between the safe custody of a room and the dangerous imprisonment of an island.

The second motif is the Wāqwāq Island which features largely in the travels of Sindbad.[3] It is the destination of those fantastic trips that Sindbad supposedly made untrammelled by the limitation of time and space. Obviously the land has no physical existence, but the reader or listener to the story, who is under the spell of its mystery, would not find its location difficult to visualise. The atmosphere of the island is one of Gothic mystery and adventure, and its remote geography and geology evoke an air of the extraordinary.

In this story one becomes immediately aware of the unpleasant sound of the repeated syllable which makes up the island's name, like the call of a crow, menacing and without meaning. The picture of the island here acquires a serious dimension and expands to accommodate the critical situation in which ‘Abd Allah Samsa finds himself caught. For example, the descriptions are strictly functional and their style is not entertaining. The first of these concludes with a reference to the fact that one is not allowed to enter into political discussions of the island's affairs. The second account tells us about a destructive foreign invasion which the islanders meet with a loud and ambiguous excitement. Later in account (b), however, the narrator makes it clear that the disaster was indirectly caused by those islanders (like ‘Abd Allah Samsa) who adopted imported ideas. The fourth account is in the form of a radio commentary and is typical of the sort of brainwashing propaganda broadcast on the mass media of authoritarian regimes.

The records on ‘Abd Allah Samsa which follow only serve to intensify the distortion of reality. Before his death, reports testify that he was caught red-handed, and his guilt, according to these reports, is not disputed. The case for the prosecution is now complete. ‘Abd Allah Samsa cannot even plead guilty. His death is an inevitable step in a series of distortions and accusations.

The story of ‘Abd Allah Samsa is essentially the story of the intelligentsia in general. It is the story of the individual intellectuals who were sent to jail in the 1960s and 1970s on false accusations followed by ready-made interrogations and a collection of reports used in psychological intimidation. All this happened against a background which is as mysterious as the reality of Wāqwāq Island itself. The difference between the mystery of Sindbad's Wāqwāq and that of ‘Abd Allah Samsa is expressed in a parallel contrast, that is, one is wonderful, the other is dreadful.[4]

The narrative effect is further promoted by the irony which characterises the gripping style of the description. The first section is given the title 'In the beginning', and the whole tone of the story is established from the very first part with extreme economy of words. 'Abd Allah Samsa wakes up from his sleep to find himself caught in a horrifying situation, and this picture is consistently presented by every structure of the narrative discourse. The distortion is apparent from the very first words. 'In the beginning was not the word, but people'.

The twisted form of reality continues to dominate the rest of the narrative after the beginning. For example, the seven main rivers flow with red and dark colours of their water into the vacuum around the earth. The name of the historian and traveller as well as his book are twisted: Gama de Vasco and his *Travels in the World Around Me.*

'Abd Allah Samsa is ferociously uprooted from reality firstly by the falsification of his geographical, historical and social environment as seen in the various accounts and the radio commentary, and secondly by the false accusations of the reports about him. The result is that 'Abd Allah Samsa finds himself living and surrounded by a big lie. He evidently finds no means of communication with his interrogator who, consequently, prepares false confessions as if they were real.

Another source of effect is the dramatised silence of 'Abd Allah Samsa which recalls Gregor's. There would be no room for his words in Wāqwāq Island. His ideas may be imported, as the accusation states, but they are strong enough to frighten the authorities and make them live with Gregor's 'uneasy dreams' even after 'Abd Allah's death.

11. 'SINDBAD' *FROM* 'OLD SORROWS, FIVE TALES FROM THE ARABIAN NIGHTS': SINDBAD ON SALE

Qandīl draws upon two previous sources of the Sindbad motif used by Faḥmī and 'Aflaq. He takes the first scene of Fahmī's story and dramatises its effect. He substitutes Faḥmī's Chief of Merchants (Shaykh al-Tujjār) with the Captain of the Ship, al-Sinān story, the ship replaces the palace of Faḥmī's narrative, but the merchants who attend the auction remain the same. In both stories Sindbad is humiliated by being alone at the mercy of those who were supposed to come to his rescue rather than run away from him at such a time of need. As in other stories which use the Sindbad motif, this story heightens its dramatic effect through sharp contrast between its events and the parallel experiences of the old Sindbad who always received the utmost help and sympathy from his fellow merchants.

The way the old Sindbad is helped at critical times serves a remarkable function in Qandīl's narrative. With the picture of the old Sindbad in mind, Qandīl is able to compress the narrative and depend on suggestive implication. This enables him to be economical, but not less effective, and this certainly justifies the dominance of the dramatic element in the narrative, which serves the purpose of exposing the sham of a vile society.

In using the dramatic element, Qandīl is obviously influenced by 'Aflaq, who was able to dramatise the main aspects of the modern Sindbad and to capture the elements of loneliness and betrayal in which the modern man Sindbad finds himself caught: 'Aflaq's Sindbad recalls Eliot's *Gerontion* (whose description early in the poem, we know, is derived from Fitzgerald's diary of his old age) 'Here I am an old man ...' 'Aflaq introduces his narrative with the following description of Sindbad:

> Sindbad, an old man with back bent and clothes in tatters, returns from his voyage, all his wealth spent. He finds all his family dead and his house sold. Weakly, he mounts a stone which lies in front of the house which no longer belongs to him. The neighbours and the youth of the quarter gather around him: they bombard him with questions, half pitying, half mocking.

Qandīl's picture, which is apparently based on ‘Aflaq's, provokes more mockery than pity on the part of the auctioneers.

However the pattern which ‘Aflaq's narrative established before Qandīl's Sindbad and other Sindbads of modern writers is a structure of an old Sindbad coming to the modern world, and the contact between the two is what determines the point of view. ‘Aflaq's dramatic narrative presents the main features of Sindbad's life which explicitly stand in opposition to the existing reality of this world. Sindbad tells people in the dialogue that his blindness resulted from the dazzling truth he saw on the far horizon, a truth which was originally in his eyes. Yet Sindbad says, ‘“I travelled to the farthest corner of the world to know the point nearest to me, to know myself.”’ His only sons are his thoughts and his faithful wife is his dreams. When Sindbad is asked about his home he answers: ‘“My home is where my desire and longing lead me,”’ and the response which comes from one youth is: ‘“His home, his home, the creditors have sold his home.”’ In this response Faḥmī and Qandīl seem to find the initial theme for their narratives.

Qandīl succeeds in dramatising the gap between Sindbad and his world and consequently in directing our sympathy towards Sindbad against his world. Sindbad emerges from the times of old with thoughts, dreams, hopes, visions and the like to articulate opposition between him (and us) and the modern world which is ours. Sindbad is in a position to see better than we do through the thick mask of present reality because of the distance available to him, and it is that same distance that serves as a protection for his creator. It is not unusual that writers who have used the Sindbad motif find themselves more protected by employing a technique of dramatisation instead of narration, for they can be more implicit in showing than in telling. Had this folktale narrative as a genre been more popular and advanced than other genres in Arabic, Sindbad would have developed an appropriate form for further dramatic adaptation.

Qandīl, for example, employs quite an effective presentation to dramatise his Sindbad's sense of betrayal. The story shows Sindbad betrayed by all those around him, from his life-long companion Shipwright (al-Sinān) to the tight-fisted merchant. Sindbad stands alone in his grief, unpitied by those around him and unjustly trapped in this hopeless situation.

The tone of betrayal is established from the first sentence. The bells which ought to ring in celebration of his return from his seventh voyage, are in fact announcing the sale of his ship and belongings. The bell is rung by the biggest auctioneer in the kingdom.

The betrayal in the story is dramatised as an auction and the author heightens the drama by having Sindbad stand helpless and tortured by the events taking place before his very eyes. When he tries to interrupt the auctioneer, Shipwright says that he and the crew must be paid their wages. This reference to the crew's wages provides the framework of the story, for it is the reason for the auction, and it is mentioned twice: once by Shipwright and again by the narrator who concludes the story with the comment, 'And for all this the goods auctioned had not realised half the arrears of pay!'

It is worth noting here that this framework is the only reference to the crisis in question. It shows how the serious design of the narrative is concealed behind the motif which forms the different components of the story, and that only a critical reading can penetrate properly into its covert design. At one level of this design, the story may be taken to imply the betrayal of the dreams and aspirations of the masses. The long-drawn-out farce which Sindbad is forced to witness is a tale of old sorrows, which Sindbad witnesses on behalf of the masses.

The auctioneer, called in Arabic *muzāyid*,* which also means an opportunist, is the agent of betrayal in this story. He is a world in himself, for he belongs neither to the rulers in power nor to the ruled. He is the type of the evil counsellor who often finds himself a place near a ruler, and initiates schemes of betrayal for his masters, presenting them as means of safeguarding the state. Typically, he has no social conscience, and his lack of humanity makes him an antipathetic character.

In this reading the ship is to be identified with the homeland of the masses. Also the books which Sindbad brought from lands of ancient wisdom and which are now on sale as used paper may stand for the ideas and culture of the intelligentsia which are not valued by the agents of the state. Sindbad, in this context, can be identified with the intellectuals whose revolutionary thinking has been encountered with great suspicion by authority.

Notes

1. *The Old Sindbad*
   1. Raymond Williams, *The Long Revolution* (London: Chatto and Windus, 1961) p. 282.
   2. J.C. Mardrus, trans. Powys Mathers, *The Book of the Thousand Nights and One Night* (London: Bibliophile Books, 1964) II, p. 178.
   3. *Ibid.*
   4. *Ibid.*
   5. *Ibid.*
   6. *Ibid.*

7. *Loc. cit.*, p. 179.
8. *Loc. cit.*, p. 192.
9. *Loc. cit.*, p. 902.
10. *Loc. cit.*, p. 203.
11. *Loc. cit.*, p. 221.
12. *Ibid.*
13. Mia Gerhardt, *The Art of Story Telling: A Literary Study of the Thousand and One Nights*, Leiden: E., Brill, 1963) p. 261.
14. Williams, p. 286.
15. *The Book of the Thousand Nights and One Night*, p. 223.
16. Mia Gerhardt, p. 263.
17. *The Book of the Thousand Nights and One Night*, p. 233.
18. *Loc. cit.*, p. 234.

2. *The Modern Sindbad*

1. The three poems appear respectively in *Ḥiwār* 2 (1963) pp. 29-30; *Shi'r* (1964) pp. 60-4; *al-Ādāb* 17 (1969) p. 47.
2. Michael 'Aflaq, "The Death of Sindbad", *al-Tali'ah* 8 (1936) pp. 422-27.
3. 'Aflaq was undoubtedly an outstanding Arab intellectual who played a very important role in the modern political history of the area. Like his own Sindbad, 'Aflaq did not speak of his predicament in his last days in Beirut in 1966. He opted to live in isolation (before he had left Beirut in the second week of October) rather than confront the ruling members of his party (*al-Difa'* 14 October 1966, p. 4).

4. *Towards a Modern Sensibility*

1. For details see Bernard Bergonzi, "*Fin de Siecle*" in *The Turn of a Century* (London: Macmillan, 1973) pp. 17-40.
2. Jabra Ibrāhīm Jabra, "Shaking the Dusty Heavy Door" in *The Eighth Voyage* (Beirut: al-Maktaba al-'Asriyyah, 1967) p. 33.
3. *Ibid.*
4. *Ibid.*

5. *Ibid.*
6. Quoted by C.B. Cox, *Modern Poetry: Studies in Practical Criticism* (London: Edward Arnold, 1974) p. 93.
7. John Press, *A Map of Modern English Verse* (Oxford, OUP: 1969), p. 202.
8. Jabra, p. 38.

5. *Sindbad the Porter*

1. One of the famous scenes in the Second Voyage is Sindbad flying with the rukh (roc): 'This monstrous bird will sometimes fly away. When he does so, I will be carried into some place where I can see others of my kind again. Wherever I am set down will be better than a desert island ... I rose and rose until I thought that I was about to touch the vault of Heaven.' (*The Book of the Thousand Nights and One Night*, p. 189)

   Another dramatic scene occurs in the Seventh Voyage:

   > One day it came to my notice that the people of the city suffered a change every year in Spring: this physical process lasted for a day, and at the end of it the men of the place had wings upon their shoulders and could fly high up into the vault of the air. During the time which this change lasted they were never out of the sky and left only their women and children in the city because these did not grow wings. Though this circumstance was astonishing enough, I soon got used to it; but in course of time I began to feel shame to be the only wingless man in the city and to have to stay down with women and children. I tried to find out how to grow wings on my shoulders, but my fellows either could not or would not tell me. I knew dark hours of mortification that I, Sindbad the Sailor, should not be known also as Sindbad the Airman.

   After much pleading he took hold of a merchant's waist 'and was carried into the air by the oars of his wings'. (p. 231)

2. For example see Joyce's reference to 'friend Sindbad and his horrifying adventures' (p. 598); to a most elaborate play on Sindbad's name (p. 697), and 'Going to a dark bed there was a square round Sindbad the Sailor roc's auk's egg in the night of the bed of all the auks of the rocs of Darkinbad the Brightdayler.' (*Ulysses*, London: The Bodley head, 1949, p. 698.)
3. In his discussion of the ethics of Sindbad the Sailor Peter D. Molan dismisses the usual view of Sindbad as a romantic hero and instead examines the disparity between his attitudes as protagonist and those of Shahrazad as narrator: 'The knowledge and values of the protagonist are almost inevitably different from those of the narrator; for she and we, know the characters as they could not possibly know themselves.' (p. 239)

   Without trying to reduce the story to 'a didactic morality play in disguise', Molan argues that the story shows the social division between one Sindbad and another. Despite the value Molan's argument has in going beyond the familiar romantic picture of Sindbad, I believe that his emphasis on the division between the two Sindbads is far-fetched. Molan's argument becomes rather superfluous when, for example, he remarks that 'Sindbad the Porter is the Sailor's alter-ego, the Sindbad who questions the distribution of wealth and the ways in which it has been gained'. ("Sindbad the Sailor: A Commentary on the Ethics of Violence", *Journal of the American Oriental Society*, 98 (1978) p. 238.)
4. *The Book of the Thousand Nights and One Night* (p. 176).
5. *Ibid.*, pp. 176-77.
6. Claude Levi-Strauss, *Tristes Tropiques*, trans. J. and D. Weightman (New York: Atheneum, 1974) p. 62.
7. Northrop Frye remarks: 'The importance of the god or hero in the myth lies in the fact that such characters, who are conceived in human likeness and yet have more power over nature, gradually build up the vision of an omnipotent personal community beyond an

indifferent nature. It is this community which the hero regularly enters in his apotheosis.' (*The Fables of Identity: Studies in Poetic Mythology* (New York: Harcourt, 1963) p. 19.)

6. *The Faces of Sindbad*
   1. 'The Faces of Sindbad' was published in the first issue of *al-Ādāb* in 1958 (pp. 62-3). Later in the year *al-Ādāb* published 'Sindbad on his Eighth Voyage' in eight parts (pp. 4-5), and the poem (a remarkable improvement on the previous one) is introduced with a prose statement telling the story of Emīr Bashīr al-Shihābī, who used to serve some of his distinguished guests with coffee mixed with poison and elegant flattery relevant to the good old days, '"One day the coffee was served ... and the Emīr died in Dayr al-Qamar where he was buried."' I believe that Ḥāwī intends to show that those who survive with decadence eventually die with it, and it is presumably a reference to the decadent present where the social ritual is abused even by dignitaries who turn out to be hypocrites. Obviously this short preface was replaced by another preface which must have appeared to Ḥāwī in an afterthought, a more comprehensive and relevant one (see translation of the poem in the selection). A revised form of the poem appears in his collection where the main shifting emphasis at the end inspires hope rather than despair ("Sindbad on his Eighth Voyage" in *The Harp and the Wind*, Beirut: Dār al-Talī'a'h, 1961, pp. 72-110).
   2. I am using the terms 'face' and 'mask' without any specific technical way, but rather in the general notion of innocence and experience which I believe Ḥāwī intends them to suggest.
   3. The image of the fog here recalls Eliot's in 'The Love Song of Alfred Prufrock':

      The yellow fog that rubs its back upon window-panes,
      Licked its tongue into the corners of the evening,
      Lingered upon the pools that stand in drains,
      ....

Slipped by the terrace, made a sudden leap,
And seeing that it was a soft October night,
Curled once about the house, and fell asleep.

7. *Sindbad on his Eighth Voyage*

1. *The Book of the Thousand Nights and One Night* (p. 234).
2. C.G. Jung "Psychology and Literature" in *Modern Man in Search of a Soul* (New York: Harcourt, 1966) p. 153.
3. In this connection Fry says: 'The human cycle of waking and dreaming corresponds closely to the natural cycle of light and darkness, and it is perhaps in this correspondence that all imaginative life begins.' *Fables of Identity*, p. 18.
4. Michael Bernstein, *The Tale of the Tribe: Ezra Pound and Modern Verse Epic* (Princeton: Princeton University Press, 1980) p. 127.

11. *'Abd Allah Samsa in Wāqwāq Island*

1. Franz Kafka, *The Penal Colony, Stories and Short Pieces*, trans. Willa and Edwin Muir (New York: Schocken Books, 1961) p. 67.

III

Shahrazad: The Eternal Perspective

1. 'SPRING IN THE ASHES': THE HOPE OF REGENERATION

The main motif of the story is apparently the Phoenix legend which seems to have inspired even the title of the story itself. The protagonist's fierce longing to become a bird immediately suggests an analogy between him and the ancient Egyptian mythological bird, the *bennu*, whose name in Greek is Phoenix. The 'great mass of red fire, blazing in the heart of the black night' is an analogue of the pyre of flames on which the fabulous bird burnt itself when it reached the end of its life, which according to the legend is 500 or 600 years spent in the Arabian wilderness. Moreover the rising sun of a new day in the story points to the Phoenix, the symbol of regeneration.[1] Even the fight in the city can be read as the symbolic death which precedes resurrection, and the sword may stand for the fanning wings of the Phoenix.

The other motif is derived from the frame story of *The Arabian Nights*, where Shahrayar emerges out of the ashes a new Shahrayar whose genuine concern for Shahrazad replaces his previous old egotistic passion. The change in Shahrayar is articulated by a motif from Adam's dream where Shahrayar goes and picks some apples for the starving Shahrazad.

However, the internal design of the story can be further

explored by examining the reality of the present before it is evoked by the legend of the past. The story presents a series of pictures which suggest that Shahrayar's surroundings before resurrection are as disintegrated as the ashes of the Phoenix. This sense of disintegration (a dominant theme in Tāmir's fiction) is expressed very effectively by successive pictorial images in the early part of the narrative. Apart from the river of abundant water the town has no identity in space or time. The difference in appearance and behaviour of the inhabitants suggests the sharp division between the poor and the rich, who are united only on the occasion of a townsman's death.[2]

More disintegration is expressed by the lack of professional ethics where workers keep themselves *busy* for eight hours and doctors reduce medical service to common sense hygiene. It is also seen by the gap between the oppressing old generation and the oppressed new one. Even on the level of friendship communication is limited to the morning greeting.

In the middle of such total disintegration, a survivor like Shahrayar naturally longs for regeneration. First he turns to nature expressing his strong desire for union with a flower or a bird, or a wandering cloud. However, since he is particularly concerned with human life, and not merely with survival in any form, his dream of transformation shifts to the Phoenix because of its specific emphasis on personal regeneration. In the use of Adam's dream a further shift is made on what may be considered a gradation of regeneration. The dream is adapted here by the suppression of the account of temptation, which would be superfluous in this context. Now Shahrayar is a new Adam who goes to pick apples for his woman, but not out of temptation. The incident thus demonstrates the difference between the old Shahrayar who once (before regeneration) bought Shahrazad to feed on, and the new Shahrayar who comes to believe that without Shahrazad's survival there would be no regeneration at all.

At their union all the elements of ritual which prepared for their regeneration are present, a bird was singing, the cries of children were heard 'and before them was the young bright sun'.

Yet if 'Spring in the Ashes' is read in comparison with Ḥāwī's 'Sindbad on his Eighth Voyage', the latter will be found to have had a remarkable impact on the former. It should be remembered that 'Spring in the Ashes' first appeared in *Aṣwaṭ* (a journal published in Arabic by the University of London) in 1961, shortly after the publication of 'Sindbad on his Eighth Voyage'. A close reading of the fourth, fifth and sixth parts of the poem will show the extent of the common ground shared by the poem and the story. The title of Tāmir's story as well as the innocent picture of the girl seem to be drawn from Ḥāwī's poem:

> Mirror of my house be washed
> of your burdensome care and the dust
> and celebrate the beautiful innocent one
> who as though in the morning
> was carved from my ribs,
> *sprang up from the lily of the seas* [italicising is mine]
> untainted the ripple of her laugh
> and the wine in her nipple,
> by the terror of sin,
> nor has she known the furtive deceit of the smooth
> serpent in the cellars below.
> Let us celebrate the beautiful innocent one,
> the brightness in the eyes
> that is the brightness of the lender shoots
> *coming through the snow in the spring.* [italicising is mine]

This obviously sets the tone for the main scene of communion between Shahrazad and Shahrayar after what is felt to have been a diaspora. Like Ḥāwī's woman, Tāmir's Shahrazad is innocent, and both women respond spontaneously to unification with their partners showing eagerness for a fresh new life, and before the men make any contact with their women partners they pass through a trying journey which is meant to be a kind of purgation.

Tāmir picks up Ḥāwī's notion of immortality in life, which is represented as the same kind of flux that Lawrence develops in his fiction. We have already seen that Ḥāwī's poem 'The Faces of Sindbad' was mainly concerned with enacting this notion of 'the life of the blood' (Lawrence's term) which was developed with further complexity in Ḥāwī's other poem 'Sindbad on his Eighth Voyage'. The speakers in the two poems as well as the narrator in Tāmir's story feel doomed to fight extinction, and they cling to their women with such eagerness because they long for survival and find women their last resort. Hence Ḥāwī's and Tāmir's references to the Phoenix, Adam and Eve, and Shahrazad, all of whom are archetypes of creation and survival.

In the absence of a positive reality Tāmir, like Ḥāwī, tends to create a new reality out of chaos. For this reason we find that Tāmir writes a story with the ideogrammic thought of poetry, and this obviously justifies the absence of plot and the sequence of narrative order. This is, for example, what the woman says to her partner:

'"I am Shahrazad. I have not fallen to the scythe of Death. Shahrayar is dead."

The man said, "Shahrayar is not dead; he is still alive.''
The woman ''O my lord!"'

The dialogue continues in a most economical manner where words, phrases, or sentences are not really an imitation of reality or a reflection of any particular situation we are already familiar with. The narrative reveals itself to us as we have contact with its language not as we follow its sequential order of events. It is the device of a process where meaning (or significance) depends on the immediacy and spontaneity of language itself. Language here is not a means of conveying subject matter, but rather the subject matter itself.

Tāmir owes Ḥāwī more in this linguistic aspect than in his subject matter, and Tāmir's innovation in the art of narrative comes mainly from his assimilation of what is known in modern poetry as the ideogrammic method. Unfortunately this is what makes Tāmir's story hard to read and difficult to appreciate (at least by the Arab reader) because of what looks like a disconnected narrative as a result of using the ideogram.

However, Tāmir does not only take from Ḥāwī but also gives to him. I believe that the ending in Ḥāwī's poem, which he adds to the revised version, came under the effect of Tāmir, who seemed to have convinced Ḥāwī that a construction should follow the destruction naturally at least to make the story of creation and resurrection plausible or complete in its cycle. Thus the ending of both poem and story comes as 'the sun also rises'.

2. 'THE BLUE CHARM AND THE RETURN OF JUBAYNAH': THE VISION OF RETURN

The 1967 war was, for obvious reasons, a great shock to the Arabs in general, and the Palestinians in particular. Suddenly the natives who had been living in diaspora had access to their brethren who happened to be able to stay behind in their homeland after 1948. The emotional effect of this reunion simply overwhelmed families that had been split up for about twenty years. Evidently the whole situation was not easy to accommodate.

Palestinians were evidently thrilled to have access to their pre-1948 Palestine. Bus trips were arranged to take them all over the country. They came back from their trips as if emerging from a dream or a nightmare: for they had trodden in places which for about two decades they had only seen from the high mountain tops or from a citadel on the West Bank or from south Lebanon. No matter how painful the experience was, it brought some kind of mysterious joy to those people going back to their home as tourists.

Emīle Habībī explored this situation in a series of stories published under the title *Sudāsiyyat al-Ayyām al-Sittah* (the *Double Trilogy of the Six-Day War*) in which 'The Blue Charm and the Return of Jubaynah' is included. Habībī's articulation of the aftermath of the Six-Day War is not a simple identification with the tale. For the implication of the tale is that 'all's well that ends well', whereas in reality this can only be so superficially. Thus, Habībī's vision pierces the overt pattern of the return to show a quite different covert meaning. He expresses the discrepancy between what is and what seems to be by making his story diverge from the traditional tale.

The story begins with the real event of homecoming. A Palestinian woman, who for about twenty years has lived in Lebanon, away from the place of her birth, is on her way to see her mother, accompanied by the narrator, who comes from the same village. Apparently he is one of the Palestinians who has continued to live in the homeland, and this in itself permits him to control the narrative, for he drives the newcomer towards her, or her mother's home and refers to her as 'our guest'. The event brings to his mind the tale of Jubaynah, which thus provides him with a link between reality and fiction, and so he calls the 'guest' the new Jubaynah.

The story derives its effect from the interaction between reality and fiction, and in the inevitable discrepancy between the two, lies the covert purpose of the story. Towards the end of the story the mother says to her daughter: '"Your father, may God rest his soul, always used to say that had you kept this charm, all that has happened would not have occurred. Wear it and never take it off."'

The fact that the new Jubaynah has lacked the blue charm all her life, and that it has been kept by her mother who stayed in the village, is, of course, symbolic. It can be interpreted as the absence of grace without which the return becomes empty and ultimately unfulfilled. This is perhaps what justifies the narrator's remark to the guest, 'the mechanical litter (*howdaj*)* is now entering the village. Will the water in the spring gush forth?' The return has the mortality inherent in time for being momentary, and this is marked by the reflection on the old mother's face, 'a vision of a bride's glory at the moment of her unveiling'.

The return, then, is a momentary vision often identified with daydream which has the transformational power for realisation. Its realism is expressed as a state of Limbo, where the narrator is caught between restrained despair and remote hope. Habībī is skilful at creating a multiplicity of perspective based on the temporary interplay of contraries. His narrator here is caught between the real and the unreal. The whole situation is as unique as the old woman's smile, 'such as I had never seen in my life; a smile that was like the traces of waves on the beach during the ebbing of the sea.' In real life people do not go back to their own homes *only* as visitors for two weeks after they have been evicted for about twenty years. The existing situation is too unreal to be grasped otherwise. It is surcharged with enough fiction to invite artistic transformation without much contrivance, and what is needed here for a fictitious account of the experience is a certain degree of detachment which Habībī evidently possesses.

It would appear that the narrator adopts a neutral stance towards the return as he sees it bringing happiness to all those concerned, even though its effect is bound to be limited by its duration of only two weeks. The narrative tone is balanced by the narrator's tempered sympathy. The narrator does not suspend his sympathy completely from the event which makes his fellow villagers happy (though he does not glorify it), nor does he extend it, because, unlike the villagers, he is not blinded to the deeper issues by the emotional impact of the event.

In the meantime, the narrator extends his sympathy to the characters, though not to all equally. He is most sympathetic towards the old mother, who represents, for the most part, the author's point-of-view as her reference to the blue charm shows. She has an air of mystery about her which colours the part she has to play.

On the other hand, the narrator does not seem to be equally sympathetic to the new Jubaynah. When she expresses her joy with a diffident, audible, but invisible laugh, saying '"Jubaynah has returned,"' the narrator wishes to laugh but cannot and his telling of the event points up the discrepancy between the two 'Jubaynahs'. In this way, the narrator's emphasis on the fact that the new Jubaynah did not carry the blue charm all her life and did not bring her daughter with her, is intended to reduce the reader's affection for her.

Yet it may be suggested that the narrator uses the folktale in his story not to decry the joy experienced by the newcomer, her old mother and the villagers at the time of the event, but merely to point out that Jubaynah has not returned yet. He finds a way out of the tension by shifting *that* return to an indefinite future. It is a depressing point-of-view, which is still effective, even if not immediately obvious. Yet what makes the point-of-view here less depressing and still effective is the fact that the suspended return is neither certain nor impossible. Hasn't Habībī been prophetic?

3. 'THE ORPHANS' COW': ALIENATION AND DREAM

Baqarat al-yatāmā, which gives the story its title, is so popular as a folktale that the mere allusion to it puts the story into a particular context. The sole source of income, for example, in a family of limited means, is often known as the *baqarat al-yatāmā*. The narrative is based on the fact that the father of a family is the breadwinner, and that therefore orphans often find themselves in a precarious financial position. The Koran pays special attention to orphans and on various occasions urges believers to give help and sympathy to them. In the *Sharī'ah* (Islamic Law) their property, both movable and immovable, is considered as sacred as *waqf* (the religious common property).

'The Orphans' Cow' is the classic story of the Arab *fallāh's* migration to the city; usually, as in this case, this brings only bitterness and disappointment. Arab cities are rarely industrialised to any great extent, and the opportunities for employment are therefore relatively limited. Most villagers find work in the construction industry when they migrate to the city, and the *fallāh* of this story refers to this when he says that workers like him only build large houses (by implication, for others to enjoy).

Prosperity in Arab cities is more apparent than real, and it is as artificial as the fat woman called, by the *fallāh, baqarah Holandiyyah*, a grotesque description not uncommon in the Arab world. The false picture of city life stems from the *fallāh's* ignorance of the origin of its prosperity and the harsh life of the village to which they compare it. For example, 'Aziza, the *fallāh's* wife, tells her husband that she hears city life is full of comfort and ease, and in an attempt to correct his wife's impression, her husband explains that he, and others like him, work like animals from dawn to sunset, and that ease and comfort are privileges to which he and his like cannot contemplate.

Abu-Isma'īl's life in the city is not only wretched and degrading but also pathetic, it runs parallel to the tale of *baqarat al-yatāmā* , and it is here that the emotions roused by the tale and the story are so interwoven that the reader finds himself moved by both simultaneously.

Having spent the best years of his life as a building labourer, and then as a gardener, Abu-Isma'īl returns to his village not, as in past years, for his fortnightly visit, but for good. He is too proud to describe his experiences in detail, and he maintains a desperate silence over anything which he thinks might be incomprehensible or upsetting to his wife and children, merely alluding to the difficulties of life in the city. In this context, he listens eagerly to the tale of *baqarat al-yatāmā* told by his son as if he identifies his own life story with the tale.

This interaction between tale and his own story arouses deep memories in him which vividly recall the details of his experiences with the city woman. Impulsively he retells the same tale to the family, but with great emphasis on the brutality inflicted on the *baqarat* by the rich, overlooking the sympathy which the narrative usually includes, and which his son Isma'īl does not exclude in the course of narration.

In Abu-Isma'īl, the tale and his story interact, and are harmoniously integrated. As he hears the tale, the past merges into the present, creating a mood of despair to which, however, he cannot give vent in front of his family. Thus, the tale serves as an outlet for his emotions, while his family finds some comfort in the fantasy (at least before they become indignant at Abu-Isma'īl's version).

Abu-Isma'il is intensely aware of the family's desperate situation and, thus, only *he* realises the implication of the tale within the context of the story. The shifting states of mind produced by this awareness increase the dramatic irony as the distance between the two narrows to the point where Abu-Isma'īl is driven to dramatise his own story through his retelling of the tale.

Dramatic irony is also provided by the character of Umm Isma'īl. She stands as a link between father and son, and she helps the child to tell the tale which eventually provokes the father to deliver the narrative. She makes casual but important remarks which may perhaps be taken as evidence of her awareness of the interaction between tale and story. The first remark is her comment, in response to the child's pleading to hear the tale from her, that she is tired of telling the tale. The other remark is her reference to Isma'īl's inefficiency in telling the tale.

Isma'īl promotes the dramatic irony to a high level. For despite the fact that he responds to the tale with the total involvement of a child and is completely unaware of its implications within the story. It is through him that his father (and possibly his mother as well) becomes aware of the interaction of the two. Yet the conclusion reveals that Isma'īl's response to the tale has also changed. The dramatic vigour with which his father presents the narrative shocks the children out of their former innocent involvement and occasions the wonderful dream, which marks the highest point of dramatic irony by linking tale and story in the children's subconscious.

Thus the irony of situation is transformed into the irony of vision. For the children's dream transcends both the dismal and humiliating reality of their father's story and the sentimental effect of the folktale.

4. 'ABU-ZAYD SURRENDERS': STRUGGLE FOR SURVIVAL

This story stands in sharp contrast to those romance stories where the picture of the country is merely a backcloth, as, for example, in the stories of Maḥmūd al-Badawī, whose Upper Egypt might as well be China or India. It also fulfils the requirements of realism which those critics and commentators (discussed earlier) found wanting in the stories they reviewed.

The first part of the title suggests the background of folktale. The second, however, goes beyond the traditional images of Abu-Zayd. It is well known, to the Arabic reader at least, that Abu-Zayd has a reputation for legendary courage. By establishing a disparity between the traditional courageous image of Abu-Zayd and the timidity of the Egyptian *fallāh* who bears the same name the writer creates a tension from the beginning. The reader thus approaches the tale with the impression that Abu-Zayd is already defeated and the story is about his defeat. It is not about *what* is going to happen to Abu-Zayd, but about how it happens to him. This shows that a short story can do without the third division insisted on by Rashād Rushdī: the moment of illumination, for example.

Abu-Zayd is the typical Egyptian *fallāh* whose sorrows are too well known to need any elaboration here; Wahībah is his wife, who steadfastly stands by him; Zainab is his daughter, who waits for the financial situation to improve so that she can marry Yūnus; and Diāb is a neighbouring *fallāh*.

The story is set at harvest time when the cotton is collected by the Inspector, to be sold for the Princess. The scene is most frustrating for all the *fallāhs* who witness this annual practice without knowing how much if anything they will receive for their crops.

The question arises here as to whether the story goes back to before the Revolution of 1952 when the *fallāh* suffered from the *taftīsh*, or whether the author is using the references to the *taftīsh* and the Princess as a cover for his criticism of the contemporary political system without intending to limit the story to a certain era.

When the story was published in *al-Majallah*, it was followed in the same issue by a review which concluded: 'The author has shown that the life of the Egyptian *fallāh* in the pre-Revolution period is still an inspiring subject.'[1] In emphasising that the story is set in the period *before* the Revolution, he intended to protect himself as editor of the journal from censorship. However, neither the author's allusions to this period nor the reviewer's interpretation should divert the reader from the covert structure of the story.

Abu-Zayd is made to believe that moving from the old *taftīsh* to the *hajj tafish* would be his salvation, but he discovers that the whole thing is illusion. The *hajj taftīsh* had been replaced by *al-Iṣlāh al-Zirā'ī*,* which the 1952 Revolution boasted of introducing, but which fell short of the people's aspiration.

The story implies a continuity in the life of the *fallāh*, and there is nothing in the narrative to suggest that *al-Iṣlāh al-Zirā'ī* put things right or alleviated his sufferings. The new regime called on writers to glorify what the Revolution had done for the *fallāh*; so although the story appears to present a picture of Egypt before the Revolution, its perspective should be seen as a rejection of 'reality glorified'.

The author can do this with impunity because he is protected by the element of folktale in the story. Only a close reading reveals the subtle implication of continuity. The lion tattooed on Abu-Zayd's arm is more than a comic folktale motif. It is his *alter ego*. For Abu-Zayd, the shaking of his arm is a form of assertion and provides some therapy.

However, life on the *taftīsh* is so miserable that Abu-Zayd is driven to despair and, as the story opens he is contemplating suicide. He feels desperately in need of resolution and the lion's fierce courage. Yet his religious beliefs make him reject suicide, for it is punished by eternal damnation.

Two beliefs help Abu-Zayd to survive: his religious conviction and his faith in traditional love; the former prevents him from despair, while the latter gives him hope. Together they give him the strength to go on living.

Thus Abu-Zayd vacillates: taking up the hope to kill himself, and putting it aside in the hope that things will change for the better.

Abu-Zayd tries to solve his problem by moving to a new *taftīsh*, the *hajj taftīsh*, where he hopes for a better life. Unfortunately when he stops to ask about this *hajj taftīsh*, he finds there is no such thing, and his journey turns out to be merely a dream. Here he creates this parallel of the Abu-Zayd of the folktale whose life was a continuous journey from east to west and yet was sheer illusion. The lion, the character of Abu-Zayd he adopts, the dreams he and the rest of his family have for the future, the journey–are all aspects of an illusory life.

Abu-Zayd lives in a fantasy world because he is divorced from reality by the *taftīsh* system. In the absence of a just reality he comes to believe in his fantasies and tries to realise them. The story ends: Abu-Zayd said groaning, '"The acre, Yūnus ..., the acre. I'll stick out my tongue at the Inspector and the Princess,' and putting out his tongue he wept"'

The use of the folktale also allows the author to give his story immediacy and involvement in the milieu of his characters. It is as though the story could have been written by Abu-Zayd or any one of the small group around him. Indeed, the author allows his characters to tell their own story through the extensive use of dialogue. This unusual technique is extremely effective, given the narrative a directness which would otherwise be difficult to achieve.

The story is told in what the sociologist Basil Bernstein calls 'restricted code' as opposed to 'elaborated code.'[2] The speech of the characters is limited in vocabulary, and sentences are limited in structure. There is no elaboration either in what the characters say or in the narrator's speech.

However, although the vocabulary of the characters is limited, their powers of expression are not. Their reactions and emotion are voiced clearly and directly and everything they say is pragmatic and relevant to the immediate situation.

The review mentioned above perhaps fails to appreciate the subtlety of the story's technique when he remarks that the author 'concerns himself more with the movement of action and dialogue than with the penetration into the psyche of character ... and that he often uses the technical device of the cinema.'[3] It is, of course, *through* the dialogue and the movement of action that the author penetrates 'the psyche of character'. The restless repetition in both speech and movement are expressive of the dreary, limited and uncertain life in which the *fallāh* is imprisoned and from which he can only escape into fantasy.

In their movement towards the longed for new *taftīsh*, Abu-Zayd and his family must have taken the *sarāb* (mirage) for water without realising that their whole life was *sarāb*, and it begins and ends with it. The author creates a sense of alienation, with Abu-Zayd and those around him forming an entity which has no contact with those who are not *fallāhs*. Through the overt pattern of action as expressed in the continuous movement and dialogue, the covert feeling of the *fallāh* is effectively presented without the need for any authorial rhetoric or preaching.

The technique of movement in action and dialogue helps the author to achieve maximum neutrality in the narrative. It is as if Abu-Zayd and his group are both actors and chorus, simultaneously acting and commenting on themselves and what is happening to them. This device and the use of the folktale motif effectively distance the author from what would be dangerous implications of this story.

5. 'SHĀṬIR ḤASAN AND THE SEASON OF DROUGHT': SURVIVING THE STRUGGLE

Shāṭir Ḥasan belongs to a long heritage of folktale which is approximately a thousand years old. Shuṭṭār (plural of Shāṭir) are groups of outcasts and outlaws who emerged at the end of the 'Abbasīde period and continued to flourish throughout history until the end of the Ottoman Empire. Shuṭṭār were the product of social and political corruption as well as economic depression. What cannot be granted by law and order, Shuṭṭār thought, should be grabbed by force and violence. That is how Shuṭṭār became powerful at times of misrule and abuse. The state, whether represented by Sultans or Caliphs considered them enemies and fought them ferociously. At the same time Shuṭṭār were in alliance with the public as they stood for the *alter ego* of people. They vaguely expressed their aspiration for justice. This explains how people in the story here resort to Shāṭir Ḥasan as a result of the drought and why he was warned against the Sultan and his followers during his search for the spring.

Some of these Shuṭṭār have acquired a public reputation more than others because of their heroism. For example, the life of Ali al-Zaybaq is considered a folktale and an account of it is recorded in *The Arabian Nights*. We know from historical records how the Caliph asked for the help of Ali al-Zaybaq to suppress the dissension between the Sunnis and Shi'ītes in Baghdad in 1051. In recent years interest in the literary history of Shuṭṭār has increased and research has shown that a whole literature of Shuṭṭār is available. A most complete study on the subject is by Mohammad al-Najjār, who sums up the literary features of the Shuṭṭār as follows:

> The tales of Shuṭṭār in folktale tradition are those of outcasts rebelling against authority, and its civil law as opposed to the

divine law. The reasons for the rebellion were political, economic and social. The rebels wanted to avenge themselves and their society with their own special bag of tricks so that they were able to threaten those with authority and money in the hope of achieving lost justice. As a result of this they acquired an important position in the eyes of the populace and their daring deeds became the subject matter of tales telling about their exploits and heroism.[1]

In drawing upon the tradition of Shuṭṭār (which Shāṭir Ḥasan belongs to) Haniyyah does not follow all the main details of the archetype, but rather adapts them to the design of his story. He obviously keeps the affinity between Shāṭir Ḥasan and the people; he also rewards his Shāṭir with the traditional prize of making him marry the most beautiful girl (we remember that Shāṭir Ali al-Zaybaq marries the most cunning and beautiful Dalīlah even with the blessing of the Caliph). Haniyyah equally introduces a happy ending at one point but only to twist it for a different conclusion, and this is where the main part of his adaptation lies. He seems to imply that dependence on Shuṭṭār, even when they occasionally proved efficient, cannot offer a crucial solution for a situation which requires radical treatment. No matter how benevolent Shuṭṭār can be, their benevolence turns out to be a casual phenomenon which cannot serve a long-term solution. Haniyyah seems to further suggest that people–all people–should make their own Shuṭṭār. A most striking analogy to this situation is the conclusion in Surūr's 'Sindbad the Porter', where 'all became Sindbad'.

Yet a discussion of 'Shāṭir Ḥasan and the Season of Drought' can be made with specific reference to the people in the story, the *fallāhs* who form a majority of Arab society and more than any other people in society waited for the emergence of a saviour, and in the absence of one they turn to Shāṭir Ḥasan.

The story has no explicit reference to the *fallāh* by name, yet every one of its details is related to the life of the *fallāh* in one way or another. First, the Arab village, which is the milieu of action in the story is, often if not always, inhabited by the *fallāh.* Second, the *fallāh's* life in the village is greatly affected by the amount of rainfall the sky yields every year. A season of drought is simply a disaster for the *fallāh* especially in areas where an irrigation system does not exist. For this reason, rain has developed a most suggestive motif throughout the centuries, and classical Arabic poetry includes well-known poems written with the romantic perspective of rain, such as that of Abu-Tammām who is known for his poetry on rain. In modern poetry the motif of rain is equally suggestive and the attraction modern poets have found in the motif of rain in Eliot's 'The Waste Land', for example, particularly shows how urgent the need is for the artist to draw on such a motif.

However, it is not the intention of Haniyyah to emphasise the romantic aspect of the motif, but rather to see it, like other modern writers, in a different perspective altogether. Haniyyah shows how flawed the romantic vision of life can be, and he does this without moralising about romance. For example, in the first part romance is enacted as being positive in consequence. The spring bursts forth and consequently the dream is realised. All this happens through the irrationality of chance and the typicality of romance. Shāṭir Ḥasan succeeds with the help of favourable external circumstances in which he serves as a knight-errant. The old man is like an oracle guiding Shāṭir Ḥasan, who, by sheer luck, is not caught by the Sultan's army on his way back to the site of the spring: and the mission Shāṭir Ḥasan undertakes fulfils the realisation of people's dreams as well as his own. Had the narrative ended there it would have been a folktale about knight-errantry.

But the story continues in a kind of counter effect which, by implication, suggests that romance may not be altogether an illusion, and that the unreal may sometimes become real. The second part of the story further suggests that romance cannot be so reliable as to be taken as a mode of life. Its credibility is evidently limited. It should be noticed here that Haniyyah's presentation is more than a moral. Rather it is a preoccupation with a typical *fallāh's* attitude towards life; that attitude is always a major issue of consideration, at least for sociologists and psychologists. In Lukacs's description the picture of the attitude is a static reality which is characterised by what Lukacs calls abstract reality. The fact that the spring gushes forth does not change the *fallāh's* life, for the spring dries up and the *fallāh* is back to normal after a while. The drought returns and the *fallāh* is disappointed once more.

What the *fallāh* needs is not an ephemeral realisation of a dream which is, in any case, incidental. We know that the main structure of Shāṭir Ḥasan's achievement is based on chance. So is the rainfall. Even the spring which gushes forth is found by the lucky Shāṭir Ḥasan, who comes across the old man and consequently manages to protect himself from the danger of the Sultan's soldiers.

The absence of Shāṭir Ḥasan from the scene drives the *fallāh* to search for an alternative. It is only the dynamic reality (the term is also Lukacs's) which will help the *fallāh* to survive; and such reality certainly needs more than a subjective abstract reality which is static by nature.

The shift of emphasis from the romance of the first part to the realism of the second one marks the crucial change in the *fallāh's* sensibility. It is a transformation from old static reality to new dynamic one, which is ushered in by breaking the deadlock the *fallāh* reaches when the drought returns. A situation like this is articulated by Williams who remarks 'that to explore a new definition of realism may be the way to break out of the deadlock and find a creative direction.' It is the reality 'which human beings make common, by work or language.'[2] Williams here relates the reality of life to the realism of art by expressing it in a most economical phrase perceptively integrating; 'work' and 'language'. The common reality of work in the story is generated by the interaction of individual potentialities. All this is lacking in the first part, where there is no interaction among the individual *fallāhs* who join together only in abstract reality: in hopes, wishes and dreams. Similarly there is no interaction between the *fallāh* and Shāṭir Ḥasan whose motivation is not pure, for he opts to undertake the mission of finding the spring in the hope of winning Sitt-al-Ḥusun; and when he tries to do the same again after the return of the drought he hopes to keep his image as a knight-errant in the eyes of other people including his wife.

The transformation of static reality into a dynamic one can be seen in the light of Williams's notion of new realism as discovery rather than recovery. It does not help when Shāṭir Ḥasan follows the same path to recover the spring. Williams articulates the process of discovery and interaction in what he calls 'the structure of feeling' (a phrase which he actually coined and made popular and useful for readers). This means that individuals have independent potentialities which can become a dynamic reality only when their potential awareness is structured together. It should be the crucial aim of the artist to discover this structure which in real life may be missing. The writer then does not discover independent individual potentialities but rather a structure of potential feeling in a community, which when envisaged interacting together in work, form the common reality that is incarnated through language.

'Shāṭir Ḥasan and the Season of Drought' is comparatively a story with a perspective. It is certainly different from the fanciful stories of the *fallāh* which Maḥmūd Taymūr and other writers of the previous generation wrote early in the century in which the aristocrat patronised the most underprivileged and saw the *fallāh* as a fantastic object arousing pathos. Also it is different from the serious stories on the *fallāh* included in this study. Abu-Zayd and Yūnus in 'Abu-Zayd Surrenders' are bitterly defeated at the end. 'The Orphans' Cow' concludes with a kind of apocalyptic dream. So does 'The Blue Charm and the Return of Jubaynah' (its setting, at least, recalls that of any story on the *fallāh*) in which the dream for the gushing spring is indefinitely suspended. The difference may be partly explained in terms of Haniyyah's approach to the *fallāh* as a community rather than as the small unit of family which we find in the other two stories of the *fallāh*, and partly in terms of his confidence in the genre as a potential for serious perspectives. Certainly Haniyyah saw the *fallāh* as bigger and more permanent than Shāṭir Ḥasan, who with all his magical power, could not survive another season of drought!

Notes

1. *Spring in the Ashes*
   1. Tāmir's indirect style and pictorial method seem to have misled critics and commentators. This can be seen in a typical review by 'Adel Sallūm who fails to see any significance for the sun in the story and remarks that it is merely ornamental description. The reviewer's over-emphasis on the *ashes* makes him see no Phoenix regenerated. ("*Spring in the Ashes: A Collection of Short Stories* by Zakariyyā Tamīr" *al-Ma'rifah*, 2 (1963) pp. 165-7).
   2. It is a common custom in Arab society to volunteer for carrying the bier when seen passing in the street. Also it is a custom to join for a meal shortly after the burial of the dead. Tāmir is ironical here as he implies that this occasion is the only one when the poor and the rich are brought together.

4. *Abu-Zayd Surrenders*
   1. Fu'ād Duwwārah, "A Comment on 'Abu-Zayd Surrenders",

al-Majallah, 10 (1966) p. 89.

2. Particular reference is to Chapter 2 of Bernstein's *Class, Codes and Control* Vol. I: *Theoretical Studies towards a Sociology of Language*, London, 1971, pp. 42-66.
3. Fu'ād Duwwarah, p. 89.

5. *Shāṭir Ḥasan and the Season of Drought*
   1. *The Tales of Shuṭṭār in Arabic Heritage* (Kuwait: *'Ālam al-Ma'rifah*, 1981) p. 419.
   2. *The Long Revolution*, pp. 287-8.

IV
Aladdin's Lamp Without Oil

1. 'NIGHT 1002': MIRROR WITH NO LIGHT

This story is a deviation from the norm of the frame story of *The Arabian Nights*. We know that the whole narrative of the *Nights* falls within the two polarities of the desire for revenge and the hope for survival worked out through the redemptive power of narrative. The two polarities are suspended until one is overcome by the other after a thousand and one nights. The revengeful Shahrayar, his sanity restored in time to live happily with Shahrazad, instead of Shahrazad meeting the death sentence planned for the same night as that of her marriage to Shahrayar. Shahrazad has survived the murderous fate met by many women before her.

The story design of al-Marzūqī's 'Night 1002' is limited to the first part of the polarity, – the original intention of King Shahrayar – without recognising the countereffect of redemption. The author shapes the narrative in the light of the grim situation he seeks to portray. He even twists the frame story by making Shahrazad follow suit in the sequence of betrayal first practised by the King's wife and so Shahrazad here goes over with the Visier leaving Dunyazad delivering the narrative in her absence with Shahrayar alone. The result is that the narrative exercises no real effect on Shahrayar, at least the effect is not enough to make him change his usual practice; yet a further twist to this practice is undertaken when Shahrayar (instead of murdering Dunyazad, who is in the story a kind of surrogate for Shahrazad) intimidates her by ordering the servant to kill the cock in front of her eyes (which serves as an expression of masculine chauvinistic superiority). (A popular folktale in the Arab world retells how a bridegroom initiates intimidation right from the first wedding night to ensure everlasting submission, if not complete loyalty.)

The story extracts the aesthetic element (which forms the highlight of the original narrative) by presenting Shahrayar, from the first words of the story, as restless and unable to sleep; and what he gains out of the narrated events, if he gains anything at all, is temporary entertainment, which may be no more than passive listening and merely the passing of time.

However the part which is particularly twisted, to complete the deviation from the original design of *The Arabian Nights*, is the mirror motif. We know that Shahrazad's crucial role in the narrative is to make Shahrayar obliquely see his revengeful face in the parallel stories which reflect the ugly reality of evil in all its guises, in anticipation of forcing him to abandon his practice. Shahrazad's success is crowned by the new sensibility Shahrayar acquires as a result of the narrative impact on him when he emerges with the conviction that women are not evil. All these positive elements which eventually lead to a positive result are inverted to produce a negative effect. The parallel mirror in this story here is made to reflect all that is bad; hence its reflection of the face of the girl (who parallels Shahrazad, the woman) and its exclusion of the face of Aladdin (who parallels Shahrayar, the man). The deviation is complete, and it is made so to reflect the grim reality of a breakdown in the whole way of life. That is how the story ends with a Christ crucified, soliciting salvation for what is around him.

What does all this signify? Is it the kind of 'fury' whose 'sound' 'signifies nothing'? Similarly the whole narrative in this story is reduced to empty rhetoric where Shahrayar asks Dunyazad to continue her narration but under intimidation. There is no need for a Christ advocating 'first was the word', and by implication no role for a genuine Shahrazad to play with the powerful word. The sense of negation is extreme; so is the living reality where negative effect leads the narrator to find no impact in the word.

There is more than one title which may express the implication of the narrative here. One would be simply made by replacing the word 'after' with 'before', so as to curb the meaningful progression of the narrative leading to redemption in the original *Arabian Nights*. This, of course, cancels the positive effect usually generated by Shahrazad, the narrator. Another title could be 'Aladdin loses his lamp in Tripoli'. But a title of this kind being explicit, would lack the functional protective mask used by the author for safety reasons. Another title may be 'The one thousand and two nights in the tunnel'. But again this title would be too explicit to serve the purpose, as it would expose the context of the narrative which is like other contexts here in this study, the main target of the author and designed to be implicit.

However a more appropriate title can be something similar to those Sindbad titles used above by Masnāwī and Qandīl.

2. 'AN OIL SLICK': A BROKEN MIRROR ON THE SEA

Finding this story beyond easy grasp, I wrote a letter to the author, Sulayman Shaṭṭi, pleading for help towards interpretation. The reply I got was not illuminating enough but satisfactory and the reading here draws mainly on the general remarks kindly offered by the author.

Shaṭṭi expresses deep concern with the spirit of the time and he proposes that history is crucial for his fiction. The two major events which deeply affected Shaṭṭī in the 1980s, the letter records, is the notorious financial market known as *Almanach* that seriously affected everyday life. It disrupted the rhythms of stability, bringing about a serious loss to a large segment of the community, trapped by its illusion. The other event is the Iraqi–Iranian War (and later the Gulf War). The title of the story finds its origins in a specific incident of the Gulf War when an oil tanker was hit, accidentally (or otherwise), and the resultant spilling of oil on the sea water in slicks scattered in large quantities. And although this story is not dependent on history as his other stories are, I am told by Shaṭṭi, in the sense that it does take history as a support, or a covert meaning, it is, Shaṭṭi confirms, an overt pattern. For example, it was obvious that the whole Gulf area and Saudi Arabia (and also other Arab countries) were taken by surprise when they suddenly found themselves confronted by Khomeini's historical triumph in Iran. In brief, the whole thing is a reworking of what is called, in the most disputable history of Islam, the question of *wilāyah* and *wālī* and it is worthwhile here to give a brief account of this issue and its bearing on the story.

Shaṭṭī's attitude is in agreement with that of Arab writers who adopted the short story to explore serious issues such as those discussed in this book. Like his fellow Arab writers, Shaṭṭi seems to believe that the genre can extend its frontier beyond the common ground already known to us. In its wide-ranging theme and sincere commitment to the public cause 'An Oil Slick' is epical in tone. It is a portrait of a most critical time of the Gulf history. Shaṭṭi says that his story draws upon the daily scene of the Gulf, literally becoming a lake of burning fire, threatening the lives of its people. He remarks that the pollution from this is man-made rather than a fate imposed from outside. The whole story demonstrates wanton acts of mankind committed against public welfare and, in particular, shows the tendency towards self-destruction. More important is the emergence of the politics of religion and somehow the whole issue of religion and state has acquired a new dimension. This explains the futile dialogue in the story which obviously yields the nemesis of the crisis.

Whether in his letter or in his narrative, Shaṭṭī expresses his preoccupation with the political and social crisis of the time, but he does not intend to render it by means of crude realism where startling events of daily life crises are directly represented or simply reported to convey a shocking effect. The result is a perspective whereby the present remains an implication shaped by a new sensibility. The story recalls William Golding's *Lord of the Flies*, where Golding removes the present crisis (the cold war of the 1950s) in time and place to demonstrate through the behaviour of the boys on the island (a microcosm of society at large) that fear or evil or both is internal, that is, man-made and that one or both are created by man regardless of time and place, cause and effect.

Shaṭṭī's story is narrated by a shaykh who survives hardship with a dark black patch on his leg, emblematic of a long history, which the shaykh has the privilege to unravel after the moon prayer. It seems that Shaṭṭī's question is similar to Golding's: what happens to a group of people (society in miniature) living in isolation and facing danger when they face a common enemy? Whatever the answer is, the traditional encounter of nature is not in perspective. In either narrative the island as milieu is quite emblematic and, in any case, is neither the romantic coral island nor one of the fascinating islands of the Sindbad, but rather an island with a modern perspective of politics and society.

What did the group of people who find themselves shipwrecked carry with them on the island? The narrative tells us that their only worry is the life of their monarch's (*wālī's*) son, and that it is his, rather than their own, life which is at stake. The fact that their life was threatened any moment did not make them abandon the notion of patriarchal society inherent in the *wālī*, that they are used to. It is not the voice of that reason that they were prepared to listen to, so as to find a way out of the crisis, but rather the voice (or even whisper) of the *wālī's* son they waited impatiently for. They are prepared to listen and to obey whatever the son's voice dictates, even in his state of delirium (and this is, of course, very ironic).

The complete self-denial of the people in favour of the welfare of the *wālī's* son obliquely suggests that such people are a long way behind the concept of the state in the modern sense. The narrator even makes it clear when he tells us that the only time they take a decision is when they decide to abandon the island and return to the sea as offering a better chance for survival, yet the decision was debated without people looking at each other as if to suggest that the decision was far from being democratic, and that it was rather solicited by circumstances, or asserted by the danger surrounding them. It is obvious here that people even in such isolation are acted upon rather than acting and they are deprived of any will.

'An Oil Slick' can be illuminated by the *Shī'ism* background, which informs the basis of the Iranian Revolution (Islamic Republic) and Khomeini's contribution to the traditional doctrine of *Imāmate*. In *Shi'ī* usage the *Imām* is the leader of the Muslim community in addition to being the leader of prayer and the founder of a major law school in Islam. All this stems out of the historical martyrdom of Hussein (Ali's son and descendant of Prophet Mohammad) which forms the most controversial incident of *Khilāfa* (succession to the Prophet).

Before the Iranian Revolution, *Shī'i*'s thought was strictly dominated by the doctrine of *Imāmate* where Muslims have to wait for the *Imān*, the *Mahdī* (a personage who will appear one day and establish Islam once and for all as a righteous force). Instead of indefinitely waiting for the *Imām* (a kind of Waiting for Godot) Khomeini introduced the idea of *Wilāyat al-faqīh* which suggests that Muslims do not have to wait for the appearance of *Imām*, but rather to seek help in the *wālī's* foresight and discretion.

Khomeini's lectures given at Najaf in 1969 and his major work *Kashf al-Asrār* show that the *wālī* is an *Imam* in proxy and that he can do the job until the *Imām* actually appears, if he ever does. Khomeini was clever enough to introduce this kind of thesis so that no opportunity will be left for opportunists who will make a sport of life and its politics. Khomeini evidently intended to break the ice engulfing the belief of indefinitely waiting for the *Imām* to appear from his long absence. The move is more political than religious, and the behaviour of Khnomeini's successors proves this in being flexible enough to manipulate the current politics with the intention that they should do their utmost rather than leaving it behind, and that they should adjust their situation accordingly. Khomeini's regime, represented by his followers and successors still surprises us by its empirical approach to the complicated issues in the history of Islam.

In brief, Khomeini, his followers and successors came to believe that Islam as a state should be the responsibility of the *Fuqahā* around us rather than the absent *Imām*. The logistics of this adaptation already developed in Iran seems to be unacceptable by Shaṭṭī; hence is his parody of *Imāmah* as well as *wilāyah*. The least we can say of Shaṭṭī's; attitude is that it is political.

As a *Shi'ī* Khomeini believed in the doctrines of the *Shi'a* concerning the question of the *Imāmah* (leadership in Islam) and what relates to it, like the infallibility of *Imāms*, who must be looked at as beyond evil, sin or any wrong doing. The strong conviction in the *Imām* is the basis of the *Shi'a's* Islamic belief and a pillar of this belief. The *Imām* should be so trustworthy that he will not be subjected to any questioning because what he does is absolute good. Hence his infallibility. *Al 'Ulama* (learners) unanimously agreed that the *Imām* is immune to wrong deeds. However, the most important aspect of this controversial belief is that the *Imām* is unfortunately out of sight and that his return is somehow indefinite. A *Shi'ī* believes that the *Imām* who is, for one reason or another, not available, will come back one day even if it happened that he is already dead. His return is thought to be a kind of resurrection.

Khomeini somehow revised this belief by introducing what is called *Wilāyat al-Faqīh*, that is, the *wālī* as a religious sovereign or leader. Khomeini's main contribution to the question of *Imāmah* (*Imāmate* in Persian) lies in making it more practical. Instead of waiting for the indefinite return of the *Imām*, Khomeini wanted to be pragmatic. He thought that it was impossible to jeopardize life and social institutions awaiting the *Imām's* emergence. Khomeini seemed to question the validity of the belief that life remains static and religious beliefs kept in abbeyance and even paradise, due to the fact that the *Imām* is still not accessible.

Khomeini intended to break the ice that engulfed the *Imāmate* for centuries and to bridge the gap between the *Sunnī* and the *Shi'ī* and even to build a rapprochement between the two. In brief Khomeini intended to liberate Islam from the fictional notion of the devout *Imām* believed to be righteous enough and beyond any questioning by people who are not allowed to trespass on his turf. Khomeini seems to believe that Islam (though he cannot afford to be explicit about it) should be flexible, and in order to be so it should be more secular and less orthodox. The *Faqīh* (scholar of Islamic law), Khomeini advocated, can do the job of the *Imām*, and in order to be accepted by the general segment of '*Ulama*; Khomeini makes the *faqīh* look as if he can undertake this task of the *Imām*, maintaining the impression that the doctrine of the *Imām* can be suspended rather than dismissed altogether.

Khomeini enjoyed much popularity after the Iranian Revolution because he claimed that Islam should be secular in order to become a unifying force for the state.

Evidently the whole enterprise did not appeal to Shaṭṭi, who made a point of parodying secular elements of Khomeini's enterprise. In any case Shaṭṭi's scepticism as demonstrated in both his narrative and his letter, a reaction apparently made in response to the upheaval caused in the area by Khomeini and his Revolution. The whole situation is perceptively rendered in an essay recently published by Jean Baudrillard where he remarks:

> The idea of a clean war, like that of a clean bomb or an intelligent missile, this whole war conceived as a technological extrapolation of the brain is a sure sign of madness. It is like those characters in Hieronymus Bosch with a glass bell or a soap bubble around their head as a sign of their mental debility. A war enclosed in a glass coffin, like Snow White, purged of any carnal contamination or warrior's passion. A clean war which ends up in an oil slick.[1]

3. "'ANTARAH IBN ZABĪBAH': FĀRIS WITHOUT FURŪSIYYAH

'Antarah Ibn Zabībah, 'Antarah Ibn Shaddād, and 'Antarah al-'Absī, is the same legendary folktale figure, who lived between *c.* 525–616. 'Abs is a famous pre-Islamic tribe and Shaddād a dignitary of the tribe. 'Antarah was born to an Abbysinian maid (known in Arabic as *amah*) where he was, in accordance with pre-Islamic tradition, to be named after his mother and never to change his social status as a third class subject. It is said that 'Abs was once attacked by the neighbouring tribes when 'Antarah's father turned to his son and urged him to take part in the defence. 'Antarah's reply was (sarcastic, of course) that a maid's son should not be able to carry arms, being restricted by society to menial jobs. Immediately his father set him free and it was due to his participation in the counter attack that 'Abs won. 'Antarah had already trained himself in the art of war (in Arabic *furūsiyyah*) and he came to be known as the bravest of the brave.

'Antarah's biographical accounts are so controversial that some modern well-known men of letters like Tāha Ḥusayn and Ḥusayn Fawzi even denied his existence as a real person. On the other hand, Shawqī Ḍeif, a celebrated literary critic in modern Arabic literature, considers him the Arabic *Iliad*, and Philip Hittī sees him as an Achilles. Whether 'Antarah actually existed or not, his impact as a folktale hero in Arabic popular culture has been particularly immense. In Arabic tradition 'Antarah is a legacy of infinite bravery and special gallantry. He is a balanced warrior rather than a dashing fighter. Prophet Mohammad once said every time an account of an 'Ārābī is mentioned before him he yearned to meet 'Antarah.

What further makes 'Antarah survive in Arabic culture with the charisma of a hero is the gift he enjoyed as a poet, and his *mu'allaqah* is one of the seven or ten most famous classical pre-Islamic poems which form the great tradition of Arabic poetry. The lyricism of the poem reveals a gracious soul of a particularly tough fighter. The poem tells us the story of his passionate love for 'Abla which apparently was a dominant motivation for him in war and peace. This is how 'Antarah, the warrior-poet or the poet-warrior won his popularity in Arabic culture throughout centuries.

Biographers tell us that 'Antarah stands for the unity and dignity of his people. His people acknowledged him on his own merit, and he deserves the social status he earned. His death marks the end of 'Abs's glorious position in society.

* * *

This is the context of the frame reference from which the story of 'Antarah Ibn Zabībah emerges. The juxtaposition made between 'Antarah of the folktale and 'Antarah of the story is designed to demonstrate the lack of potential in Khartāsh's 'Antarah whose portrait is comprehensive enough to include a most critical crisis in modern Arabic history.

The title of the story is intended to keep 'Antarah in the position he found himself born in, so as to show his lack of potential for change and development. Contrary to 'Antarah of the tale, 'Antarah of the story stays in the abyss despite all the attempts he makes to become another 'Antarah Ibn Shaddād.

Hence the title of the story: 'Antarah Ibn Zabībah is meant to suggest all that 'Antarah Ibn Shaddād is not. 'Antarah in the story is mere evocation. This 'Antarah survives with the illusion that he is that 'Antarah, and the title itself satirizes this illusion. 'Antarah Ibn Zabībah is a superfluous title. The story demonstrates that this 'Antarah is a distorted picture of that one and that his whole career is a desire which is never fulfilled. He is a kind of Don Quixote without the human grace of weakness the Don enjoys.

The 'Antarah of the story is mainly the portrait of the sovereign who stands behind the disastrous war against Iran followed by a more disastrous one: the Gulf War. The narrative shows that the two wars in the area are Don Quixotic in nature and far from bearing the heroism of that, 'Antarah. For example, this sovereign claims that he is a descendent of the prophet, and to assert this, a family tree of the prophet is prepared and hung on walls in many public places in his country. The least the title suggests is that 'Antarah Ibn Zabībah can not be mistaken for a descendent of the prophet especially when his deeds drag him in the end into the abyss.

In its overt pattern 'Antarah's triumph in wars runs parallel to the sovereign's triumph against Iran; yet the covert meaning goes beyond the association between the two wars. 'Antarah's *furūsiyyah* is different from the sovereign's *'antariyyah* (an idiom used in Arabic to mean the opposite). The first was highly appreciated at the time, the second looked down upon. It was natural that the 'Abla of that 'Antarah would value her warrior's triumph and appreciate his courage and gallantry, but the 'Abla of the story, as we see in the text, is very critical of him altogether. The 'Antarah, who was once hailed as a hero returned from the battle is now received as a villain. This is ironical, of course, but such irony is realised once we remember that 'Abla (and her sister Lamya) stand in the story for the West who, no doubt, tempted the sovereign to fight Iran. For totally different reasons Iran turned out to be a common enemy for both the West and the sovereign whose self-conceit and egoism (a main theme lurking in the background of the story) made him believe that his triumph would satisfy the West. Whether the sovereign had the intention of playing a game with the West (at one time he actually did and perhaps was allowed to win in accordance with the rules) is something which needs contemplation. In any case the consequence is miscalculation on the sovereign's part and the story particularly dramatises this effect.

It is the sovereign's misfortune that he did not realise that the complex machinery of Western order gave him a role to play in the area and that his triumph against Iran simply meant to the producer (the West) an end to the first act.

The second act is heightened by 'Antarah's other encounter with 'Abla and her sister Lamya whose role this time demands becoming obliging and submissive in order to tempt the sovereign to get involved in another war game. A close reading of the story along with the political context of the Gulf War will identify 'Abla's (and her sister's) with the notorious story of the sovereign's consultation with an ambassador, who seemed to trap him in one way or another by not objecting to a perspective war against the neighbouring Arab country, in case the sovereign decided to do so. After the war began the intriguing incident has become too well-known to need elaboration here. Thus the second act of the two-act play begins with a dark comedy and ends in 'Antarah's defeat and humiliation in cold blood.

Who is this 'Antarah of the portrait? He is self-conceited, self-righteous, egoistic, a demagogue lost to history. During the Gulf War a reporter commented that millions of words were written about him but the words of this story are expressive enough to make up for a lot of them. In Arabic tradition the real 'Antarah is an exceptional example of bravery, decency, honesty, gallantry, sensitivity and so on; this 'Antarah is the opposite. The narrator records his dream early in the narrative:

> The mountains surrounding the tents of Banī 'Abs sent out their voices to him, calling his name, and repeating it across the reverberating desert sands. 'Antarah swayed with joy, as everything in nature chanted the name of the hero, 'Antarah, vanquisher of warriors. He held his head high and that slight smile of which he had always dreamed appeared on his face, heralding his triumphant entry into a new era called: The Time of 'Antarah Ibn Shaddād. Today, that new page would begin, and he would announce a new history of his life. Many people before and after him had written their histories as they pleased, so why should he not write the history of this life with his own hand, and by the sword?

Also the narrator records towards the end 'Antarah's devastating adventure, showing how the dream was never realised:

> Years later, he was released, and took to the corners of walls, tying his head with a coloured band to protect it from the winter cold and the summer heat. In his hand, he held a piece of coloured chalk, and he entered the cafés to recite poetry about wisdom and people's morals, then going outside again, and scribbling everywhere 'I am 'Antarah'.

The whole character of the sovereign 'Antarah is perceptively summed up in one stroke which concludes the narrative: 'I am 'Antarah'. This says everything about the man who led his country and other brethren countries to disaster. Had the narrator chosen to be explicit he would have substituted 'Antarah with *'Antarī*, the adjective for the noun *'antariyyāt*, and this will establish a sharp contrast between the two 'Antarahs of the past and the present.

The problem with the sovereign 'Antarah is that he confuses fact with fiction, concrete with abstract reality, imagination with fantasy and prose with poetry. All his references to 'Antarah's great poem are incoherent, fragmented and made to fit his own rhetoric. For example, the first verse (considered the most beautiful line of any poetry) which the *mu'allaqah* begins with is misrepresented when remembered and sung by the sovereign 'Antarah, who sees it as rhetoric, failing to observe the profound, inspiring rhetorical question the verse poses to posterity in its original context.

* * *

The narrative, however, does not restrict the point-of-view to 'Antarah in the story so as to see him the only party responsible for what happens. The irony is further worked out in the story to show the discrepancy between one 'Antarah who led his people to glory and another who caused them infinite misery – this irony extends its sphere to Lamya, who stands for the sovereign toadies ('Abla being a representative of foreign intervention and Lamia its agent). Here is Lamia's reply (full of irony) to 'Antarah which implies at the end that other Arab sovereigns are partners in the responsibility:

> 'But we are negotiating with them, and there shall be peace between us, and there shall be no work for the likes of you after that. Come back to us after the peace negotiations. You may be of use to us in teaching the Arab tribes a lesson because, thank God, you only fight Arabs.' So said Lamia to him.

Other partners or sovereigns are portrayed as observers, and this is ironically dramatised:

They signalled each other to subdue him, then pulled him out of his chair. Then ensued the following scene, which you watched at Cinema Cairo: ''Antarah shackled in irons, roaring in the face of his tormentors.' That was on the first day. On the fifth day, most of his bones had been broken, and his moustache had been plucked.

Like Sulayman Shaṭṭī and many other short story writers Faysal Khartāsh has succeeded in making the long story short, and the small canvas of the short story accommodate big issues involving the life of people in the area. It is here where the modern Arabic short story tells much more than what it actually says and in similar manner to what the great tradition of the folktale can capture of life at large as has already been demonstrated.

Notes

2. *An Oil Slick*,

1. Jean Baudrillard, 'The Gulf War: Is it Really Taking Place' in *Postmodern Debates* ed. Simon Malpas, (Palgrave: Basingstoke, 2001), p. 65.

V

Conclusion

The Arabic short story is a special case and has a comparatively special situation. When Katherine Mansfield, Katherine Ann Porter, A.E. Coppard, Maupassant and others wrote short fiction they were already convinced that the short story with its particularities or limitations was the genre they wanted to adopt. Similarly when H.G. Wells, Henry James, D.H. Lawrence and Joseph Conrad–to mention only a few of a long list–wrote short stories they were evidently masters of the longer fiction; they turned to short fiction with the intention of writing in a different genre altogether. All these writers wrote with enough clarity in mind about the relative limitation of one genre and the freedom of another. The fact that the novel had a longer history made it possible to establish some tradition for the short story, at least on the basis of comparison and sense of relatedness between the two genres. When, for example, some outstanding short-story writers like Maupassant, Mansfield and Coppard were urged to write novels their immediate response was that the longer fiction was not a simple expansion of the shorter one, and this obviously suggests that these writers were fully conscious of the technique of the genre they did not or could not write in. This does not mean that some writers like Mansfield were not sorry for not having written one of 'the "big" things'.

Writers, then, wrote short stories with certain attributes of the genre already established. Such attributes are: the short story as an impression like one of Sargent's pictures, as James remarks; as a 'mood of aesthetic restlessness', to use Elizabeth Bowen's description; or as an attempt to capture the flying moment, according to Sherwood Anderson. Throughout its literary history from the late nineteenth century onward the short story has acquired a large number of phrases identifying its generic structure. In a most perceptive study of the short story Valerie Shaw quotes and draws upon some of these phrases as the 'supreme moment of perception'; 'a sort of over-to-you (reader)'; 'the objective demonstration rather than personal narration'; 'a fluid composition of primary colours and intermediate shapes'; 'a sense of the moment's drama' and so on.[1] One can almost compile a dictionary of literary terms for the short story even without being able to lay down a definition for it.

The Arabic short story, on the other hand, has a different background, where, in his critical account, Hussām al-Khatīb points to the similar circumstances which both short story and novel passed through in their short histories.[2] Somehow this particular situation has worked to the advantage of the Arab short story writer. By this I mean that the Arab short story writer was not suffering from an obsession with what might have been a rival genre, which could curb his artistic bent in one way or another. I do not think the Arab short story writers such as the ones chosen here, for example, were really concerned with the dilemma of form which preoccupied Western writers, who experimented with technique in the hope of establishing a tradition independent of other similar genres like the novella and the novel. Similarly they were not seriously involved in the status of the genre in comparison with that of the novel which in Western literature has been obviously favoured, at least in critical evaluation. An Arab writer can gain reputation by publishing just one or two good short stories. Maḥmūd Shukair published a small collection of short stories (in which 'The Orphans' Cow' is included) which established his reputation as a writer. Zakariyyā Tāmir was first launched in literary circles by 'Spring in the Ashes'. Similarly Emīle Habībī's reputation was promoted by 'The Blue Charm and the Return of Jubaynah'. In other words the short story is as respected a genre as any other related or interrelated genre, and one reason for this may be due to the fact that different genres (in the Arab world) such as the short story, the novella, the novel and free verse emerged almost at the same time. We can assume that the short story proper is not more than four decades old.

Whether the short story has been influenced by the visual arts, photography, metaphysics of time or psychology is something almost beside the point to the Arab writer. Arabic short story writing has been undertaken within the context of pioneering conditions. The Arab writer found himself surrounded by critical issues at stake which demanded a writer to express. In simple terms the Arabic short story is generally an act of expression rather than impression. Its motivation is comparatively different.

Arab writers, as might have been demonstrated from this study, entered into a writing experience which can be identified with that of Virginia Woolf who, on seeing Walter Sickert's paintings, realised that they were 'full of pictures that might be stories.'[3] Similarly those writers looked into different folktales (Sindbad and others) and found them full of tales that might be stories. Instead of the visual element as a source of impact on the short story, Arab writers turned to the verbal form of folktale as a starting point with no urgent need for relying on objective demonstration.

Also Arab writers wrote short stories with the notion that 'content determines form', Lukacs's well-known critical statement. We have already seen that the content is not a light subject-matter made entertaining by revealing its intricacy, subtlety, invisibility or mystery as is the usual practice of the short story. The Arab writer has found his life immediately determined by the issues at stake and he has had no choice but to start with and from them; this is how content gains preference over form, at least in the sequential process of writing. The special nature of content seems to decide the kind of epical form the Arab writer draws upon from the folktale motif, which appropriates the form. Figures like Sindbad, Shahrazad, Abu-Zayd, Shāṭir Ḥasan and ‘Antarah have a sense of dimension large enough to accommodate the situation and help the writer manipulate the normal gap between author and his subject-matter. Such figures have national characteristics which, because they are so discernible, save the author right from the beginning the trouble of working out a form surcharged with the necessary allusions and implications which are usually needed to make up for the brevity of form. No matter how much an author here would labour towards creating a form by personal narration or by objective demonstration the artifice may not have the same potential as the form of the folktale motif.

By exploring the heritage of the folktale, Arab writers have made a remarkable contribution towards establishing a modern tradition in short fiction, and any further research into the modern Arabic short story will show that there are ample short stories which have been written in the vein of this tradition during the last five decades or so. For this reason I find Denys Johnson-Davies's critical review of modern Arabic fiction rather unfair, especially when he says in the course of a reappraisal of al-Ṭayyib Sālih's fiction as we have seen above how ‘Marxist commitment and existentialism are two attitudes which continue to bedevil Arab fiction today.’[4]

I believe that such an outlook bedevils Johnson-Davies's enthusiasm for Arabic fiction, despite all his invaluable work on the subject particularly in the field of translation. I also believe that al-Ṭayyib Sālih himself would not appreciate an assessment intended to appraise him and, at the same time, discredit his fellow Arab writers with whom he shares a deep concern for the existing political and social situation. No Arab writer in modern times can escape the public events which immediately affect his daily life. Even the most Bohemian contemporary Arab poet, Nizār Qabbānī, found himself fully involved in public affairs after the 1967 war and consequently wrote his most extended public poem which was censored in most Arab countries despite all the popularity the poem enjoys among Arab readers. As mentioned earlier in this study, the situation of the Arab writer is similar to that of English writers who, in the 1930s found commitment to public issues inevitable; and some outstanding writers found themselves drifted towards fascism and communism.

Yet Arab writers have not been deviating from the norm of the short story–at least its basic feature of locality which is often considered a characteristic concern of the genre. Most serious Arabic short stories leave the reader (who is familiar with the milieu, at least) with the feeling that only in the Arab world could this or that happen! It is, however, a special locality which is distinguished from the common locality of the short story at large by being public rather than private, human rather than provincial, communal rather than having the kind of individualised character seen in 'objective correlative'. It is the kind of typicality where individual emotions are expressed by means of socially meaningful patterns. In a sense it is a complex locality because it moves towards universality by using folktale motif which gives the typical situation a bigger dimension.

The shift from the exotic to the realistic is what may be viewed as a major development in the short history of the Arabic short story. The early generation of the Arabic short story writers draped their local figures in fantastic colours to make them eventually appear out of proportion in this world. It did not matter to those writers whether, for example, the picture of the *fallāh* in their stories had no authentic ground, because what they aimed at was the fantastic element. It is this picture which seems to be most appealing to Arabists like Johnson-Davies, as his interpretation of al-Ṭayyib Sālih shows and the Arabic short stories he selected for translation may demonstrate. However a devoted and sincere Arabist like Johnson-Davies should have the privilege of being selective in his outlook at the Arabic literary scene using the common ground of the genre in his reading of the short story.

The situation of the writer under the regime of the Revolution has been so much in focus in current literary journals and supplements, and one wonders whether Johnson–Davies, who has been living in Egypt for many years, has changed his views about Arab writers whose fiction, he comments, is bedevilled by their commitment to 'communism or existentialism'. This is, for example, one of many accounts which retrospectively captures the relationship between the writer and the authoritarian regime of the Revolution. In his essay 'Nostalgia for the Leader: the Democracy of the Just Dictator' Mohammad Shu'ayr says that 'we are not nostalgic about 'Abdul-Nasir, simply because nostalgia, by definition, is brought about by incidents which, with the passage of time, become a memory'. He then quotes the well-known reformer, Mohammad 'Abdu, who says that undeveloped societies are always in need of the just dictator transitional era, implying (not without irony and sarcasm) that the leader of the Revolution was a just dictator. Shu'ayr adds, (supported by Baha' Ṭahir, the novelist) 'that in dealing with the intelligentsia the Revolution followed the policy of what is called 'the rod and the carrot', a reference to crime and punishment. Shu'ayr concludes:

> The intellectual [the writer, of course] has to observe his limits and leave the officers of the Revolution alone so that he will be equally left alone. Those officers may bestow on the intellectual whatever artificial honours and favours they want and whenever they want, but most important is that the intellectual should not go beyond the role already set for him, and even when he decides to collect his courage and cross the limit he still should abide by the binding limit and its maximum margin. The intellectual may be allowed to be critical of social conditions and institutions, but he should be so general in what he says or writes. For example, he can refer to the Sultan's duty towards his subject urging him to go back to them for the sake of democracy, but no specific reference should be made to the identity of the Sultan or the identity of the subject.[5]

What could Arab writers do when faced with 'the just dictator' whose mandate over his subject, in different parts of the Arab world has not vanished? Some writers such as included here opted to join the flights of Sindbad (the Sultan Sindbad) or the similar flights of folktales. Others seem to prefer staying on ground and resort to 'existentialism and communism', an option which is initially, a kind of flight.

What those 'just dictators' and officers failed to realize is that the Sultan and his subject do not really need to be explicitly identified when they are effectively presented in writing.

In approaching the modern Arabic story we need to realise the awareness of the positive function of the genre exploited by some Arab writers drawing a portrait out of Arabic folktale, incorporating current politics and fiction, and consequently creating social consciousness moving from 'silence to sound again' to use the tittle of an essay by Edward Sa'īd.

Notes

1. Valerie Shaw, *The Short Story: A Critical Introduction* (London: Longman, 1983) p. 13.
2. al-Khatīb, p. 28.
3. Quoted by Valerie Shaw, p. 15.
4. Johnson-Davies, *Azure*, p. 16.
5. Mohammad Shu'ayr, "Nostalgia for the Leader: the Democracy of the Just Dictator", *Akhbār al-Adab*, July 23 (2000), p. 9.

Part Two

A Selection of Texts

The Death of Sindbad

A Narrative in One Act

by
Michael 'Aflaq

The curtain rises on one of the quarters of old Baghdad. Sindbad, an old man with back bent and clothes in tatters, returns from his voyage, all his wealth spent. He finds all his family dead and his house sold. Weakly, he mounts a stone which lies in front of the house which no longer belongs to him. The neighbours and the youth of the quarter gather around him: they bombard him with questions, half pitying, half mocking. The children pelt him with stones.

Youth of Baghdad: Sindbad! Sindbad! Give us news of foreign lands.

Another: Tell us of the lands you have seen.

Another: Tell us of the hardships you met.

Old man: Speak, Sindbad. Tell the people what happens to him who is not content with what God decrees for him.

Another: Speak, Sindbad. You are on the last step of your journey. Why do you not speak the great word which you have won after weariness and voyaging? Tell these young men of the fate of one who mocks tradition and order, who leaves family and country, who follows only his own desire: what does destiny do to him?

Another old man: Speak, Sindbad, you are surely dying. One profitable word from you will make good your offences of excess and passion. Speak, one word, one word before you pass. Disown your life and past. Advise these young men to respect what is sure and guaranteed and not, like you, to cling to impossible dreams.

Sindbad: *(Laughing bitterly)* Ha, ha, ha. A profitable word from me? How can he be of profit who has spent his life mocking at profit, squandering all he accumulates! You seek profit even from one whom you hate and slight; you think of profit even in the hour of my death, my failure, my ruin ...

Old man: What does he say? He talks of mocking profit when he has worn himself out seeking wealth!

Another: Destroyed himself in pursuit of riches in far off lands!

Another: Dived for pearls in the depths of the sea!

Boy: *(Throwing a stone)* Look at his hands: they're worn with all he has collected.

Another boy: *(Attacking his legs)* Look at his legs faint with the way he has travelled.

Another boy: *(Spitting in his face)* Look at his face and eyes: sea-monsters have eaten his eyes.

Youth: *(Driving the boys from him)* Don't grieve, Sindbad. Tell us news of foreign lands.

Another: Tell us of the wealth you amassed.

Another: Tell us of the horrors you have experienced.

Another: Tell us of the pearls you have won and sold.

Sindbad: My hands are not worn with piling up wealth: they are worn with giving. My feet are not faint with walking, but with desire and distress. Sea-monsters have not eaten out my eyes, but the blazing light. I have journeyed from pole to pole to hear the sound of my own voice, and I have sailed the farthest seas to see the colour of my own eyes.

Youth: The colour of his eyes, the colour of his eyes! He wants to see the colour of his eyes!

Another: To see the colour of his eyes, he encircles the earth with his arms!

Old man: Close your eyes: close them, Sindbad: for if you open them you will see nothing but black. You wished to serve your own soul, and to see nothing but yourself in all creation. And you are dying, defeated, a failure. For the eye exists to see only what is far from it, to see other people.

Another: You are dying, Sindbad. And it is best for yourself and for the people that you die. There is a lesson in your failure, and an example in your death.

Sindbad: What greater failure have I, than that you should seek a lesson in my life? What death harder than that you should try to profit from my death!

Another old man: Die, Sindbad. It is best for yourself and for those young men that you die, and that they learn that you have returned bankrupt. There is compassion on their eyes for what you have seen and witnessed, and a desire which they cannot conceal, for what you have learned and discovered. Tell them that the far horizon conceals from them nothing but disappointment and delusion.

Another old man: Tell them that you were blinded by the shock of disappointment and the gloom of emptiness.

Sindbad: Rather I was blinded by the dazzling truth I saw.

Youth: Blind from the dazzling truth? Then is there truth and light beyond the horizon?

Another: Is its light bright enough to blind the eyes?

Another: Tell us, Sindbad, of the truth which blinds.

Sindbad: It was in my eyes before it was on the far horizon.

Youth: Why, then, did you seek it beyond the horizon?

Sindbad: I travelled to the farthest corner of the world to know the point nearest to me, to know myself.

Old man: To know yourself and to forget others! Did you find yourself, while your children were dying of hunger and cold?

Another: Did you find yourself while your wife was selling your house and her body to your creditors? You ought to have known your duty towards your fellows.

Sindbad: I have no duty but my duty towards myself.

Old man: And your starving children?

Sindbad: My thoughts are my only sons.

Another old man: And your faithful wife?

Sindbad: I have no wife but my dreams.

Another old man: And your strong, secure home?

Sindbad: My home is where my desire and longing lead me.

Youth: His home, his home, the creditors have sold his home!

Another: His home is where desire and longing lead him!

Youth: Tell us, Sindbad, about your homes which desire has raised and love has built.

Another: Your homes, which are built by night and demolished by day.

Another: Your homes, which dance now on the mountains, now on the sea.

Sindbad: I have carried my home, all wealth on my back. I have left all that is heavy, all that cannot be carried on the back or lifted with the fingers. But my hands can hold the world in their ten fingers.

Youth: Sindbad! Sindbad! He carries the world in his fingers. Look, do you see the world, as a mouse-hole?

Another: Now you see his hands, hands of *jinn*: now you see mountains of wool!

Sindbad: I took from life all that a man's hands can hold; but I took and threw it away, I took and gave till my hands and touched everything and my heart held every living thing.

Youth: Tell us Sindbad, how your hands hold the world?

Another: Tell us how your desire wandered away from all living things.

Another: Tell us how you took and threw away, and took and gave and how you grew rich by giving!

Old man: Look, now, at his riches: he owns nothing but water and air!

Another: Look at his generosity and his giving: he piled up wealth for himself and left nothing for his family!

Sindbad: I went to give people what is better than wealth, more costly than pearls.

Old man: But you piled up wealth for yourself.

Sindbad: I went to seek a new world, built of freedom and beauty.

Old man: But you return loaded with chains.

Sindbad: I went to search the world for news of a secret which will restore its sons to happiness.

Old man: You went to pile up wealth for yourself.

Sindbad: I have ransacked the world from east to west, from south to north, in search of a magic point which will restore hope to mankind.

Youth: You went from south to north for the sake of a word?

Sindbad: For its sake, I went down into the depths of the sea. I scaled alone the heights of the mountains.

Youth: And is it now far to seek?

Sindbad: For its sake, I went down where none had dared go, and mounted to where none go without giddiness, dancing upon places where danger lurks.

Youth: Then tell us what you found.

Another: Tell us the word that restores hope to the heart.

Another: Tell us the new secret word, which is above all secrets.

Another: Tell us, Sindbad, speak!

Another: Speak!

Another: Speak before your journey's end.

Old man: Hush: do not speak the word!

Another: Say nothing!

Another: Do not speak what God has forbidden to be known.

Youth: Speak, Sindbad. Tell us the word which disperses doubts.

Another: Tell us what is the truth which has been before our eyes since all eternity.

(Sindbad is about to speak the word but falls to the ground and lies motionless: from his mouth emerges a black snake ...)

Youth: Silence has killed him.

Old man: He has given us life!

Sindbad And His Mistress

by
Michael 'Aflaq

Most lacking in modern Arabic literature is the story [by which the speaker here means the short story]. *It is the various aspects of narrative including the psychological, the social, the philosophical, the symbolic, the pragmatic, and the historical. Many attempts have been undertaken to promote this genre: only a few have been successful, but the majority have been flat, superfluous, dry and marred by the flaws we generally find in our modern Arabic literature as a whole.*

However, we introduce our reader today to Michael 'Aflaq, a new man of letters who is a short story writer. The following short story demonstrates how imaginative 'Aflaq is for the profound psychological mood he presents in this story. Despite its brevity and economical language the story expresses the articulation of theme and form [This editorial Note is obviously written by 'Aflaq himself].

* * *

Night extended its wings over Baghdad. The great city lay asleep in the shelter of darkness, as if it were an exhausted traveller. Sindbad walked towards the window of his room and opened it extending his eyesight to the wide horizon as if he was overlooking a destiny already settled there. The sky of that night was crowded with soft clouds transparent enough to reveal ethereal boats carrying dreams on their way to the stars. Sindbad inhaled the fresh air with whatever strength he had, but the gentle breeze provoked in him great yearning. Sindbad pressed his heart strongly and continued walking in silence.

In one corner of Sindbad's room was his mistress floating on silk waves and swimming in perfumed mists, leaning over her breast as if suppressing the beatings of her heart with a black question mark of hair coming down of a hair lock over her pale brow.

O Sindbad, that strange traveller! What makes you travel? Don't you have in my eyes what makes up for the clearest sky and in my hair what gives you the most protective shelter?

You are my darling two flowing streams on whose banks I take rest against my restless soul and longing heart. Your hair is my new haven of peace where I find in its comfortable shades the quintessence of my real existence. But my soul is in need of harsh experience and my heart is after illumination brought about not without wounds in the course of quest for truth. All this is to make me appreciate my final resort to you at the end.

Aren't you, my dear, afraid of dangerous adventures across the seas?

My dear, without the smell of death, life is tasteless for me. I have never been elevated to the stars except on the wings of storms. My life, dearest, is wealth subject to daily loss and gain.

You are a strange creature, Sindbad. I can not understand you. What wealth you are talking about to urge you to travel while you live already in prosperity.

Mere wealth, my dearest, is not the driving force, but rather the quest. It is not the greed which drives me to go away from home, but my feet which insist on moving. My arms never rest without struggling against wares and rocks!

Sindbad stopped talking as he was growing nervous and more restless as the time of the caravan departure was getting closer, and it was just before dawn. He felt a hot suffocating wave was blowing over as if he was prepared for a rendezvous. His whole existence, he felt, was diminishing and melting in a bottomless space. He could hardly bear the few minutes to pass before he can cross over to the new life calling him from behind to horizon. He looked at his mistress lost in the corner of the dark room and whispered in contemplation: in what way am I attached to this woman? She stands for laziness and immobility. She belongs to the past. The ropes of the night will rap her along with my past. He looked towards the promising dawn wavering in the distant horizon. He sensed the prospect of the future, of the coming life. He nodded and smiled sarcastically at himself. Let life go on with all its regeneration and magical surprises. What matters which way he should take. Let his legs take him wherever they want.

In silence Sindbad's mistress cried bitterly in the middle of darkness. She stared at her lover's yellow bare muscles glittering in starlight and felt a big barrier standing between her and the man she lived so close to as to make her imagine life impossible without him. It dawned on her that she had lost him though he was only a few yards from where she lived. She continued staring at those yellow muscles as if they were the reason behind the mysterious barrier which suddenly emerged between them. How strange the situation of this man is! Every time he looks beside the window and is patted by the dawn breeze he is upset and agitated: his sympathy is transformed into apathy and his peace into worry. As for the Sindbad's mistress the situation is different. Every time she stands beside the window to explore the mystery of life she suddenly senses in the stars nothing but peace and the dewy morning breeze convey to her only comfort and longing for sleep.

Sindbad turned to his mistress's bed to say farewell to all his past with her as if he were having the last glance of a dear departed. He made her sit on his lap and kissed her. With his eyes closed he embarked on the following narrative:

'In the north, my dear, have you ever heard of the north? It is a place in the middle of nowhere surrounded by mysteries. It is said that dawn in that country is so peaceful and serene that it climbs down the top of huge mountains to dance at the banks of the stream and sings with country women. Also the sun in that country is so intimate with the night and darkness is consequently minimised for months where the dull light of the night becomes a screen which increases its mysteries. I have been told this by an Indian sage, a travelling companion I met on my last voyage. He spoke to me at length. I didn't at the time pay attention to what he said because I was bored of travel and wanted rest. But now I hear the Indian sage with his magical voice saying: imagine the earth and the mountains made of snow and that all of them melt quickly as snow does. Then they all appear as mountains of dream ... .'

'Sindbad! Sindbad!'

That was the voice of a man from the caravan. Sindbad freed himself from the arms of his woman and hurried towards the door. His mistress called:

'Aren't you going to take your luggage?'

Sindbad replied as he was on horseback:

'I am going to dispose of my garment in the river '.

Sindbad the Porter

by
Najīb Surūr

Shahrazad said: 'I have heard, O Happy King, that there was during the reign of the Caliph and Prince of the Faithful Hārūn al-Rashīd a man called Sindbad the Porter and he was impoverished ... .'

Night (524) of the *Thousand and One Nights*
1 *The Final Melody*
....
So the Prince begot ten sons
and ten daughters ... like full moons,
all revel in content and joy,
the years roll past, O my Happy King
pristine clear as the eyes of a cock
along comes Fate, scattering the beads
parting friend from friend
and cutting the path,
he buries lips in the snow
and consumes the balls of the eyes,
the eyes drink of the earth
and in the darkness the worms feast
the tale of life is at an end
like a tender song dying across the sky;
My Happy King
short and sweet is the tale of life
like the smile of a child

like a drink of milk
like the kiss of a lover to the beloved
like the tale of the amazing Sindbad!'
And morning caught up with Shahrazad.

2. *The City of Agony*
'It is said, O my Happy King
that long ago did Sindbad live
he was a man who drank of sweat
and was clothed in rags
and dug his thick fingers into the flames
to force forth a loaf
and chewed '*alqam* * from morn till night
he was like a wind-ravaged salt
that is left in tatters and shreds.
It is said he approached the sea one morn
and left his children with hunger howling,
the scent of nectar from the water he breathed,
exhausted he made his way to a rock
whereon he laid his heavy sack,
he cast his sight far and wide
the Sun Goddess weaves a golden tent across the sky,
the Ocean Goddess swallows '*aqīq**
and washes up shells,
a wave boils and churns up foam,
it lashes the rocks with its veil,
a call from eternity are the sands,
riddles like graves are these hills,
pitched on horns by an old magician
who hid treasures within their heavy ribs.
Sindbad wondered what the seas concealed!
And where the journeys of the birds did end!

And where the horizon did begin!
He asked the sands for the tale of life
he asked the waters,
bewildered an hour he was by the images of life
for in this world is food
and within the seas and hills is wealth
enough to satisfy humanity
so why starve we?
Why does the Sun Goddess burn the naked
and tenderly caress the affluent?
Those thousands within the City of Agony
are captive-like women behind a wall,
are chewed by eagles and hawks,
their hopes are still-born,
tormented, their feelings are strangled by despair
they curse heaven.
In the City of Agony my Happy King
for a few pounds are the women sold!
The women are eaten
the men are crucified behind its impenetrable gate,
the young are buried alive,
blood is drunk
the hands of thieves are severed,
heads are strung into necklaces
and skins are ripped off,
lions crouch at its great gate,
guarding hell,
he returns not who enters hell!
Sindbad was fleeing from hell,
his children abandoned,
in his grief he dug in the sand
to bury the tears,

like a ray came a call from the dark,
then the grieving Sindbad smiled..'
And morning caught up with Shahrazad.

3. *Sindbad's Dilemma*
'My Happy King,
–like a ray came a call from the dark,
then the grieving Sindbad smiled–
a ship there along the horizon
like the shining wing of a bird ...
–its sail–waving ... or a bride ...
gliding daintily like a breeze
beneath it the blue ocean for a carpet.
Sindbad picked up some straw
and almost sent the ship a smoke signal
to leave hell behind to those who remain,
far beyond that horizon,
it is said, in the country of Wāqwāq,
are cities like paradise
overflowing with treasures, fruits and seeds,
overflowing with spices,
with no Caliph for a Lord,
without chains to fetter humans,
nor are hands there cut off
for there are none there who starve!
–Sindbad almost issued forth the smoke–
'May he who dies die
may they who drown
Noah appears not twice
and salvation is for those who board!'
Like wolves before him the images swarmed
digging their teeth into his head ... like wolves

tore his feeble ribs ... like spears;
the heap of children in the City of Agony
bite the earth,
quell their bellies with mosquitoes and flies,
hit their heads against the walls;
there a weak wife ... a rabbit
chased by hounds
solitary in the hawk's landing space ... a skylark
the rosaries of the hand and neck
taken by the Caliph of God .. a chain
to bind the slaves to heaven
he savoured flesh like a monster
–the Caliph of God–
children he ate for breakfast,
adults he ate for lunch,
women he ate for supper;
and the wife of the impoverished Sindbad,
a chicken easily preyed on by a monster,
for she was full of flesh!
Like wolves before him the images swarmed,
digging their teeth into his head ... like wolves–
would he abandon the thousands in the City of Agony,
amongst them his feeble children,
and his wife an easy prey to the monster!
Would he seek life in the country of Wāqwā ,
whilst here are the treasures, the fruits and the grain.
'Whilst here the spices are
locked up in the palaces!'
A true call appeared like the morn,
pointing to salvation ... the way:
a flock of birds after a winter's journey
returns home;

why does it return?
So Sindbad returned ...'
and morning caught up with Shahrazad.

4. *Salvation*
'My Happy King
Sindbad returned to hell
to bring about prosperity,
to make life fit to live,
deep and wide like that ocean,
so that Fate would be mocked by life,
though it be brief like the smile of a child;
Sindbad set forth blowing his bugle
–the Caliph of God imprisons life
and spreads disease and ruin;
–Where lies the way O Sindbad?
Sindbad told the tale of the raven
'... And he was wont to rob the nests of the birds
strangle the chicks,
the birds lament or weep;
in calamity wherein lies the good of weeping!
For that raven loves tears.
The birds said: Wherein lies the way ...?
Then a wise bird advised:
to the raven and kill him,
destroy his resplendent nest;
we are naked ... while the raven is in silks!
Our silks ... our labours from morn till evening
are plundered by the raven ...
Like rain they pelted him with fire
hanged him as a tale to be told to the chicks ...'
All became Sindbad!

The City of Agony they destroyed
the raven they hanged,
they built the city of 'steadiness and plant',
wedded the youths and the girls,
carried on the joyous nights,
kept songs going till morn;
the years roll past my Happy King,
pristine clear like the eyes of a cock,
like a drink of milk,
the kiss of a lover to the beloved;
short and sweet is the tale of life,
like the tale of the amazing Sindbad ...'
And morning caught up with Shahrazad.

Sindbad on his Eighth Voyage

by
Khalīl Ḥāwī

It had been his intention not to bestir himself from his sojourn in Baghdad following his seventh trip. However, he heard one day of sailors who had undertaken adventure in a world hitherto unknown to him; and so it was that a yearning to set sail an eighth time overcame him. One of the things that is told about Sindbad on his eighth voyage is that he sailed through the universe of his self and that here and there, he stumbled on heaps of old luggage and worn-out concepts, all of which he threw into the sea without regretting the loss in the least. He stripped himself naked until his nakedness reached the essence of his natural self. Then he returned, bringing us a treasure unsurpassed by the treasures of which he had availed himself on his previous trips.

This poem is a chronicle of what he suffered over the period of his emergence from the labyrinths of his self until he experienced the dawn of resurrection and the certitude of his knowledge was complete.

1

O my home that has sailed away and become estranged
to me. You have been the best refuge
in the tumult of the seas.
In my estrangement
and my room

with dust growing on its doorstep,
in cities petrifying the night in my nerves
I throw myself onto the train but the night goes with me.
My seven voyages and my treasure amassed
through the bounty of the Almighty and trade,
the day I slew the monster
and the devil, ... my burial,
then that crack in the cave,
I have told the tales they usually tell about me,
I suppressed what cannot be rendered in words,
yet I continue to go in pursuit of it
I sense it within me yet I do not grasp it.
How can I survive knowing that I
am being driven in pursuit of nakedness and loss?
I strive to empty my house in the hope
that when it appears it will be tempted to claim it.
I sense him within me yet I do not grasp it.

2
In that home there was a hall,
images embellished its walls.
Moses sees a fiery chisel with searing flames
engraving into the rock
the ten commandments of his Lord.
Pitch, sulphur and salt on Sodom.
That was on one wall.
On another wall a picture
of a priest in the temple of Ba‘l
raising a scotched viper, an owl
preying upon the secret of fertility in virgins.
The drunkards celebrating,
the wombs and the vines bear fruit,

the wine foams in the jars.
On a third wall a fresco:
that shows al-Ma'arri,
behind his eyes
and in his deep cavern
his world the intrigues of a woman unwashed
of her blood ...,
knowing not though the banks of the nectar-coated bay
the roundness of the breasts coming later of its foam
and lily crowned forehead.
The ancient culprit
and the bitter fruit after which he lusted.

From these images
flows a stream
laden with gas and poisons
it is absorbed by the viper in the female
and the gypsy race that is in her blood
and the blind tiger and the fever of his hand
in his male jealousy:
Lorca and *The Wedding of Blood in Spain*
and the sword of the Cock of the Jinn in Hamah,*
the ivory neck is a red river
what horrors has death frozen upon the lips!
This congested explosive blood in the veins
is bitten, seared by a thousand burns
in the corners of a stair
in the darkness of the alleys
a choked gurgle and a gasp.

A city on the opium stage awakens
to the echo of the earthquake in its guts,
a wall of flames

blinds the night and the road,
the underworld bursts and from its lairs
springs a monster which lashes creatures
with curses and flames.
This congested explosive blood in the veins.

3

I experienced that pavilion
a child in whose blood flowed gases and poisons
in whose breast images were engraved
I was in it with old friends
bringing it tidings of malice, sweetening its taste with hypocrisy
with a dose of 'the Caliph's honey
and al-Bashīr's coffee'
my silken speech
cuts like the keen edge of a dagger
through the silken coils of your beauty, my beloved.

I striped that pavilion
I turned it into an old shelter for old friends
I exorcised my house from the echo of their ghosts
by day and by night
from my own spite my feebleness
soft as a slender serpent, a dagger in my heart.
I lived waiting
in the hope that if he passed by I would tempt him
but he did not pass
nor did he send his thunder and lightning towards me.
I begged for the brightness of morning and rain, O my Lord,
why has my house become clouded?
Why is it choking with silence and dust
a calcified salty fallow desert?

After the taste of arid limestone,
darkness erupted from
the corridors, damp
rotten and fevered
as though the city's channels of filth had gathered there
and poured forth,
overflowing by night and by day.
The taste of arid limestone returns.
One night the darkness foamed
eating away the ribs of the ceiling and wall,
and the ceiling folded and wall folded
like a wet old rag,
like a sail that is flung
on seas of deep darkness
chafed by the black winds around it
gnawed by the black waves
which threw it to the wind.
The white swoon closed my eyes
I left the battered body
soaked with wounds
to the waves and the winds.

4

On the shore of the islands of ice
I was seeing as one drugged and demented
a desert calcified, salty and arid,
shimmering as with snow or the blossom of fruit-trees
My house that had collapsed
arises from its ruins,
the logs tremble
and gather into a living green dome in spring.

I shall not claim that the angel of the Lord

poured holy wine and live embers
into my body imprisoned by ice,
drained my veins of the blood
congested with gas and poisons,
wiped from the panel of my breast
the imprints and images,
I shall not claim
a deep awakening rocked by the cradle of the stars,
Nor do I know how it came to pass,
no, perhaps it was the wounds
perhaps it was the sea and the chafing of the waves and wind
perhaps it was the white trance and the ice
that sealed my veins to the veins of the earth,
the white shroud was a shield
under which the spring fermented,
my heart grew verdant,
throbbed with the tender-winged sails of the lilies.
A child sings of innocence in my veins,
I am naked and the morning does not abash me,
the first pulse,
and a vision that could find no word,
choked, tears shone and trembled.
Is it an invitation to love this voice
the phantom that shone in the sun
took on flesh and scooped from my body
bread and salt,
wine and fire?
Alone I wait
I have emptied my home a second time
I live on tender sweet *'ambers* and hunger
as though my organs were birds
that crossed seas
I wait alone.

5

In the city square
her steps were
a boat that brings songs
from the joy of the waves in the bay,
breaking the sunlight
on the crystal, filling it with shadows
of green and tranquility.
Was she not seen by others
in the city square
was she not seen by other eyes?
This Life would not cry
'if only the years
filled my hand and my arm,
the sweetest pride of the seasons
in the vine, the spring and the fields'
this Life will not cry
'if only the years.'

6

My home suffers the last vigil
the echo of the daring steps
breaking the coral patterns
in the floor home and the wall.
Mirror of my home be washed
of your burdensome care and the dust
and celebrate the beautiful innocent one
who as though in the morning
was carved from my ribs,
sprang up from the lily of the seas
unstained the ripple of the laugh
and the wine in her nipple,

by the terror of sin,
nor has she known the furtive deceit of the smooth
serpent in the cellars below.
Let us celebrate the beautiful innocent one,
the brightness in the eyes,
that is the brightness of the tender shoots
coming through the snow in the spring,
celebrate the breast and waist.
Is this scent of the soil
tender and warm?
Is this threshing floor of wheat and the fields?
Is this ripeness of summer in the fruits?
Is this taste of spices?
Is this as I have related it to the others?
I have left the treasures of the world,
it suffices me that today I have had my fill.
The beautiful innocent one
gives and knows whenever she gives,
the wine foams in the jars,
she is innocent and daring,
daring and innocent.
The wine in the vessel is purified.
Morning shall not forsake us
at the end of the day.

7
Last night was the night of the *jinn*
and the black storm.
In the forests and the paths
the naked lilies leaned towards us
we warmed them with touch and they were enriched with scent,
the birds came to us for refuge

from their wrecked nests.
We went with the departing caravan
to the archipelago of the 'whale islands',
we turned, rested and covered ourselves with the night and the unknown
a stranger and like her a stranger.
Where we descended
a dwelling arose for us
and a thousand weary neighbours hastened to that dwelling
in the tumult of the seas
and the exile away from home.

8

I continue to go in pursuit of it
I sense it within me yet I do not grasp it
I strive to empty my home in the hope
that if he passes he will be tempted and claim it
I felt it within me yet I do not experience it.

She goes to her room.
She breaks in on my loneliness,
through all my darkness,
through my long sleepless nights.
My heart beats like black droplets
eroding the silence
increasing the blackness.
I had experienced what is not
usually related:
a dried up well that overflowed,
and a lighthouse that erupted from darkness.
I contemplate the vision that occasionally overpowers me,
and I cry.

'How can I lack the strength to spread the gospel?'
Two months, the silence has been long,
my lips have gone dry,
when, when will the word come to my rescue?
Long have I rebelled, lashed the monster
and his toadies in my land.
I spat out the poison and the curses,
words flowed from my mouth
a torrent of packs of wolves.
Today, as the vision sings in my blood,
with the tremble of lightning and the brightness of morning
with the instinct of birds that smell
the intentions of the forests and the winds,
that feel what is in the womb of the season
that see it before it is born into the seasons.
The vision overflows, and what then!
There shall come an hour,
when I say what I have to say.

9

My eyes are filled with perfumed fields,
and a god part of whom is a fertility Ba'l
and a part of whom is coal and fire.
A million and one houses like mine,
blossoming with children, the branches of the vine
and olive trees; the *'ambers* of spring
swallowed the nights of ice.
My eyes are filled with a pavilion whose towering
ribs are knotted into
the wrists that build it, build the epic
and from the richness of our soil grow
crystal and marble,

crystallised from the visions of eyes
that lit up and burned out in the depth of darkness
and sprouted pillars of marble
from the mud of the dark cellars,
that absorbed the floods of tears,
absorbed the hills
of crushed flesh and bones
and fermented for a thousand and one black years:
so how could it not sprout snow-white marble
pillars that grow and are overhung by a green canopy
standing firm before the wind and the snows,
the tranquil centre and the tower that
stands fast in the whirlpool that swallows up towers?
A certain vision realised by the eye and the touch
not a tale invented by tellers.

I would not have been able to celebrate
the sun had I not seen you all bathing
at morning in the Nile, the Jordan and the Euphrates
freed from the stain of sin:
every body a hill bejewelled by the sun,
a sweet shadow, an innocent lake.
The crocodiles have departed from our land.
Our sea rose up against them and fell upon them:
they left some remains
their skins were flayed,
new skins did not grow to replace them.
Their present is in the decay of the past which
has been banished and will not return:
their names are burnt by the vision in my eyes
into smoke and exist no more.
Lord, why is the vision permeated by
red smoke and fire?

I wished my hand had held a mass
of snow to wipe away the sins
of yesterday's decay and to increase the vines and the herbs.
The crocodiles are lost in my sea
and the hatred of the muddy rivers.
Balm springs from a wound
on Golgotha.
I loved! No, my love is as yet a shower
falling on the green in my land,
all around it is wood for fuel
burnt by the vision in my eyes into smoke
that has no existence.
There will come a time when I shall embrace
the land and purify her heart,
wipe away the borders.

10

My seven voyages are tales of
the monster, of the devil and the cave,
of tricks that outwit cleverness,
I repeat what they say to no avail,
impossible to regain,
I have lost the capital and the profit:
what the torrent said
to the well and the dams,
to a pen that adeptly falsifies and hides
the meagerness in the vessels of the word
I have lost the capital and the profit,
I return to you a poet with a gospel in his mouth
saying what he says
with an instinct that feels what is in the womb of the season
sees it before it is born into the seasons.

The Sindbad City

By
Badr al-Sayyab

1.

Hungry in the grave with no food
Bare in the snow without a rag
In winter I screamed:
O Rain, let not the bones, the snow
the dust, the rock-hard stone beds
Sleep;
Let the seeds grow and flowers bloom,
And burn the barren threshing flowers with lightning;
Let the stems burst forth
And the trees droop with their burden.

And so did you Rain come
You burst down from the sky, and the clouds
And the rocks cracked
Murky, Euphrates overflowed with your gifts
The graves awoke, Death shook himself and arose
The bones cried out:
Blessed be the God
Who gives Rain to the Blood
Ah Rain!
Would that we sleep again,
Would that we could die again,

For our sleep is the beginning of awakening
Our death conceals life;
Would God that we might return
to his deep, clouded invisible domain
Would that the road might move us back
To its distant beginning.
We roused Lazarus from his sleep,
To feel the morning and the evening
Summer and winter,
To feel hunger and the burning of thirst
To fear Death
And count the minutes fast and slow,
To praise ruffians
And shed blood
Who has sent us back, clutching our fears?
Who is the god in our homes,
Whose fire feeds on our candles
And his grudges on our tears?

2.
Is this Adonis, this emptiness?
This pallor, and this draught?
Is this Adonis? Where is the light?
The crops?
Scythes that reap nothing
Buds that will never bloom
Black fields are unwatered
Is this what we waited for years?
Are these the shouts of men?
Are these the groans of women?

Fie Adonis! Fie for the rout of the hero!
Death has dashed out all hope in you
And you have come with dazed eyes
and an empty fist:
A fist that threatens,
A scythe that reaps nothing
But bones and blood.
Today? Tomorrow?
When will he be born?
When shall we be born?

3.
Death in the streets,
Death in the fields,
All that we love is dying
Water is locked in the houses
And the streams gasp for dryness
The Tartars are coming, there is blood in the distance
Our sun is bloody, our food is blood on the plates
Orphaned Mohammad they burnt, and the evening
Is alight with his fire.
Blood gushed from his feet, his hands, his eyes.
And the god burn on his eyelids
Mohammad, the Prophet, they chained him in the Cave of Hīra
The light of day was nailed where they nailed him
Tomorrow Christ will be crucified in Iraq
And dogs will eat the flesh of al-Burāq*.

4.

Spring!
What has befallen you, Spring?
You came without rain
Without a flower
Without a fruit
You ended as you began
Wrapped in blood ...
Summer came with black clouds
The day was full of care
And we pursued the night counting the stars;
Until, when the ears of corn
Were ripe for harvest
And the scythes sang
And the threshing floods covered the lowlands
The starving imagined that Ishtār
Goddess of flowers, had returned the captive to manhood,
And adorned his luxuriant brown with fruits
The hunger thought that Christ's shoulder
Had rolled away the stone from his grave
And that he had come to raise the dead
To heal lepers or to restore sight to the blind.

Who has loosened the wolves from their bonds?
Who has given drink from the mirage?
And hidden pestilence in the rain?
Death is born in the houses
A midwife is born to tear
Life from earth's womb, and from the springs of water
For tomorrow will be dark

And women will abort in the slaughter house,
And flames will dance on the threshing floors
And Christ will perish before Lazarus.
Let him lie,
Let him, for Christ has not called him!
What do you want? His flesh as jerked meat!
To sell in the city of sinners
The city of ropes, blood and liquor
The city of bullets and rocks!
Yesterday the brass knight was removed
Yesterday the stone knight was removed
Its sky seemed drowsy
And boredom set heavily on it.
A human knight roamed the streets
Killing women
Painting cradles with blood
And cursing fate decrees.

5.
As if Babylon with its ancient walls
Has risen anew
In its high steel domes
A bell peals like the groaning
In a graveyard; the sky is like a scene of carnage
The Hanging Gardens are planted with heads
Severed by axes
And the ravens pick at their eyes
The sun disappears behind the dyed hair on the branches
Is this my city?
With 'LONG LIVE LIFE'

Traced on these ruins
In the blood of the murdered
For here there is no god, water, or fields!
Is this my city? The daggers of the tartars
Are embedded over its gate, and the desert
Gasps around its roads, and the moon is never seen!
Is this my city, these craters
And these bones?
Only darkness looms from the houses
And blood is covered with dark dust
Mislead to the tracker:
Is this my city, with its wounded domes
Beneath which Judas dons red robes
And sets his hounds
On the cradle of my baby brothers ... and the houses,
To eat the flesh. In the villages
Ishtār dies of thirst, no blooms upon her brow
In her hand a basket without flower but a rock
For the stoning of all wives
While the palm trees wail upon the shore-line.

'Abd Allah Samsa in Wāqwāq Island

by
Mustafa al-Masnāwī

1. In the beginning:

In the beginning there was a people, and the people were free to die of hunger and silence or from the damp of prisons and secret concentration camps. When 'Abd Allah Samsa woke from sleep one morning, after a disturbing dream, he found that he had not been transformed into an amazing insect, but that a thought had been imported into his head.'

2. 'Abd Allah Samsa:

He said, 'Speak.'

3. The Island of Wāqwāq (extract from the Great Pharonic Encyclopaedia):

The borders of the Island of Wāqwāq are internal, not external as some imagine. To this is to be ascribed the failure of geographers to define its position on the map, and the fact that some go as far as to deny its existence. In fact it exists, as may clearly be proved from its name with its two very cogent syllables 'Waq-Waq'.

'The Island is bounded by two mountain ranges, the first of which is known as 'The Great Buildings of Goliath', and the second 'The Peaceful Villas of the Tempter'. The two ranges were formed in the third era. Despite the small area which it occupies, geologists attach great importance to it, greater indeed than that accorded to the extensive island which certain anthropologists term 'The Valleys of Bedouville'.

'There are seven principal rivers apart from tributaries, all of which spring in the fortresses and castles of which the above-mentioned valleys are full. Their red-black waters flow mainly into the desolation which surrounds the disc of the earth.

'Concerning its history, Gama de Vasco states in his book 'Travels in the World Around me' (p. 517) that this island was in ancient times connected with the mainland, until the famous conqueror Alexander 'the one-horned' severed it with one stroke of his sword in the first century after the disappearance of the continent of Atlantis under the sands of the frozen West Pole. The descendants of this conqueror have continued to rule in the Island until the present time, by means sometimes of the sword, and sometimes of the rod.

'The politics of the Island are forbidden as a topic of discussion and for this reason, we will pass over them here.'

4. 'Abd Allah Samsa:
He said, 'Speak.' He said, 'What shall I speak?'

5. The account given by the noble Shaykh Aḥmad al-Nīsābūrī concerning the Island of Wāqwāq (a):

'... on one of the days of Sha'ban in the year four hundred and zero and ninety-five, I was at the traveller's inn in the city of Wāqwāq, when there arose a great commotion outside. So I went out by way of the gate of entry to find out what was the matter and behold! The black wagons of the land of foreigners were running through the streets while before them raced a large crowd of the men and maidens of the Island, shouting something which I could not understand till their throats almost burst. And suddenly the wagons of the land of foreigners opened, revealing persons like scarecrows holding the trunks of elephants and they brought them down on the backs and sides of all whom they met, leaving them with ribs broken and blood flowing. One who stood beside me and saw that I was watching, kicked me and I looked where he pointed and I saw one of those scarecrows of the land of foreigners approaching us, waving its truck as one looking for trouble. Then I besought the protection of God and turning tail I ran to my room.'

6. 'Abd Allah Samsa:

He said, 'Speak.' He said, 'What shall I speak?' He said, 'Speak.'

7. An extract from a radio broadcast from the Island of Wāqwāq:

'... our deliverance, brothers, is in the spirit, not in matter. Let the materialistic nations land on the Moon, or Mars, or the Sun; let them show the nakedness of their sons and daughters, and drive them to prostitution in the streets. Let them invent theories of atheism and anarchy, claiming that the economy is the basis of society, and that society is divided into warring classes, and that the source of men's troubles is their ownership of land; theories which claim—shamelessly—that the pure origin of mankind goes back to apes (which can be applied to its proponents in that he who says this is the descendant of an ape while our ancestor was Adam, upon whom be peace, and he who will not accept this may opt to bang his head against the wall ...) Leave them all that, brothers, and let us return to the real world, the world of the spirit, in which there is no conflict, no disturbance, no trouble, but bliss eternal and absolute, and boundless peace, and dominion real and everlasting, in this world and the next.'

8. 'Abd Allah Samsa:

He said, 'Speak.' He said, 'What shall I speak?' he said, 'I have nothing to say.'

9. Part of the account of the noble Shaykh Aḥmad al-Nīsābur (b):

'... On the evening of that day, when I questioned the innkeeper, he told me that the Island had for two generations suffered from terrible famines which were devastating and widespread, and that the learned men and lawyers and men of consequence had conferred and discussed the matter at length, and had concluded that the cause of famine and chaos in the land was the dissemination of strange foreign ideas which had been imported and their corrupting influence on the minds of men; for which reason the rulers of the land had fixed and resolved to combat and to root out these ideas. The innkeeper further informed me that what had happened that morning was only one of the many wars waged in the Island to wipe out those ideas. I found this strange and said to him, 'Many people were killed, while I was watching.' He replied, 'What you saw was not people, but imported ideas which to the onlooker appear to walk and talk and stand and sit like other people, but are in fact quite insubstantial.' So I concluded that among them the words 'imported ideas'' were the equivalent of the words 'devil' and 'fiend' and the like among us.'

10. 'Abd Allah Samsa:

He said, 'Speak.' He said, 'What shall I speak?' He said, 'Speak.' He said, 'I have nothing to say.' And a strong fist which was descended from the first father of mankind came with the speed of light and lodged itself below the middle of the bottom rib and from his mouth burst forth the howl of a wolf and a trickle of blood, and his body flew backwards and he cried, 'You have killed me.' He replied, 'Not now; but if you refuse to confess, we will.'

APPENDICES

Appendix I. Extract from a report by the quarter sergeant:

'I solemnly swear by Almighty God that he has turned a heathen and with these two ears—may God cut them off if I tell a lie—I have heard Mr____, the Imām of the mosque, accusing him of missing prayers, for no good reason and urging him to return to the good old folk. And with these two eyes—may God gouge them out if I have strayed from the way of truth—I have seen him indeed I have—shrug his shoulders in contempt and hurrying away leaving the sage and learned man open—mouthed and goggle—eyed ... I was informed by *al-Hajj* _____, keeper of a shop selling foodstuff, that he had spoken to him at length about the rise in the prices of God's bounty, and he had said that the reason for this was the existence of many poor people, and a few rich who consumed the wealth of the poor. When *al-Hajj* ____ pointed out to him that God was more generous with food to some than to others, he replied—God protect us—that the purpose of food was the mind, not money or coin ... I did my best to strike up an acquaintance with this unbeliever to learn what his purpose was, but he was very short with me and looked away whenever he saw me approaching in the distance or if I greeted him.'

Appendix II. Report:

'On the morning of ____ at ____ o'clock, we raided the house of the accused 'Abd Allah Samsa. We found him alone, fast asleep. We arrested him in compliance with our orders dated ____. After an examination of his house which lasted one day, we seized the following: a book entitled 'Plato's Democratic Republic'; a coloured picture of a large number of people smiling; a wooden box, black in colour. We seized the articles of evidence and brought them with the arrested man to ____.'

This report was compiled in the presence of ____.

Appendix III. Inquiry:

'Why did you not return the sergeant's greeting? A private matter, I suppose. Why have you ceased to attend prayers?' Also a private matter, I suppose.

'And keeping books and pictures which are forbidden, and boxes in your house? Also a private matter? And the poor and the rich and the mind? All private matters, of course.

'Well, suppose we arrest you for a private matter—ha, ha—what do you think of that?'

Appendix IV. Extract from a secret report:

'Despite his refusal to speak of his leaders or his fellow conspirators, though we employed various methods on him, we have strong evidence that he is a bearer of imported ideas, *viz.* the book and the pictures and the black box, the making of which has been forbidden since the Greeks finally left our land and we gained our absolute independence.'

Last Appendix. Evidence of a person who has refused to give his name:

'They brought him one night. I did not see his face, but his body was swollen. He was placed in the cold—storage for corpses and they ordered me to guard him. I guarded him for two whole days until they returned. They asked me, 'Has he moved?' I was amazed and said, 'No,' They seemed alarmed although they tried to conceal it. They fell on the papers and the doctor in charge said to them. 'Aren't you going to leave him for the anatomy students?' They said, 'No', and were already worried. They ordered the assistant nurse to remove him and they hurried away with him. I noticed only his feet; the toenails had been pulled out and the soles were torn. I think I could see through the red lacerations and the black, dried blood, the yellow of the bones. I think so, but whenever I looked an appalling nausea and giddiness came over me from which I have not yet recovered ...'

Sindbad *from* Old Sorrows: Five Tales from *The Arabian Nights*

by
Mohammad al-Mansī Qandīl

The bells of Baṣra were ringing in honour of Sindbad, the conqueror of sea and storm, on his return from his seventh voyage. But the man who was ringing them was the best-known auctioneer in the land, and his harsh voice, well known to all merchants, was intoning '*Alla una, alla due, alla tre.*[*]'

In the great port of Baṣra Sindbad's ship was moored, his faithful barque, worn out by the billows of the sea and the troubled fretting of ebb and flow. It stood garlanded with flowers in honour of its never-to-be-forgotten voyage, but on the bows was fixed a small blackboard, on which was chalked 'for sale'.

To the right stood Sindbad; to the left stood the crew; in the middle stood the merchants of the land whispering confidentially. Directly in front of them was the famous auctioneer, ringing his bell and spacing his phrases to fit its rhythm.

'A great opportunity, the greatest ship ever seen in this country ... the great ship of Sindbad.'

The merchants muttered audibly, 'A superannuated ship, worm-eaten, ought to be broken up and the timbers sold retail ...'

Sindbad gazed at the faces which seemed to be wearing strange masks, as if a long-drawn-out farce were being played. Two guards, one on either side, prevented him from slipping away.

'We will start with four hundred *dinars*! Now, have we any advance on that?' The merchants murmured; one of them shouted, 'Not for four hundred *dirhams*! What's the point of buying woodworm?'

Sindbad called out, reviling the merchants. The ship was the dear friend of his lifetime; it has existed before this country came into being; he himself had stood at its helm before the creation of the world.

The auctioneer shouted, 'Quiet please! Let's get down to business!' and he glanced towards the crew. Shipwright, the leading seaman and companion of the seven voyages, came forward and said, 'The sale must go ahead. We want our wages.'

The bell rang: 'Three hundred, then? Two hundred? A ship in first-rate condition, ready to sail at once.' One of the merchants, as if his interest were aroused, said, 'A hundred and fifty, then.'

The auctioneer looked around the company and said, regretfully, 'Is that all?'

No one replied. Shipwright accepted with a nod of the head and the auctioneer registered the agreement in the merchant's name.

During the morning labourers had opened the hold and unloaded the cargo. The auctioneer beckoned to them and they placed in front of him four large boxes. The bell rang.

'Now we come to the cargo: books collected by Sindbad on his voyages.' Again, Sindbad cried out, but no one heard him. This had been the real voyage of his life, this dream of one day finding an Earthly Paradise. He had collected books of philosophy from Greece; of wisdom from Persia; of magic from India; and of law from Rome. Old yellowing books, but still profit of thousands of men who had suffered torment, crucifixion and death.

The auctioneer shouted, 'One hundred *dinars*?' The merchants burst out laughing. One of them, controlling himself with an effort, said, 'Come now, this is just so much waste paper.'

Sindbad managed to free himself from the two guards. He faced his old crew. 'I appeal to you, remember what we have been through together. We're life-long friends.'

Shipwright said, 'That was before you went mad. We always used to come home with loot, with gold. But this time you filled the ship with foolish things.'

Sindbad replied, 'With the exception of the last voyage which was in quest of truth, all other voyages were false and illusory. Still do you not understand?'

The auctioneer rang his bell and said sarcastically, 'Truth has no value, it is virtually no more than a drop of salt water. Fifty *dinars*? Thirty *dinars*?

The guards brought him back. One of the merchants agreed reluctantly to buy the boxes for ten *dinars*. The efficient auctioneer managed to raise the price for fifty *dirhams*. Sindbad studied the faces of his crew, perhaps for the first time: his comrades in the hard nights who had come across distant lands when the trackless desert had woven together threads of high destiny across the ocean and the sea of darkness. Their looks showed carelessness and stupidity, cold as death.

Labourers set down a number of large boxes and began to unpack the contents: strangely shaped instruments of iron and glass. They scattered them carelessly, instruments for observing the sky and stars, astrolabes and sun dials, measures of salinity and depth, of heat and pressure, vessels all of glass for distillation and perfume, alembics and storage pots.

The bell rang harshly. 'A great opportunity, strange instruments, a must for magicians and conjurors, in fact for all the clever men in the kingdom.'

A merchant came forward and said with an air of finality, 'Listen! Don't exaggerate. They are just so much iron. I'll buy them at so much a kilo.'

Ding-ding went the bell.

A strange cloth, neither wool nor cotton.

Ding-ding! 'Coloured fluids with a penetrating smell!' 'Pickled skeletons!' Ding-ding! 'Plants in a special glass case.'

An amazing heap of odds and ends, not worth the trouble of selling and bargaining. The price fell from *dinars* to *dirhams*, to half *dirhams*. The faces of the crew were unyielding. Ding-ding! The auctioneer shouted 'The last lot: a plush case with silver studs.'

Sindbad cried out, a harsh, wounded cry, 'Leave them: they're mine.' The auctioneer looked at him contemptuously and opened the case. Inside were a withered red rose and a small letter, carefully folded. These he tossed aside carelessly and offered the case for sale. Sindbad tried to wriggle free but one of the policemen held him, while the other hurried to trample the withered rose and the letter in the mud.

Sindbad cried out and then broke into tears, long and continuous. And for all this the goods auctioned had not realised half the arrears of pay!

Spring in the Ashes

By
Zakariyya Tāmir

Once upon a time, there was a little town, built among wide green fields, which were irrigated by a river of abundant water. All the citizens carried in their pockets a piece of thick paper, on which was written a name.

Some of the citizens were rich, some poor. The rich were cultivated and considerate. They wore white robes and shiny shoes. They were proficient at dancing and polite conversation, at bowing gracefully, and at kissing ladies' hands, and their children called their mothers, with excessive refinement, 'Mama.'

The poor would laugh coarsely in their moments of joy, spat much on the floor, believed they would be given hospitality in heaven after death, and used to call out to their mothers in a rough, drawn-out voice, 'Mo-ther!'

Rich and poor alike felt intense respect for the dead: when a funeral passed by, men would halt, with grief and fear shining in their eyes: some would help to carry the bier of an unknown man for a considerable distance. As they opened their mouths for the first mouthful of a meal, they would say humbly, 'In the name of God, the Merciful, the Compassionate.' At the end of the meal, they would murmur, 'Praise be to God, Lord of the Worlds.'

If a girl sinned sexually, her head was cut off from her body, at once, with a large-bladed knife.

The workers were busy for eight hours in the day; lovers would meet secretly in the dark of the cinemas, and embrace passionately.

The doctors would tender their advice continuously; 'Chew

your food thoroughly; go to bed early; keep off tobacco and alcohol.' And the older men would shake their heads sadly, muttering. 'The world is going to the dogs: women are wearing trousers, children do not respect their fathers. These are signs foretelling the end of the world.'

Friends would greet each other at the beginning of each day with 'Good morning.'

Though the town was small, it had a sun which rose at an appointed time and set at an appointed time. It had a night which was studded with many stars, and which was dazzlingly bright when the white moon came forth.

Now there was a man with a name living in that town. His face was skull-like where the pale, dry skin clung to the bone. He had a fierce longing to be a flower, or a bird, or a wandering cloud. Discouragement could never get the better of him, though he knew that he would never be a flower or a bird or a wandering cloud. But he was tired of living alone in a silent, melancholy house, and saw, one ash-grey moment, that he would buy himself a wife, a wife who would be a companion and whose voice would clean away the rust which clung to his days. So the man went to the nearest market and chose a woman with two large eyes which were sinking into their sockets with a grief mingled with particular mystery. The man paid her price, saying to himself, 'Perhaps she can kill the hedgehog which weeps in my blood.'

The man spoke not a word to the woman as they made their way home, but when they reached the house he asked her, 'What is your name?' The woman answered in a quavering voice, at once soft, and a little condescending, 'My name is Nada [dew].'

One day, the man was sitting by the woman; on his knees rested his coarse hands which trembled with the boiling of fierce blood in his veins. He fancied that the woman was at that moment naked on a sandy shore, facing a blue sea which wetted her breasts with its warm, salt waters. He said in agitated tones, 'From what country do you come?'

'I have no country.'

He contemplated her carefully; then he said, 'You are beautiful.' Her mouth, live, a little dark and crimson, seemed to him exceptionally unusual. His fingers contracted and a relentless shudder ran through them and he said, slowly, 'Your name is beautiful, too.'

The woman said, with a dark smile, 'My real name is Shahrazad.'

Gripped by amazement, the man shouted, 'Are you Shahrazad?'

The woman said, 'I am Shahrazad. I have not fallen to the scythe of Death. Shahrayar is dead.'

The man said, 'Shahrayar is not dead; he is still alive.'

The woman said, 'O my lord!'

'My kingdom collapsed, O Shahrazad.'

'We were parted.'

'We wandered over the great earth.'

'I sought you everywhere.'

'Hunger made me weep.'

'I was imprisoned in a room with locked doors.'

'I was led astray.'

'I have walked the streets wrapped in a black robe.'

'I have dug the earth with my nails.'

'I have lived as the only woman in towns of men.'

'My face has been spat upon.'

'Rich men bought me.'

'I am a poor man. My God, why have you deserted me?'

'Oh, how we have suffered.'

They embraced, fiercely, and wept long. The man murmured in a trembling voice, 'I love you, I love you.'

She looked up to him with eyes bedewed with tears in the

depths of which screamed a desire which reached out to his flesh claws which he could not escape. Eagerly he embraced the woman's body. His lips had no sooner touched hers than there reached his ears a cry which came from the street, 'The enemy is attacking ... kill, kill, ... to war!'

The beating of a drum arose, rhythmical, urgent, angry, which the man could not ignore. He pushed the woman's body from him with a stern movement and the woman cried, imploringly, 'Do not leave me: don't fight; stay by my side.' The man said, 'Be quiet ... the alleys of the town ... my mother calls me.'

So he took his sword from where it hung on the wall, and went down to the streets where men were fighting in the darkness of the evening. He was drawn into the heart of the struggle and he began to thrust with his sword at every breast which he found before him. He felt joy as the long, firm blade sliced into the yielding flesh with its vicious and savage movement. When the battle was over, he stood, his body wet with sweat and blood.

He felt a sudden panic as it seemed to him that he was the last man left alive: the bodies of the others were scattered on the asphalt of the street, in heaps of torn flesh. He threw himself down on the bloodstained ground and began to sob bitterly as flames consumed the house of the town and its dead.

When the fire drew near him, he stopped weeping and ran swiftly out of the town to the distant fields. When he looked back at the town, he saw that it had turned into a great mass of red fire, blazing in the heart of the black night, and he collapsed onto the grass and surrendered to a deep sleep, and he did not wake till the sun of a new day had risen.

Silence reigned everywhere; the town was a great black pile, from which smoke was rising. The man heard a low moaning voice and turned his eyes about until they fell upon a young girl lying in the grass. He drew near to her and asked, 'Why are you weeping?'

The town has been burnt: everyone is dead.'

Then no one remains!'

The girl did not reply, but renewed her weeping. Again he asked her, 'Why are you weeping?' Hiding her face in her hands, she said, 'I am hungry. 'The man left her and went to look for food. He was delighted when he came upon an apple tree whose branches were loaded with ripe fruit. He picked some apples and took them to the girl. He bent over to watch her as she greedily ate the apples.

He felt the old longing to be a flower or a bird or a wandering cloud. He asked himself, 'Is the girl's name Shahrazad?' The girl wiped her face with the edge of her robe. She gazed at the man with deep longing. Her face was calm; the man remembered the past days of his childhood and he said, sadly, 'So we alone are left alive.'

The girl remained silent but her lips parted a little. The man saw a red rosebud, which he plucked and presented, with embarrassment, to the girl, who accepted it with a shy smile. She awakened joy, and made it sing its loveliest songs in his veins.

The man helped the girl to arise and they went together with slow steps towards the dead, blackened town.

Suddenly, they heard a bird singing and they stopped, and their eyes met in a long gaze, and it seemed to the man that he heard the cries of children mingled with a distant moaning.

The man and the girl went on together and they embraced in love and harmony, and before them was the young bright sun.

The Blue Charm and the Return of Jubaynah

By

Emīle Habībī

Thou dweller of Heaven
Allow thy gaze to fall
Bring back our brethren

Look down from on high
on us and on our lands
and restore out kinfolk

We have homes and terraces
With doors open wide
O dweller of Heaven
Give wing to the doves
Grant us sweet repose

Upper room upon room
to sunlight and to freedom
look down from on high
to span the days and nights
that is the fruit of peace
(song by Fairūz)

The young men were returning from their usual evening stroll and darkness had just begun to fall as our car approached the charcoal kilns of our Galilean village. The fragrance of the submerged wood in the kilns filled the air, and our guest exclaimed joyfully, 'We have arrived.'

I sounded my horn to warn the young men returning from their evening stroll to stay clear of our path. They were in need of no such warning, and I was actually blowing the horn to announce the arrival of our guest. She was returning to her village and her old, crippled mother for the first time for more than twenty years. She had gone to live in Lebanon with her husband and children and now she was returning twenty years later. She had crossed the bridge over the sacred river with permission to visit her mother's home for two weeks.

She asked, 'Is the spring still there like the charcoal kilns?'

'It is still there at the other end of the village, but it has dried up,' I replied.

Our guest gave a diffident laugh that was audible but invisible and said, 'Jubaynah has returned.'

It was my turn to laugh, but I could not.

Do you know the tale of Jubaynah, or has it sunk into oblivion among the ruins of Damoun and Igrith?

It is the tale of a childless village woman who used to make cheese and pray to God on high to give her a daughter with a face as round and fair as the cheese in her hands.

God answered her prayer and sent her a daughter whose beauty put the moon itself to shame.

Hugo named her Ezmeralda; but the village woman named her 'Jubaynah.' She nurtured her and pampered her and clothed her in brocaded silk. She entwined her wrist with a beaded blue charm to protect her from the evil eye. Her anklets rang out to the graceful rhythm of her body as she walked, alerting pedestrians to make way for her as she approached.

To cut a long story short, she, like Ezmeralda, was kidnapped by the gypsies. Her mother continued to search for her and weep for her loss until she collapsed and lost the light of sight in her eyes.

As for Jubaynah, she was transferred from one master to another until she ended up herding geese in the pastures of the prince of a far away land. She was separated from her mother and father by seven seas and seven years.

As she tended the geese, she sang a sorrowful song:

> O birds that fly
> Over mountains high

Tell my mother and father
That precious Jubaynah
Tends geese
And walks thorny paths
On mountains high
And weeps.

A young prince overheard her song and was touched by it. He returned next day, and the song seemed even more enchanting to him. He returned for seven more days and he fell in love with Jubaynah. Seven long nights he spent without sleep until he poured out his heart to his mother. And so it was that he took Jubaynah from the pasture and brought her to the palace as his wife and princess.

After spending one year in comfort, Princess Jubaynah gave birth to a bonny boy. A second year elapsed, and Princess Jubaynah said to her husband the Prince, 'My country yearns for its own.'

So he set her upon a camel litter and gave her perfumes, silks and gifts to take with her. She travelled until she came to the village spring. Her child became thirsty. Seeing the village women quarrelling and jostling one another around the spring, she asked them for some water for her child. One of the women answered, 'There is no water in the spring. Ever since Jubaynah disappeared, the spring has been dry.'

Jubaynah answered, 'Go and look, and you shall find water in the spring.'

And so it was. The pent-up water gushed forth from within the broken-hearted Earth.

One of the women whispered to her sister, 'Jubaynah has returned.'

The news spread. Girls and boys ran about shouting, 'Jubaynah has returned.'

A boy ran impulsively to the house of Jubaynah's mother and approached her like a goat at full tilt. Shouting so that she could hear him and panting so that she would believe him, he said, ‘Grandmother, grandmother; Jubaynah has returned.’ But she would not believe him, so he returned to Jubaynah's litter abashed. Jubaynah gave him the blue charm that encircled her slender wrist and said, ‘Tell Jubaynah's mother that this is from Jubaynah.’

The boy took it to her and placed it in her hands. She smelt it and rubbed her eyes against it; and the tears welled up in her eyes and the light of sight was restored to them.

Then they were reunited.

However, I said to our guest, ‘The mechanical litter is now entering the village. Will the water in the spring gush forth?’

Our guest smiled an inaudible, invisible smile.

We entered the village alleys. I asked her to guide me to her mother's house if she still remembered the way.

She did.

As she continued to guide me, I drove the car up a steep alley. Suddenly, she astonished me by crying out, ‘Beware of the ditch to your left at the beginning of the next alley’, for there was the ditch in the very spot where Jubaynah had anticipated it.

She became aware of my amazement and said, ‘No, not everything has remained the same. We have grown older and the alley arches have aged; but the children fill the plain and the mountain. I do know them and they do not know me; but I think they know that my crippled mother has a daughter abroad.’

In this matter as well, she was right. A young man was shutting the shop beneath her mother's house. He saw that we were strangers, accompanying a strange lady in modern clothes as she alighted from the car at such a late hour in that congested alley. No sooner had he seen us than he ran towards us. Without a word from us, he turned round and shouted to his neighbours, ‘So and so's daughter has returned. So and so's daughter has returned.'

The women neighbours quickly ran out to welcome her. I saw the crippled old woman at the bottom of the stairway, standing on her own two feet. She was trying to hear, trying to see, trying to understand. They said, 'Here is her mother.'

It was pitch dark, and the men were shouting to the women to bring a torch.

The old woman standing at the bottom of the stairs was smiling such a smile as I had never seen in my life; a smile that was like the traces of waves on the beach during the ebbing of the sea.

Through the commotion, a shrill cry of joy could be heard, which froze every movement and silenced every voice.

The old mother was uttering exclamations of joy. We did not understand any of the verses she recited. Perhaps all we heard of her cry was the rustling of her lips; but her face reflected a vision of a bride's glory at the moment of her unveiling.

Then, they were reunited.

We were still helping the old mother back to her bed, when she pushed us aside and sprang like a lioness towards an old wooden chest. Raising its lid, she rummaged in it and brought out some old clothes for a seven or eight-year-old child. She whispered hoarsely, 'These are your clothes. I have kept them for your daughter. Why didn't you bring her with you?'

Then, she brought out a blue charm attached to a golden pendant and said, 'Your father, God rest his soul, always used to say that had you kept this charm, all that has happened would not have occurred. Wear it and never take it off.'

As I took leave of our guest, she said to me diffidently, 'As for the new Jubaynah, it was not *she* who kept the blue charm.' I answered her, 'My way lies past the water spring at the other end of the village. I will visit it. Perhaps it has overflowed with water.'

As I passed the water spring, I raised my hand in salute. No one could see me, so why should I not salute the spring?

As for visiting the spring to see whether life had returned to it, I decided to postpone that until some other day.

The Orphans' Cow

By

Maḥmūd Shuqair

His ears hung loosely as he idly wandered about the garden, weakly holding the long rubber hose, as the water splashed out and seeped away under the moist stems of the roses. From time to time, out of the corner of his eye, he looked towards the balcony; perhaps, even then, she was sleeping on her bed like a Dutch cow and would remain there asleep, till the sun was high in the sky. And when she rose, she would loom over him with her hot body, watching him provocatively. He had only to slacken his efforts and she would scold him bitterly, rush out and abuse him, threatening him, 'I'll throttle you, I'll be after you.'

His thoughts wandered off into foolishness. He heard a faint sound from the balcony, and started; it was the dog, wagging its tail. He let go the hose and it fell twisting from his hand. He stood, with feet apart, neck stretched forward. Taking the tip of his nose between his fingers he blew it. Suddenly there was a voice, scolding. He jumped in alarm. She rose, like a venomous snake.

He said, pleading: 'Please, for my children's sake I haven't rested all morning: I've cleaned and watered the garden and pruned the roses.' She examined him attentively; something obscure was hiding in her eyes. She turned away muttering. 'Dirty *fallāh*, always coughing.'

He took hold of the hose with a trembling hand and turned the tap. The water gushed forth. He looked resentfully at the balcony and muttered, 'God damn you, you bitch. So I look dirty, do I?'

He continued his work, the sun's heat beating on his skull. Since he had begun work in the town, people had called him nothing but '*fallāh*'. It had not been so in the village: since he was a boy, they had called him 'Abu-Isma'īl'. He used to feel pride as he swept along in his *qunbāṣ** through the lanes of the village, with his fine *kufiyyah** about his shoulders, with its top at a jaunty angle, a lock of hair escaping from under the head-cloth. How he danced and sang at wedding feasts! All the girls had envied 'Azīza, because she had got herself such a husband. In the fields, none had worked as he. How the young folk of the district had talked about him. What good looks! He would lift a sack of wheat as if it were a basket.

But drought devoured the land, and there was no more work in the village. When he decided to travel to the distant city for work, some of the young men of the village went with him. Though they were all about his age, they always called him 'Abu-Isma'īl'.* And 'Azīza, how she wept, and tried to prevent him from leaving the village.

The distant city ... the old man of the village used to say, 'He who goes to the city is ruined; he abandons his wife and forgets his children .' 'Azīza had only been pacified when he promised that he would not abandon her, that the city would not corrupt him. And, indeed, he had kept his promise. He went back to the village once every fortnight or three weeks ... and, on the bench, in the evening,the family would gather round, and 'Azīza would press him to tell her about the town, and of its wonders and stories. Doubt lay behind her insistence. Then his eyes would cloud over and his concern would show itself; he would shake his head and say, in a low voice, 'All life is misery: we work from morning till night, like beasts.'

'But they say life in the city is all pleasure and happiness.' 'Pleasure and happiness for some, 'Azīza. But for us, we have to build houses and that's all.' 'Yes, but when you worked on the land you tasted your share of bitterness.' 'True enough, but in the city, people say odd things which make us discontented.'

Then 'Azīza would shake her head in sympathy, and the tea would gush gurgling from the pot into the cup, and Isma'īl would shiver and say, 'Mother, tell us a story, please.' She would try to ignore him but he would insist and would rub himself against her, like a cat.

'Please, a story: tell us about the orphans' cow.'

'Oh, Isma'īl, I'm tired of telling it.'

'It's nice; do tell it.'

Abu-Isma'īl would feel a sudden exultation. He has an idea: 'Isma'īl, tell it yourself, and your mother and I will listen.'

Isma'īl laughs shyly, and hides his face.

'Please, no: I won't tell the story.'

'Here's a penny: now tell it.'

Hesitating and shy, Isma'īl begins:

'Once upon a time, there were some orphan children, and they had a cow ...'

'Go on.'

'Their next-door neighbours were rich ...'

'Go on.'

'Mother, you tell it; I won't.' 'No your father will say you aren't very clever.'

'One day, the rich people said, 'We want to slaughter the orphans' cow'

'And then?'

'And then, when the orphans heard this, they began to cry. So the rich people began to chase the cow and she ran away. They were tired when they caught her. When the time came to slaughter her, the orphans cried and said, 'Please God, don't let her be killed.' The rich people, who were cutting the animal's throat, grew tired of this, attacked the orphans and beat them, and they drove them away, saying, 'The cow is ours, let her die.' So they slaughtered it but when they began to eat it, they could not chew the meat. So they got up and again beat the orphans, who said, 'O cow, be tender under their teeth,' And so they ate it and lived happily ever after.'

Isma'īl's father gets up, laughing and goes inside the house. His mother laughed and said, 'You don't know how to tell it properly.'

Abu-Isma'īl wanders off, gazing at the distant stars ...

Again a threatening voice is heard, stammering with rage: 'Sleepy? You should go to bed ... go off to your village and sleep ... I'll make him sack you today ...'

She continues, 'A useless old man ... We'll get a sturdy *fallāh* ... the garden is ruined in your hands.'

Her face coloured: her hot body was almost spilling out of the tight dress. She went in again, singing in a harsh voice. Abu-Ism'īl rubbed his eyes and gazed vacantly at his feet, planted in the mud.

'Confound you: your blood is hot and I cannot quench it.' He decided to throw his emotions into his work, and not to allow his feelings an opportunity to distract him. He looked towards the tank at one side of the garden, in which young flowers were growing.

'Today, I will dig up those flowers and distribute them about the garden.' He coiled the hose and laid it carefully by the wall. He looked closely at it: it was old and full of cracks. He had owned it for years and now here it was, crumpled like a living body, torn. When he began working in this garden, he had been in the prime of youth, his arms knotted with muscles, like iron chains. His neighbours had envied him. When he gave up building work, and began working in the garden, they said, 'A man who works as a gardener or a waiter in a restaurant or a cafe, is protected by God: the gate of Heaven is opened for him.' The mistress of the house had cooked for Abu-Isma'īl food he had never tasted before, and given him more attention than necessary. At first, he could not understand it. And when she began to flirt with him from the balcony and laugh at him, he thought she was angry with him till there came a day ... It was morning and the sun's heat was warm. Abu-Isma'īl was in the garden, holding the hose in both hands: the water gushed out clear and whispering. The mistress of the house was standing on the balcony, leaning on forearms like two fish. Abu-Isma'īl was engrossed in watering the baking hot earth. She spoke in a drowsy voice: 'Bravo, *fallāh*: you're good at watering.' He replied, carelessly: 'The need to earn a living can teach anything.' His coldness angered her, and she tried to draw him into conversation.

'But you are amazing! Have you a garden of your own?' He snorted like a bull, and said, in pungent tones, 'There's a patch in front of our house: it's nothing but dirt.' She gave a ringing laugh as if she wanted to give him the feeling that she savoured his conversation. The deep cleft of her half-naked breasts was plainly visible. She said, 'Everything needs watering, even the garden.' 'I love watering the garden, especially when the earth is hot.'

'Why, *fallāh*?' 'Because it sucks in the water greedily and the air is filled with a sweet mist.'

She laughed, coarsely, and said, 'What a low fellow you are, *fallāh*.' He felt rage, and a desire gripped him to spit on her: wretched woman, always angry with him, always irritated. What if his neighbours back in his village should hear that a woman thought him stupid, and that he was afraid of losing his livelihood. His thoughts ran on, and he raised his eyes towards her. Her open bosom disturbed him. He tried to turn his eyes to the ground, but he could not; an invisible rope of desire reached out from her eyes to his. He thought, 'This woman is one of my betters: I won't desire her, and she cannot be attracted to a *fallāh* like me.' The hose fell from his hand: the water splashed away. He stood, confused, and a wanton smile played on her lips. He didn't know if she was enticing him or not, but he heard a lustful voice saying from somewhere, ‘Come on, *fallāh*, enter.’

The water throbbed through the hose and splashed over the burning earth of the garden. He shuddered and sent a furtive glance towards the balcony: she was not there. He gazed sadly at the decrepit hose, and then moved off slowly towards the nursery bed, and began to uproot the flowers so as to plant them in their appointed places. The mistress looked cautiously from the balcony and observed him uprooting the flowers. She leaned out and called in a loud voice. He was baffled: his eyes opened wide and his lower jaw dropped. She shouted angrily, ‘Fool! Who ordered you to uproot them?’ ‘I'm going to plant them in the garden.’ ‘They're only little seedlings, you idiot! They'll die if you uproot them now, die.’ ‘They won't die, lady: trust in God.’ ‘Confound you, you won't go on working here.’ ‘Please, lady: what will happen to my children?’ ‘Away with you!’ He ran like a dog from the garden. Since he had begun working in the garden, he had been contented and enjoyed peace of mind, and had always known his place and kept to it. He thought of waiting for the master of the house, but despair got the better of him: she was in command and the master would not restore him to the garden.

That night, in the village, the dogs barked distrustfully. His family gathered in silence on the bench. Abu-Isma‘īl was telling sadly the story of the orphans' cow, as his children listened. ‘The orphans had a cow ... the rich people seized it and slaughtered it and flayed it, and ...’ One of his children interrupted him eagerly, ‘No, father; they tried to seize it.’

His father shuddered: ‘No, they seized it and slaughtered it and flayed it and ate it and stretched out and slept.’

The children were indignant. They fell asleep and dreamed of a cow with horns like spear, which charged defiantly across the fields, while, in the distance, skulked the wolves.

Abu-Zayd Surrenders

By

Hasan Muḥassib

‘Only one stroke with this hoe, and it's all over,’ said Abu-Zayd to himself; but he was shaking as he said it, and so was the lion tattooed on his right arm. His moustache was moist with sweat. A raven croaked, pecked at a worm, spat it out and ruffled its wings. Its shadow lay on the waters of the irrigation ditch. It appeared dispirited.

Abu-Zayd looked at his hoe and the lion on his arm shook. His eyes, seeking out the borders of the *taftīsh** lands, say only the *jazūrīn* trees standing silent beneath the blazing sun. Before his gaze could return to the hoe, he saw the Inspector's trap returning from the administrative building.

Suddenly the lion on his arm grew calm: its shaking ceased. He would not see the Inspector till tomorrow: now at last he would stand firm; he bent to pick up the hoe. As he did so, his backbone cracked and a painful sigh was stifled in the dryness of his throat.

Abu-Zayd walked along the bank of the irrigation ditch; his arms, folded behind his back, held the hoe. He tried hard to understand why he should be deprived of his cotton. He had often tried to console himself with the thought that he was not the only one to be caught in such a dilemma. But for all that, he could find no relief from worry.

Yesterday, his wife Wahībah had said to him: ‘Abu-Zayd, are you crying like a woman?’ The baby had cried, and his daughter had made to wipe away his tears with the back of her hand.

'How can one put it?' he said. 'Is there any honesty left? What with Shaykh 'Abd al-Malik praying in the mosque, 'God save the Princess!'

His wife gave him a piece of bread and a small lump of *mish** on another piece, saying, 'Good sense and religion, Abu-Zayd.' His daughter Zainab, her eyes red and swollen, toyed with a lock of hair, and said, 'Six years! six years!' Then she buried her face in her *damūr** and sobbed. Abu-Zayd took a mouthful of bread and swallowed a large draught of water from the jug filled by Wahībah from the ditch.

A frog jumped in front of Abu-Zayd as he was reaching the end of the ditch. He laid down by the irrigation-wheel.

'Man proposes and God disposes,' his neighbour Diab said. Abu-Zayd, his head bent heavy on his hoe, made no reply, and his dull gaze fell on the branches of the sycamore tree. Diab struck the buffalo a light blow with the whip, and the wheel groaned a little louder. Diab repeated, 'He who slanders God ...' Abu-Zayd wished he would smile and he reminded Diab of Shaykh 'Abd al-Malik in the pulpit in the mosque when he prayed, 'God save the Princess!' Abu-Zayd knew that people on the *taftīsh* were aware of the fact that Shaykh 'Abd al-Malik lunched and dined at the *taftīsh* guest-house. Diab whispered again and said: 'Leave the land to the landlord.' The whip cracked on the hide of the buffalo. Then Diab sat down beside Abu-Zayd and, taking off his woollen hat, and pressing it against the crown of his head, he said, 'I vow, and a vow is a debt till it's paid, that had I the land I would leave the cotton for the people ...'

Abu-Zayd spat on the ground and wiped his mouth with the back of his hand. The head of the lion on his arm flashed.

Diab said to Abu-Zayd, 'Zainab won't be able to marry Yūnus, six years is a long time to wait.' 'Six years!' murmured Abu-Zayd, 'Yūnus and Zainab engaged!' Then, sitting on his haunches with his chin resting on his palms, he began to gaze at the wide cotton-lands.

His breath came heavily, as he said, 'Acres and acres, Diab, we planted them, we picked the dirt and the worms out of the cotton-leaves by lamp-light. And the crop ripened and the Inspector fools us and keeps us away from getting the cotton. For six years Zainab and Yūnus have been engaged.'

A sigh came from his throat, but was drowned by the crack of the whip as Diab beat the buffalo, and the wheel went slowly round.

And again a raven croaked on a branch and the heat still stifled breath; there was no breath of air to ease Abu-Zayd's cares.

'One stroke and that will be it.' His wife Wahībah beat her breast anxiously, 'Abu-Zayd, are you out of your mind! Would you condemn yourself to eternal hell! What applies to the *taftīsh* applies to us ...'

Zainab hid her face with the edge of her garment and blew her nose. Yūnus had not shown his face for months, and some of his friends left for the city, found themselves jobs and came back to marry.

'One stroke of a hoe would release us all!'

'Be sensible, Abu-Zayd,' said his wife.

'Our cotton, Wahībah!'

'Remember that the *taftīsh* is backed by Government!'

'What can we do, then?'

'Not a thing.'

'But they'll take all our crop, and the result: I will be in debt. What sort of a state of affairs is that?'

'Patience, Abu-Zayd!'

'One stroke would release me.'

Abu-Zayd went out to the field early carrying his hoe on his shoulder. As he approached the cotton, the watchman,

Abu-ʻAṭiyyah, prevented him from entering the fields and threatened to beat him and lock him up in the compound like ʻUways Ibn Zīnātī. Abu-Zayd moved away but could not retreat far. He sat down on the bank of the ditch. The Inspector's trap passed in front of him. Abu-Zayd's eyes met the Inspector's and the lion on his arm shook. He never noticed before how fat the Inspector was. ... The trap went past, retreating into the distance. Several times it passed in front of him: he could not move. He began to compare the fat Inspector and the thin buffalo which he had sold to pay the debt of the last season. At last the carriage, having taken the Inspector to his house in the administration area. returned. 'There is no hope.' Diab spoke as he urged on the buffalo and the cow, walking behind them around the wheel. 'And Zainab, Yūnus will leave her, he'll go to the town, and when he comes back, he'll marry someone else.'

The raven croaked.

On the following day Abu-Zayd was unable to carry his hoe, nor was he able even to leave the house. He sat on his haunches, leaning his back against the water-jar. Suddenly Yūnus arrived, and Zainab rushed sobbing into the empty stable. Zainab's mother welcomed Yūnus, and Abu-Zayd called to him to sit down beside him. Yūnus told them that he was leaving for the city. Abu-Zayd did not reply, but Wahībah said, 'It is a hard thing, Yunus, being away from home.' Yūnus heaved a sigh, scratched his head, fiddled with his hat and said: 'Six years I have been ...' He fell silent with embarrassment. After a while, Abu-Zayd said: 'There is no life for us here, son.' 'We must go. We must leave,' Yūnus spoke quickly and eagerly.

'But where, Yūnus?'

'God's land is wide.'

'Masʻūd and ʻAbd al-Hafīz went to the town, Yūnus.'

'I know they came back poorer and more down-trodden than

ever.'

'So you know this, Yūnus.'

Silence engulfed them. Flies droned furtively. Zainab cast a frightened glance from behind the stable-door: she was dismayed to see how emaciated Yūnus' body had become.

'Diab said to me, if he owned the *taftīsh*, he would leave all the cotton to us,' Abu-Zayd said.

Yūnus smiled and began to fiddle with his stick in the yard.

'A hungry man's dreams, Abu-Zayd,' said Wahībah.

'My mother used to say if she owned the *taftīsh*, she would divide it among the people for nothing,' Yūnus said.

'The watchman stopped me from getting into the cotton fields.'

'They are going to bring in labourers from outside and collect the cotton,' Yūnus said.

'And they'll take it to the storehouses and sell it,' Wahībah said.

'And after all that, I'll be in debt,' Abu-Zayd said.

'And that means I won't get married this year,' said Yūnus, and he stood up.

'I told you that I would like to leave this place and go to the city,' he continued.

'It is a hard thing to live away from home, son,' Wahībah said.

And behind the stable-door, Zainab wept.

'But why don't we collect the cotton ourselves?' Abu-Zayd said.

'It's because they don't trust you with their own share,' replied Yūnus.

'But what about my share?' Abu-Zayd said and hid his thin face in his hands weeping with despair.

'Are you crying, husband?' said Wahībah, and she herself broke down with grief.

'All houses are in distress,' said Yūnus, and he went out.

From behind the wall of the stable Zainab tried to catch a

glimpse of Yūnus, but he had disappeared around the bend in the alley.

By evening half of the *fallāhs* in the *taftīsh* were prisoners in the compound. Sacks of cotton went to the storehouses. The tally clerk weighing said as he weighed a sack 'One quintār* and a half.' The Inspector said 'one *qintar* only', and warned him not to be careless and to keep his eyes open! He shook his whip menacingly, and the tally man grew flustered. Sitting on the bench, Diab said, 'Patience is sweet, Yūnus.'

'I'll leave the *taftīsh*,' Yūnus said.

'It is a hard thing living away from home, Yūnus, and Zainab is a nice girl,' said Diab.

Shaykh 'Abd al-Malik, the preacher of the *taftish* passed by; Yūnus rushed up to him and, kissing his hands, said, 'Speak to the Inspector!' 'Speak to him yourself,' the Shaykh answered, and went on his way repeating, 'God save the Princess.' Yūnus came back and sat at the bench.

''Omar Ibn al-Khattāb* used to go among his subjects,' said Diab.

'And Abu-Zayd was the knight of his time,' Yūnus said.

'The Princess comes here every month riding on the grey horse,' Diab said.

'They say she is pretty, Yūnus,' Diab said.

'Haven't you ever seen her, Diab?'

'I'm afraid to look at her, Yūnus.'

Diab's wife approached and said with tears streaming down her bony face, 'My father is a prisoner in the compound.'

'There is One above, my dear,' said Diab.

'Do something,' Yūnus said.

'Shall I risk eternal Hell-Fire?' Diab replied.

His wife, weeping, entered the house. Diab was silent, and Yūnus wondered about the *taftīsh*.

Zainab said, 'When do we leave, Father?' and he replied, 'Before sunrise, Zainab.'

Wahībah busied herself making a bundle of things they would need. Their little child was sitting beside her father. Abu-Zayd said to himself, 'People will say that I am a coward.' His glance came to rest on the hoe standing in the corner: 'One stroke of this hoe and it's all over.' The child cried, 'I want a drink, Father.' He raised the metal jug and poured her out a drink. She fell asleep and her fingers crossed the tattooed lion. 'The coward has run away; that's what Diab will say,' crossed the tattooed lion. 'The coward has run away; that's what Diab will say,' Abu-Zayd said to himself. The lion shook on his arm.

Zainab said, 'Mother, what about Yūnus?' Wahībah said, 'Perhaps he has found someone else, Zainab.' Zainab fell silent; she went out. Her mother did not call her; he knew she was going to Yūnus. He did not dare look at the hoe.

The grasses along the irrigation ditch were wet with dew. The dawn breeze was fresh on the faces of the two men. The mother and her daughter walked in silence along the canal.

They stopped the Delta Railway line and gazed at the train whose smoke and whistle mingled with the morning air around them and made a cloud which frightened them. Yūnus said, 'The Princess made the railway cross the *taftīsh*.' Abu-Zayd said, 'She had had the station pulled down because it was built on her land.' Wahībah said, 'Let's get on, before the mid-day heat.' Yūnus said, 'It's a long way.' Abu-Zayd remained silent; his hand clutching the hoe which rested on his shoulder. The drops of sweat ran down Zainab's legs and she raised the tails of her dress showing the edge of her pale trousers. Her mother said, 'Yūnus is here, child!' She allowed the tail of her dress to fall and sighed. The sun climbed higher. The dust of the road burned. The child walked on the grass of the canal bank. She cried when a thorn pierced her foot. Yūnus picked her up and walked along beside Zainab. Wahībah waited for her husband to overtake her.

'Say something, husband,' she said. Abu-Zayd sighed.

'There is no god but God,' he said.

'Fate is written on the forehead,' said Wahibah.

'One day we will get married,' Yūnus said.

'What a relief it will be, Yūnus!' Zainab said.

They sat down beside a sycamore tree and wiped away the sweat and dust from their faces. Zainab and her mother prepared supper. Abu-Zayd did not eat. 'We shall find another *taftīsh* to work in,' he said. Yūnus said, 'whose owner would be a good man, and who would already have made the *hajj** to Mecca.' 'And we'll be paid wages,' Abu-Zayd said.

Yūnus said, 'We will be able to save some of our wages.' Abu-Zayd, smiling, said, 'Will we be able to?' And patting him on the shoulder he said, 'If that happens, we'll go back to the *taftīsh*, buy an acre and plant it.' Yūnus laughed and said, 'With God, all things are possible.'

Abu-Zayd was lost in wishful thinking, and cheerfully he said, 'We'll cut our expenditure and pile up money; then we'll go back and buy an acre in the *taftīsh*, buy it and plant it, and I'll cock a snook at the Inspector.' 'And at the Princess,' Yūnus said. Abu-Zayd laughed until his eyes were full of tears. Yūnus said, 'We'll plant the acre with cotton, and save the profit to buy another acre.' And Abu-Zayd said, 'We'll buy two calves and two sheep and Zainab will keep some chickens and ducks, then we'll sell them and you and Zainab will marry on the proceeds.' 'Are we going to postpone the marriage until ...' cried Yūnus, '... Oh, no ... I can't wait for six more years.' 'And are we going to own an acre in six years' time?' Abu-Zayd said.

A sad silence engulfed them. The chirping of crickets on the bank of the canal grew louder. Finally Abu-Zayd said, 'If only the allotment administration had given me my due ...' 'If only my father hadn't died ...' said Yūnus. 'Can't we buy an acre in less than six years?' Abu-Zayd said. 'God knows!' Yūnus said. Abu-Zayd wondered whether the new owner of the *taftīsh* was a genuine *hajj*, to which Yūnus said, 'So I've heard.' Abu-Zayd said, 'Shaykh 'Abd al-Malik stands in the pulpit of the mosque and prays God to protect the Princess and the Inspector. But who knows?' Yūnus yawned and said, 'Let's sleep on it.'

All slept except Abu-Zayd who remained awake all night on the bank of the ditch engrossed in calculations, as he sought some way to shorten six years. Yūnus would get one *ryal*,* so would Zainab, so would he, so would Wahībah. The child ... if only she could do something. They would spend nothing, cling tight to everything. His thoughts came to a sudden stop: he wondered, 'Is the Inspector completely heartless? The land belongs to the Princess; the Princess comes only once a month. However, the Inspector prevents me from gathering the cotton and imprisons the workers in the compound. They say he sleeps with the Princess. God help us. They are foul. Oh, if only the owner of the new *taftīsh* were a genuine *hajj*!'

In the morning they walked like a caravan beside the canal which extended further than the eye could see. On the fourth day, the feet of Zainab and the child were swollen, and Yūnus said that he was exhausted. The child cried and asked for a drink of water. Her mother brought some from the canal and gave it her to drink till she grew quiet. Abu-Zayd said that he could walk no further.

An old man riding on a bicycle passed them and Yūnus asked him about the *taftīsh* of the *hajj*. The man said stupidly as he adjusted his dusty glasses on his mutilated nose, 'The *taftīsh* of the *hajj*!' Don't you know it, the *taftīsh* of the *hajj*?' Yūnus said. 'There are no *hajjis* here,' said the cyclist. Abu-Zayd shouted, 'The *hajj* who made the pilgrimage to Mecca seven times.' The cyclist laughed derisively. 'You've lost your way,' he said, and cycled away.

Wahība beat her breast, and tore up her faded black garment. Zainab cried. The child screamed. Yūnus ran after the cyclist, still asking, 'Do you know the *taftīsh* of the *hajj*?' But the man did not stop and continued to cycle away, laughing derisively, 'There are no *hajjis* here, you fool.'

Yūnus stooped, gasping breathlessly. Abu-Zayd looked at the lion drawn on his arm and looked for his hoe; and for Wahībah, and for his two daughters, but he could see nothing. Zainab cried out, calling for Yūnus, but her cry died. She called to Yūnus, but her voice was an incoherent rattle. She stretched out her arms to Yūnus. The child fell crying between them. Abu-Zayd said groaning, 'The acre, Yūnus ..., the acre. I'll stick out my tongue at the Inspector and the Princess,' and putting out his tongue he wept.

Shāṭir Ḥasan and the Season of Drought

By

Akram Haniyyah

The sky would yield the people no rain... . The trees and crops withered and the animals perished... . The earth cracked as it thirsted for water, and the men sat and thought in bewilderment and impotence about how to irrigate their lands and provide their families with water... . Everyone relinquished the habit of bathing. And women invented new ways to distract their children. The heavens would not heed prayers for rain and urgent supplications and hot tears. After several weeks, hunger spread throughout the land from village to village, a terrifying monster that left its mark on faces, bodies, crops and the earth.

Shāṭir Ḥasan alone sat down with his head bowed and cupped by his hand in sorrow and bewilderment... . He surveyed the cowed, impotent crowds with pity and said, 'I must do something.' He jumped with a nimbleness not much affected by hunger onto his black horse, for whom he used to save every available drop of water, then turned to the crowds that were awaiting rain and called out loudly, 'I will bring you back some water.'

Everyone raised a cowed head, but made no comment ... . Some smiled and others felt pity for the dreaming young man; but there were some who whispered suppressed prayers that the miracle would occur. As for the owner of the vast lands, he said to Shāṭir Ḥasan, 'If you bring back water, I will give you my daughter, Sitt al-Ḥusun, for a wife.'

The horse neighed and Shāṭir Ḥasan was intoxicated by the promise. The two of them sprang forward and set forth across the far-flung deserts. Eyes followed them until they disappeared into the horizon.

The distance was long ... the way was hard and wearying... . And the goal was difficult, if not impossible. Shāṭir Ḥasan knew what he wanted, but he did not know how to go about getting it. But everything was made to seem easy, for glory awaited him if he was successful; Sitt al-Ḥusun was also waiting.

After journeying for several days, he reached the large sea... . He sighed with satisfaction, but very soon was bewildered by a question. How would he transfer the water home? Shāṭir Ḥasan looked from side to side, then was able to distinguish a man sitting on one of the rocks on the beach in the distance. He dismounted and led his horse towards the man in a hurry. When they drew close to the man, Shāṭir Ḥasan stood face to face with him and beheld a visage weathered by the years. The man's voice rang out with the greeting, 'Welcome, Shāṭir Ḥasan.'

Shāṭir Ḥasan was baffled. 'How did you recognise me?' he asked.

The old man answered, 'I have watched you since you left your country in search of water. Have none of your people come with you?'

Shāṭir Ḥasan hung his head and said that his people were powerless and poor. 'But show me how to take water back,' he added.

The old man nodded and said, 'Very well, I will show you. Follow the line of trees that leads back to your home, and there amongst the deserted rocks at the bottom of the hill, dig into the ground and water from a plentiful spring will burst forth.'

As Shāṭir Ḥasan sprang onto his horse and made ready to leave, the old man warned, 'Beware the Sultan's men. They do not like you to know these things, nor do they like you to know the secrets of the springs beneath the earth.'

Shāṭir Ḥasan heeded the advice carefully, and avoided the main roads, making his way home along alternative paths at night until he arrived at the outskirts of his land.

Awaiting him was more thirst, hunger, death and dim questioning eyes. He did not say a word, but went towards the rocks, took up an axe and began to dig amongst the cracks... . Everyone waited in breathless anticipation, and Shāṭir Ḥasan's heart was beating fast as he felt all eyes, certainly including Sitt al-Ḥusun's dreaming eyes, riveted to him. The minutes passed in agonising slowness and drops of perspiration began to run down Shāṭir Ḥasan's forehead. Suddenly, he felt that his axe was no longer striking the rocks. And in a few moments, the spring burst forth, and water gushed forth, a fountain of coloured joy, sprinkling its wholesome drops onto faces, bodies and earth. Laughter broke out in hearts and on lips long visited by gloom and despair.

So Shāṭir Ḥasan became everyone's hero and the centre of their attention. He married Sitt al-Ḥusun in a celebration unprecedented in its splendour and lived at his father-in-law's palace happy with the loyalty offered to him by the people and their willingness to obey his orders.

The years passed in affluence and content. The produce was plentiful and no one complained of hunger. Shāṭir Ḥasan was able to solve many of the daily problems confronting his people because his opinions swayed influence. However, when a new drought hit the country, Shāṭir Ḥasan looked for the springs, but was unsuccessful, for they had all dried up, and he was forced to voyage once again to find new springs.

His people bade him a warm farewell and asked him not to stay away for long. He was not assailed by any strange feelings when Sitt al-Ḥusun embraced him with unusual warmth, with her son in her arms, and asked him to return soon.

He journeyed for many a long night.... . It was bitterly cold and the roads were dirty and lonely. He and his horse felt weak and tired and their strength collapsed. It was imperative for them to reach the sea. He dismounted and led his horse along narrow pathways to escape the eyes of the Sultan's soldiers. He reached the coast and left his horse to one side to look for the old man, but found no one. He searched several times amongst the rocks and trees and in the caves, but to no avail. He called out loudly, 'This is Shāṭir Ḥasan calling to you, my dear old man.' He got no answer save for the echo of his own voice. He called out once more. He felt some movement a short distance away. A group of riders was approaching rapidly. Shāṭir Ḥasan experienced fear for the first time in his life. He tried to run towards his horse, but the soldiers had surrounded him like a wall before he could move. Several contradictory images intertwined in his mind, and shadows that had always inhabited his fancy vanished. He felt the need to weep as the soldiers led him off to the Sultan's city.

A cramped cell. A small window blocked by steel bars. Sorrow was almost choking Shāṭir Ḥasan. He called out with sorrow and longing, 'What are they doing at home in my country?'

He wiped away a tear trickling down from his eye with the edge of his shirt. 'And Sitt al-Ḥusun and my son ...'.

Before his eyes loomed the shadows of the waiting wife, the son, the children, the land and the powerless eyes. He jumped to the window and trees and houses could be seen in the distance. He shouted, 'That is my country,' then sighed, 'but my country is far away.'

He clasped the bars and called out to Sitt al-Ḥusun, but was only answered by echo and threats from the guards.

Shāṭir Ḥasan's people awaited the return of their hero for a long time until they despaired of his return. They said, 'We can do together what Shāṭir Ḥasan used to do alone.' They began to dig every inch of the ground. They organised themselves into small groups and used axes, rods, sticks, hands and nails to dig. The work was back-breaking, the wind was strong and the cold brutally assailed their tired bodies. And the thirsty earth would not yield its secrets easily, but they persisted.

The work took a long time. Some stopped trying, but those leading them continued. Suddenly the secret bloomed forth and scores of spring burst forth out of the thirsty earth. The current of joy flowed through the fields, the women's wombs, the children's eyes and the men's faces. Everyone observed the bathing ritual in the drops that carried the secret of life, and a full festival celebrating water and life was completed.

And Shāṭir Ḥasan was no more than a memory and a shadow flitting across the sky.

Night 1002

By
Riyād Al-Marzūqī

Shahrayar could not sleep on the second night after the thousand, and he rang the bell.

'Where is Shahrazad?'

'She has gone out in the darkness, sending her thoughts out in the quiet, and listening to the song of the crickets'.

'She has gone out?'

'And your minister went out with her, my lord'. The King of kings was tormented by a headache: eddying wings danced before his eyes and a thousand drums beat on his head. After a few minutes, he asked for iced water, and for Dunyazad, and he smiled.

'It is told, O King of the Age, that a poor woodcutter, called Aladdin, lived in the city of peace with its thousand lanes. He went to market every Friday to sell his firewood and to buy a loaf which he would divide into seven pieces; each day he would eat one piece, and praise God'.

Her eyes were like the pool in the garden, clear and sweet; her hair was black as a winter's night; her forehead was like dawn in Springtime.

'One day, O my Lord, while he was eating his accustomed share, a skinny dog, weak with hunger, emaciated with disease, nothing but skin and bones and a little spark of life, looked at Aladdin. The woodcutter threw his portion to him. The dog gobbled it up and looked at him, begging for more; so he threw it his portion for the morrow, and his portion for the day after the morrow, and for the rest of the week. The dog shook itself, and turned into a great and dignified Shaykh.

'O Aladdin, you are a kind man, despite your poverty. Take this mirror: in it you will see everything except what is simply good'. Then the Shaykh vanished.

Her cheeks were like fresh roses, her neck like a column of wax; her mouth fragrant as vintage wine.

'Why are you looking at me so, O my Lord?'

'Oh, nothing, Go on, go on'.

Aladdin looked into the mirror, but could not see himself. He looked and he saw marvellous worlds. He saw a golden fish in a sea of quicksilver. He saw the Library of Shiraz, with its hundred thousand manuscripts. He saw a palace of crystal with stairs of marble. He saw a wounded Messiah calling down salvation in a far country. He closed his eyes and sighed'.

Shahrayar sighed.

'O my Lord!'

Aladdin was simply good and so the mirror could not contain him. He loved one of the peasant women who came from the bye ways'.

'O my Lord, she was fascinating, enchanting, and intoxication flowed from her every limb, and she caused wonder and amazement all around her. On market day she would bring marvellous fruit such as we do not know in our land; it is said that it grows among tombs'.

Shahrayar said, 'God forbid! God is most great! What is the name of this fruit, O Dunyazad?'

'Orange, O my Lord. All who know it agree that its taste is delicious and its scent excellent'.

Her bosom was a dome of marble, her waist like a statue of gold, her gown a halo of colours.

Aladdin's love for the maiden was hopeless because he had no claim on her and could not reveal his love to her'.

'Poor man!'

'My Lord, he was penniless. So he formed a resolution. He took his mirror on market-day, and stood waiting until Magic, which was the name by which people knew her, had sold all but one of the oranges in her basket. She came. 'Do you want to buy this orange? It costs a *dirham*'. And her laughter was like the water of a brook, Aladdin stammered, 'No, but I want...' 'Then it will cost you a *dinar*'. And she threw it, laughing, into the air, and gently ran past. He ran after her: so began the race under the sky of Spring. Breathless, he caught her at the edge of the wood. She laughed and laughed, and he caught the infection and laughed and laughed too. They fell exhausted on the grass.

'I wanted to give you, I mean to sell you, not to give you this ... this thing'.

'O God! How lovely this mirror is! It is as if ...'

Aladdin interrupted her with amazement: 'Look, this is you!', and he hid his face in his hands. What was there was evil; no, she was evil, as her features and lineaments appeared clearly in the mirror.

'Thank you. But what has come over you. You seem to be ill?'

'No'. Slowly he got up and turned away.

'Wait! Take your mirror!'

'It's a present:

She caught up with him, and opened his hand and put something into it. Then she kissed him on the forehead, and turned away.

He opened his hand and looked. He saw an orange of gold'.

Shahrayar took Dunyazad by the hand and made her sit down beside him.

'Servant, slaughter the cock, and hang black curtains over the windows. Now continue your tale, O Dunyazad'.

An Oil Slick

By
Sulayman al-Shaṭṭī

Noon prayers were over.

The Shaykh leaned his back against the large cylindrical column and surveyed the crowd that had gathered around him. He stretched out his leg and felt it. The people crowding round did not see the green piece of cloth that usually covered that part of his leg. A dark black patch with remnants of dust at its edges appeared. He pointed at his leg, then fingered the patch and said, 'This is a memento of the tale which I will tell you today'.

He did not wait to hear the usual questions. He was brimming with the tale, which rushed up to his lips:

At the beginning of the month of Safar in the year four hundred and two after the Hijra, we were on the outskirts of the city of (...). For several days, we had endured a sandstorm followed by locusts, which seemed to devour life itself. We encountered a land that was full of marshes and was covered with a thick black liquid. Despite this, we felt that it was a safe town, and we made our mounts kneel and dismounted below its walls.

The mud wall stretched out a long way. It had a large, high gate, and was topped by two small towers. We rested against our baggage throughout the night. At dawn, the large gate opened, and we came alive, rushing to pass through the gate. Amidst the excitement and glamour, someone shouted, 'O people! Not one of you move! The Ruler's messenger will address you'.

The messenger approached, bringing his horse into our midst. He surveyed us, then shouted: 'O people, is one of you a doctor, a soothsayer or a wiseman?'

He fell silent for a moment, then added, 'If anyone amongst you is of that ilk, his presence is required by the Ruler'.

There was commotion and muttering followed by a wary silence. A few glances were directed at me and my friend and I sensed that they were expecting something of us. They were merchants fearful for their caravan and hoping to gain something by winning favour with the Ruler. The silence became worrying, and I touched my friend's hand and whispered to him, 'Let us put our trust in God'.

Then I proclaimed, 'I will go with you'.

Exclamations of joy burst forth amongst the travellers in our caravan.

* * *

I overcame the embarrassment of that moment, and spoke first, saying, 'Sir, I am neither a wiseman, nor a physician nor a various peoples and commit it to memory so that we may put it to use when it is needed. It is neither our wisdom, nor our medicine. Rather, it is experience that we have stored and hope to put to good use, with God's help. We are at your disposal, and we put ourselves at your service if you feel that we may be useful'.

I raised my eyes timidly and looked at him, but I sensed that he was not with me. He was brooding, deep in thought, and he pointed at the minister. The latter spoke.

'Perhaps news of the very strong winds which hit us a few days ago has reached you'.

I said, 'Yes, it caused us some hardship as we travelled towards you. Had it not been for God's mercy, we would have been scattered in all directions'.

He went on speaking as though his ears had not picked up my comment.

'A great calamity has befallen us. As you can see, we live along this coast. Our lives are linked to the sea, and we are aware of its nature, but that which must be must be. When the storm began, all our boats were at sea. Divine providence protected the fishermen and sea merchants, and saved them, but ...'.

'Thank God', I responded.

'But oh, the great catastrophe!'

He turned his gaze obliquely towards the Ruler, whose limbs quivered.

'Our Ruler's son and two of his companions were on a fishing trip when the storm struck. After the sea had thrown out everyone who had been in it except for our Ruler's son, we searched for him and his companions, but we grew desperate, and our eyes grew weary without detecting any hopeful signs. We checked every trace and every illusion of a trace'.

Only yesterday, after the locust hoards had cleared, the waves threw out one of the companions of our Ruler's son. He was unconscious and barely alive. His body was completely covered with black tar, and the only part that showed was a small bit of the white of his eyes. A terrible tar. We did our very best to remove it, but we only had slight success'.

He fell silent for a few seconds, and pulled up his sleeve, revealing his arm.

'Look. Like that!'

His arm was covered with black tar that was visibly thick.

'We tried. We used everything we had to remove that black substance, but we failed. At the same time, we were trying to find out from him anything that would lead us to our Ruler's son. We laid him down, and we did our best for him.Yesterday evening, his lips moved, and he became strangely agitated. We tried to listen to what he was saying, but his words were unclear and we were unable to do any more. My master has sent out many letters asking for help and summoning the most famous of wiseman, but we fear that it will be too late. Therefore, we are looking for any help that we can get. Perhaps you will cure our helplessness. We want to understand so that we can do something.

A man who had just entered bowed to the minister and whispered something to him. The minister nodded, then said, 'This man tells me that the words of the man rescued from the sea have become clear, but their meaning escapes those around him'.

He turned to the Ruler.

'Does my master allow me to take them to him?'

He nodded his assent.

* * *

The Shaykh continued: I had nothing more than what I had given him – some left over stimulant herbs which had been given to me by a Yemani trader whose energy and lightness of movement had kindled my amazement. I had asked him about this, and he had given me a bundle of those herbs, which I had kept.

I awaited his response after he had swallowed the portion which I had prepared. I began to feel successful as he exhibited the first signs of wakefulness. The fleeting signs of consciousness could not be missed by anyone who had carefully watched him as he lay there, his blackened body covered by layers of tar. Hoping to limit his unfocused mutterings, we decided to question him. I took his slimy hand, swallowed hard, and said, 'Come on now, tell me, what happened to you? Where is His Highness' son? Speak. Do you remember anything?'

His eyes shone and his features relaxed into a smile as though he was seeing something or remembering a beautiful early morning vision. The shining of his eyes amidst the thick blackness indicated that he had become distant from us. He was there, from where he had come. The words within him welled up, overwhelming and possessing him. The lines across his forehead came closer together, and he began to tell his tale. We began to understand as the mutterings and brief words became more certain and better linked.

* * *

He began to speak, saying, 'We were caught between the devil and the deep blue sea: that barren island which inspired an expectation of death, and the sea which had thrown us before it. We did know what lay beyond the sea. After facing the storm, we had become naked before it. We were frightened, filled with dread and our will-power had disappeared. There was no strength in our arms. We waited, surrendering to fate to do with us as it pleased. The moments we experienced at sea as we surrendered to the insane anger that surrounded us are still present. During those moments, we did not even dare to stretch out our hands to one another, or to embrace one another as one would do out of fear or in quest of security. Our darting glances seemed to escape from around us. Our boat seemed devoid of any human life, and we were surrender personified until suddenly, we all started simultaneously at the sound of a strong blow at the bottom of the boat.

Land once again. We jumped up involuntarily, and in the darkness, we threw ourselves into the water, making a distinct sound as we waded through it. After we arrived and lay down for a while, we remembered the boat. My colleague and I returned to it, whilst His Highness' son lay down on the sand. From the quietness surrounding us, we realized that we were in a state of siege. Although our sense of impotence remained, we decided to move since each of us had a pair of legs. Exploration became an urgent necessity, and our mental procrastination could not be justified. We realized that we were in the midst of barren sand that stretched out into the sea, and that our attempts at searching were doomed to failure. Our feet once again began to feel the chill of the water to which they would inevitably return. So our eyes looked out towards the water, but we sharply curtailed our glances, once again becoming aware of the sand particles, which drifted apart, then came together again, forming a world that was both connected and separate.

Our fingers sank into the sand, then started nervously because the sand was calcified and we were troubled by a fear that shook us strongly deep within. Were we to sentence ourselves to returning to the sea? I looked at His Highness' son as he lay on the ground. We wanted a decision, but the eyes of the body lying there told us that he was unable to utter a syllable. If only he would give an order. At that point, we would have been happy to accept any order he might give, but all his ability was obscured by the dryness in his eyes. No decision. If he had uttered something in a voice as muffled as an echo, we would have accepted it without argument. There we were amidst a vacant universe, wrapped by the beginnings of darkness, each of us unable to think individually, yet unable to unite. And we saw it!

* * *

It captured our scattered gazes, and we stared at it. It's power of attraction was clearly overwhelming. The attraction was encountered by our importance, and so it conquered us.

It flashed a second, then a third time, then its reflection grew stronger with the setting sun. Not one of us said, ‘Look’. But our eyes were constrained to stare at one spot, the shining point. Something new surrounded us. Our chests were inflated by a great deal of air. The saviour had come, and for the first time, we felt that our bare feet could no longer bear the particles of hard sand that were entering the cracks in our heels. They longed for the flow of water once again. A state of attraction for that shining thing permeated our cells. In the midst of our affliction, we perceived it as precious life buoy, a familiar face appearing between one wave and the next, multiplying and filling our eyes so that we could see nothing else.

We looked at one another, as though the thought had occurred to us simultaneously, or we had heard it uttered by the same voice. We were governed by one clear decision. Nevertheless, we had a discussion to confirm that decision. It never happened again.

'Shall we remain on this barren island, or shall we return to the sea?'

I said to the other two, 'but shall we return to the midst of the storm?'

One of my companions said, 'The sea means death. The ground is firmer and more secure'.

'But the sea offers more hope'.

'Shall we exchange the firmness of the ground for a hope that is liquid?'

'That is better than being sentenced to oblivion'.

'We might be saved'.

'We might perish'.

It was strange that we were having a discussion without looking at one another. Our eyes were drawn to that shining crack, and we were talking after our throats had gone dry for several days. My friend even told a joke, as was his habit. Instead of remembering old poems, as I used to do, I felt that I was becoming filled with a new poem, and my thoughts wandered with it. Would we be saved? At that moment, the particles of fear broke. Hope, joy, the possible and the probable prevailed. They all entered the realm of fact, and there I was reciting my poem before new people. Their clothes were embroidered, and their eyes were wide open with energy after a long slumber.

We decided! Our boat made its way forward towards the shining glow, which began to disappear very gradually in unison with the downward movement of the setting sun.

The sound of the water as it hit the sides of the boat gradually disappeared, and we felt an increasing slime in the water around us. We no longer spoke or consulted one another. Each of us did as he pleased. His Highness' son dozed off and awoke, my friend remembered a joke, told it, fell silent, rowed once more, then threw down his oar. Rowing became impossible, and tiredness got the better of us, and we slept.

I became aware of the daylight on my skin like a flame splitting it open, and I felt unable to move. One of my companions poked me.

'Look'.

I sat up and touched the side of the boat with my hand to remove the remains of a tired sleep. Slime. I looked. My hand was covered with a thick layer of black oil that resembled tar.

'Do you see what I see?'

The black layer stretched out as far as the eye could see. The sunlight refracted at its edges, reflecting lights of varying colours. I responded. 'Do I see?'

My friend's question and my answer were full of obvious panic. He added, 'Is that black thing the light that we saw yesterday, or is it something else? Did we get lost during the night?'

With a faraway look, His Highness' son said, 'There is nothing but this'.

'Perhaps this is the Sea of Darkness advancing on us'.

What were we to do? The question presented itself, but we did not articulate it. Talking was no use. However, we asked, 'Shall we return?'

'Where to?'

'To the island once again'.

'The two of you have forgotten that we would have surely died there'.

'The problem is, how would we return to it again?'

The sun was burning us, and the limbs which had been covered by the oil were becoming more painful. It was necessary to move, because immobility meant certain death. We rowed on in the hope of leaving the oil slick behind. I said, 'We are heading in the opposite direction to the island, which means we are heading towards our country. Perhaps we can leave this behind and arrive there'.

His Highness' son said, 'And we would be rescued. My father has doubtless raised heaven and hell'.

'Ah, we forgot, sir, that we have the Ruler's son with us!'

* * *

We were no longer able to forget the burning sensation that almost on fire from the heat of the sun. Our strength was drained and our heavy eyelids felt as though they were being pulled shut by ropes. We could only see a narrow line in which vision was confused. The afternoon brought us a transient breeze, and we repeated our attempts at looking around us. Our eye movements allowed us to see the entire oil slick and take in all of its four quadrants.

An ominous calm prevailed amidst the first signs of darkness. It seemed that our eyes had become familiar with the colour black. Our gazes roamed, for the loss of hope does not rule out roaming.

All of a sudden, our gazes became fixed in the direction of the north!

Six eyes were fixed on the same point of convergence, a spot around which our visions interlocked. It was magically beautiful. With one heavenly stroke, all exhaustion drained away, as though the abscess that had burdened us had been lanced! Each of us relaxed in his place, as our fixed stares surveyed and swam in that new world that had opened up before us.

After an indeterminate length of time, I said, 'Do you see what I see?'

I heard nothing. The two of them were in worlds of their own and were not responding to any external motion.

'How strange! Do you see what I see, or am I alone in my dream?'

I put my hand on my forehead, I rubbed my eyes, I dipped my hand into the oily water and splashed it onto my face to be sure, and the vision became clearer. What I was seeing was incontrovertible and true. I looked at the palm of my hand, and it was definitely black. As for the apparition on the horizon, it was clear and could not be doubted:

At the very centre of the sea, the oil slick gradually rose, going upwards with one's gaze like a prominent mountain on a flat desert plane. Its colours were graduated, beginning with dark black, then lighter black, then dark green. The colours gradually took on a bright hue until they arrived at a transparent brilliance. Forms became more distinct with each new phase of colour, presenting a special world. The horizon turned into solid land, and water ran through it. The fresh, tender colour of plants could be felt between one's very fingers.

That hill took over my whole concentration. A thought occurred to me. 'Is this possible? The grave is one of Heaven's gardens, as the saying goes, so am I really there? But I know myself well. If I were to go to Heaven, it would not be that early. Perhaps I did do some good in my earthly life, but when and where?' Then I remembered her. It is true that I had taken care of her children. She had embraced me and taken me beneath her wing, restoring lust, which I had been unable to keep at bay whenever I was in her company! My lust had dripped heavily. Can actions be dissociated from intentions?

But this was a real world. I could almost touch it. The top of the hill had brought me back to her once again. She cancelled what was around her, for every time my gaze rose, what had gone before was cancelled. My gaze stopped at the summit, fixed to its revealing transparency that showed everything beyond it: several storeys of large glass rooms, some leading into others. One was aware of their limitless space, which gave the feeling that they were empty. Nevertheless, they were full of a countless number of objects which could not even be named. They were new and their forms, colours and decorative inscriptions, the like of which we had never seen before, were immeasurably beautiful. Every object within those rooms had a life of its own, but they all betrayed their distant origins: India, China, and the land of the Francs and Gauls. A strange and faraway world had deposited all its art within them. They were surrounded by springs and streams, and the sound of running water over pebbles. Within them were raised couches covered with rugs and cushions.

I swallowed my nearly dried up saliva when I saw transparent bottles that differed in shape, size and colour. I felt the sharp taste of their contents on my tongue, and my mouth was refreshed, although what was within the bottles never left them. At the same time, it poured down into one's very insides.

In the middle of that large room, there was a main hallway. Along its sides sat men, leaning on the cushions. Their beards were as white as the desert sand. Their clothes were not decorated, but their flow indicated that they were expensive. Prayer beads resembling sandalwood slid between their fingers, and the odour of their perfume was almost suffocating. One was captivated by the brilliance of white and blue rings too shiny to look at. It was a new world with which I was unfamiliar, but I knew the faces well.

They sat round in a circle, dignity reigning over them. The Koran was being recited, although I could not see anyone reciting or chanting it. The heavenly voice bounced around the large hall, making it more transparent, and it almost flew off, taking us and them with it.

I said to myself, 'This is a spiritual world, there is no doubt about that'.

I was overcome by a sense of pleasure that blotted out all else, as I concentrated on the world that was before me. One of the seated men moved, and my gaze followed him. The Koranic voice began to disappear. The man walked to the centre of the hall, climbing down a ladder as my eyes followed him. His bottom half. Oh! What is that?

The lower he descended, the more his body was revealed. I began to see his nakedness. His clothes remained on, but they were as transparent as a bottle made of white glass. There was no cover to conceal anything. The leg, the pelvis, the genitals and the face were all covered by a shiny, oily colour. His legs carried him, but their motion was one of trembling pleasure.

The objects in the lower hall became intermingled. A mixed world. The bottles disgorged their contents, and groups of women appeared. All that they wore was shining, creating a dazed wonder in the observer. They were lying down in positions that were too numerous to be counted. I do know why my mind jumped to the figure of three hundred and fifty-five years epitomized by sexual positions. Yes, the odour of sexual pleasure dominated any other sensation. The women were clad, but nothing was covered. Their bodies were clearly revealed despite their luxurious, shining, flowing clothes. They were as clear as anything beneath the sun, and the brilliance revealed the dark corners, which shone before every gaze.

A modest, covered outward appearance, but what was within was clear and cheap.

The two rooms, top and bottom, intermingled. I saw the modest men in the upper room, descending one after the other. As they passed the threshold separating the two rooms, their clothes became transparent, revealing what was beneath them. The Koranic voice grew fainter, then mingled with a song which I knew well. I knew it by heart because I had heard it many a time when I had given in to the night and to drink. Now, here was that voice shouting it out loud. Had it not been for my previous experience, I would not have been able to make anything out because everything became intermingled, and bodies lay prostrate like flayed sheep. They were possessed by their moments of wallowing on the green carpet, and the atmosphere was saturated with pleasure. It was a world that enticed you to watch it while at the same time you felt strongly drawn to enter it, and you did not know which course to follow.

I could no longer make out the two rooms, because the differences between them had vanished, and the threshold separating them had collapsed. Those at the top were like those at the bottom, and everyone was both dressed and undressed. I saw a meeting being held, and papers spread out, and they were suddenly covered by a woman's body.

The voices of my two companions diverted my attention as they spoke together. His Highness' son said, 'That is exactly what I want. That is my world. I know it well!'

He threw himself into the oily water, as my other companion said 'That is exactly the world I long for. That is my final goal ...'. He followed His Highness' son.

A few moments later, there they were, climbing the hill. They rose gradually, their wet clothes stained by black. They stretched out their hands and were in the midst of the room, their bodies clearly visible beneath their clothes. They were completely naked, but their oily blackness remained, and they merged into that world.

I was seized by a terrible fear. I wanted to wake up, but I was pulled back by some movement in an upper chamber. A perfume that was spreading filled my nostrils, and my heart gently settled as thought it had expected what it was seeing. I saw her, and whispered as though I were speaking to someone nearby, 'It is her and no one else. Maymounah. I have found her at last. Can the past reawaken, can it return without the moments of sorrow which sent me into ruin? This could not be a fantasy. Her moonlike face had no defects. We would not be able to preserve this magical state, or record that condition of magnetism inherent over there. I shall never forget her. The shadows of the face in the early days of fantasy when weakness overcame me, when her lips and the light of her eyes were the world in which I got lost, the old moments of calm when I contemplated her.

There she was before me after we had been separated by a long interval, after her husband had taken her with him far away. Then had come the news of her body that had been hidden and covered by the cruel earth. After that, I had sunk into the mud of life which I had discovered along with the other world in which I had wandered. But there she was!

At that moment, a trembling feeling took hold of me. My inactive body shook strongly and was covered with a thick perspiration. I saw her clearly. I felt her touch with a tangible clarity. I stretched out my head and saw her becoming transparent before me. Squeezing that body was equivalent, on its own, to possessing a spirit whose elements melted within one's veins. I stretched out my neck and the exposure, cohesion and intermingling increased. The whole of me rushed forward and pushed, lightly rising, and everything before my eyes vanished. No scenery, no gradations, nothing except for that glass spot.

The age-long deprivation disappeared. I now possessed a great deal. When I possessed her, I had what I wanted out of this world. There I was.

I threw myself into the oil slick, I slid into it, and it came between my eyelid and my eyeball. The world slid about me, and the darkness of oil blotted out all visions.

* * *

The Shaykh continued: The prostrate body was panting, and its parts moved violently. His hands pressed his body as though he were trying to bring out what was inside it. The blackness of his hand merged with the blackness of his body. He trembled, then became still. The rising and falling blackness over his chest indicated that he was breathing weakly. I wanted to say something, anything, so I said, 'Is that the last you saw of His Highness' son?'

He wanted to overcome his weakness, as though the fever of his previous vision was burning him. He raised his finger and warned, 'Do not underestimate the oil slick'.

I threw a question at the group of people, who had crowded around in increasing numbers. 'What will you do now?'

The contagion of my question seemed to take hold of them. They no longer surveyed the long beach onto which large pieces of oil were being flung. The heels and legs of some of them were smeared with it. They looked at one another and muttered. An eager voice yelled, 'We must save His Highness' son'.

A voice whispered, 'We must try to protect our shores'.

A third said, 'Rather than doing that, we should await the help for which our Ruler has sent. Rest assured and do not worry. Do not spread panic. Everything is fine. All you need worry about is

His Highness's son. He is the only one in real, not imagined danger'.

One of them whispered in my ear, 'Could you arrange for me to travel with your caravan?'

I looked at him, and promised to do my best.

As morning broke, our caravan headed out of the city. The dark remnants of the night were wrapped in the first rays of light, which revealed the chunks of advancing tar. Outside the city, we lowered our camels, and each member of the caravan picked up a piece of rough cloth with which to remove the oil that had stuck to him.

I looked into the distance at the black cloud surrounding the city. It seemed like a custom-made turban.

I wondered, 'What will I find if I return in twenty years time?'

I have never returned to it, but its memory is represented by that remaining black spot. And he pointed at his leg.

‘Antarah Ibn Zabībah

by

Faysal Khartāsh

Things had gone exactly as he had planned. The battle had ended with the defeat of the neighbouring Arab tribes, and ‘Abs alone ruled supreme. All that was left for ‘Abs to do was to await its returning warrior, who was covered with blood, and to open before him the gates of honour and supremacy, and line his path to welcome him with decorations, songs, chants, banners, flags and the branches of trees. Rejoice for one day, for two days, for seven days and nights on which the drums shall be beaten, and sheep shall be slaughtered. Lords and gentlemen shall come from every corner, horse races shall be held, and horsemen shall play with the stalks of palm leaves. Would all that not befit ‘Antarah, the desert warrior and slayer of heroes? Only a few hours lay ahead before he would be proudly seated amongst the masters of ‘Abs, eating and drinking, and exchanging conversation with them. He would regale them with accounts of the battle and of how the enemy's warriors had fled before him, of how he had thrown them dead to the ground, leaving them to the beasts of prey to "chew off their bonny fingers and wrists." He would relate how he had stormed enemy lines, breaking them up with his sword and spear. All they would have to do would be to acknowledge him as a hero and saviour because they had recognized his deeds to be those of an unsurpassable warrior.

He entered the haze of the desert heat, and glimpsed the mirage of a green oasis in the distance. He wanted to pay it a visit, but he decided that he preferred to travel on so that he would arrive before sunset to see ‘Abla awaiting him outside her tent. He wanted to get there before the other warriors, whom he had left behind to fight over the spoils of battle and capture the fleeing horses.

There was nothing that could distract him from reaching her as fast as possible. The heat melted his helmet, and he felt that his brain was boiling within his head. The horse was streaming with blood and sweat, and ‘Antarah soothed him with tender, compassionate words, urging him to swallow up the road that lay ahead as far as the eye could see.

‘Good fellow, if you gallop on and do not let me down and we arrive before the other fighters, I shall wash you and feed you with these two hands of mine.’

The horse snorted and tossed his head, and ‘Antarah laughed, saying, ‘Do you not believe me? It is true that I shall become one of the masters, but I love you dearly, and I shall do this to keep my promise to you, and I won't mind if they say that ‘Antarah washes and feeds his horse as though he were a slave.’

He stroked the horse's neck with his palm, and it felt soft and moist, and ‘Antarah said in a voice that travelled through the hot wind, the pale sky and the dry air:

If argument he mastered, he would complain
if a speech he knew, my interlocutor he would be

‘Antarah arrived in the homeland of Banī ‘Abs, entering it in the evening before nightfall. He rode down the road alone, holding his head so high that he was unable to see the notice to the right of the road, which said, ‘LAND OF BANĪ ‘ABS: PHOTOGRAPHY IS PROHIBITED’. The shepherds a long distance away welcomed him, waving their staffs and handkerchiefs at him, but he looked away. The mountains surrounding the tents of Banī ‘Abs sent out their voices to him, calling his name, and repeating it across the reverberating desert sands. ‘Antarah swayed with joy, as everything in nature chanted the name of the hero, 'Antarah, vanquisher of warriors. He held his head high and that slight smile of which he had always dreamed appeared on his face, heralding his triumphant entry into a new era called: The Time of 'Antarah Ibn Shaddād. Today, that new page would begin, and he would announce a new history of his life. Many both before and after him had written their histories as they pleased, so why should he not write the history of his life with his own hand, and by the sword? The bastards had made out that their own mothers were paragons of virtue. The Arab ravens had turned their own faces into lighthouses to guide those who were lost in the labyrinths of the desert, so for how much longer would he continue to be the black 'Antarah, Ibn Zubībah? He had found his way, and he would wipe out that history, and chronicle his new life through many wars and slain enemies.

The mountains, the desert, the wind, the sky and the horizon responded to his dream, sending him tunes of victory that repeated his name. They banged the tambourines, beat the drums and played the cymbals for him, and he swayed on the horse's back, entering the camp of Banī 'Abs. Where are you, O 'Abla, to welcome your noble knight, your husband who comes over the bodies of warriors?

Everything was quiet, and life proceeded normally. The women chattered outside their tents as they picked okra off its stalks or chopped eggplants and courgettes. The idlers had managed to get the buxom young girls all to themselves behind the tents and at the water springs, and were chatting to them about the *souks* of Al-Yamāmah, Al-Hīrah and Damascus, giving them cheap earrings, chewing gum, bustards and mirrors as gifts, while the girls listened with open mouths to their enervating talk. The road into the Land of 'Abs was not bedecked with decorations, nor were there any drums. No one stood by the roadside to welcome the returning warrior with ornaments and ululations. Men walked up and down the *souk* buying goods, vegetables and children's school things. The warriors were buying, hunting deer, and throwing it into their Nissan and Chevrolet cars as they made ready to go off hunting and shooting a short while later.

'Antarah ignored all that, held his head high, and continued to surge forward with the rustling sounds that reached him through the air, saying to himself, 'Perhaps there is a conspiracy.'

Outside her tent the black horse came to a halt. He did not take one step further. He neighed, but no one came out. 'Antarah's weapons clanged, but still no one came out. He rolled his eyes, cleared his throat and coughed, but no one appeared. He said, 'She's playing hard to get. Come out, we did it all for your sake, so say 'Good evening, O bravest of warriors.' We ask nothing more of you than that, O lady of the bewitching eyes. Is it not time for you to soothe the heart's painful burning?'

He remembered that he had not stopped to mourn over the traces of an abandoned encampment on his way to 'Abla's home, so he postponed doing so until 'later on.' He could stop to mourn over the traces of an abandoned encampment after he had met with 'Abla and could change the order of the verses without anyone finding out, especially since the poem had not been published yet.

He pulled his horse three steps backwards, pulled out his sword, struck his shield several times, and began to hum and haw, renting the air with his sword and yelling. Then he suddenly calmed down, took a deep breath, and said:

Will you not ask the horses, O daughter of Mālik,
if you are ignorant of what you know not
He who the battle has witnessed shall tell you
that fiercely I fight, but of the spoils I partake not

He heard a tender voice coming from inside the tent saying,

'Deal with him.'

'Antarah ignored the voice and stared at the horizon. The flap of the tent opened slightly, and a beautiful face, lighter in colour and thinner than 'Abla's, appeared. It was that of her sister, Lamya. She came out of the tent, and placed her hand on her waist, and said, 'So, why have you come to us, then? So that we can look at your black colour? You don't partake of the spoils, do you? And why do you smell so rancid? Could you not have passed by Zabībah's to wash off all that blood with which you have coloured yourself and to perfume yourself before coming to us?'

'Antarah stammered slightly, and was unable to finish the rest of the verses, so he asked her as politely as possible, 'Where is 'Abla?'

She answered that she did not know, and that he should leave them and understand that 'Abla was not suitable for him, and that she had no reason to marry him since he had no money, influence or good looks.

He told her that he had done himself proud in battle, that he had beaten back the enemies and protected the women all on his own, and that had it not been for him, she and her sister would have been taken as war captives by the other tribes.

She told him that this would be better for 'Abla than to marry him.

He ignored her answer and told her that the other enemy tribes, which had designs on the lands, wealth and water of 'Abs, made it always necessary to have a warrior to deter them and foil their designs.

'But we are negotiating with them, and there shall be peace between us, and there shall be no work for the likes of you after that. Come back to us after the peace negotiations. You may be of use to us in teaching the Arab tribes a lesson because, thank God, you only fight Arabs.' So said Lamya to him.

'Antarah's eyes seemed as though they were choking, and they grew yellower. He asked her for some water, and she shouted at a slave standing next to her to give him water so that he would not accuse them of being stingy. The Ethiopian slave took the water to a spot that was far from the tent, and 'Antarah followed her, leading his horse by the reins. He took the water from her, drank, washed his face, and wiped the neck and chest of his horse, who was bleeding. He left him there, allowing him to drink, and returned to Lamya, who was still standing outside the entrance of the tent, holding the rope.

'Lamya, I beg you to call your sister, 'Abla.'

'My lady Lamya. Do you no longer distinguish between masters and slaves? I told you she is not here.'

'My lady Lamya, can you tell me where I can find 'Abla?'

'My lady 'Abla. Are you unable to understand?'

'My lady 'Abla!!'

'Your lady has gone to her sister in al-Hīrah. She went with your master Mālik to offer congratulations. His wife has given birth to a son, my God protect him from the evil eye. Do you want anything else? Be so good as to depart.'

'Antarah withdrew disappointed, sad and distracted, but hid his feelings until he reached his horse. He led his horse by the reins, and walked forward accompanied by soft sounds coming from afar. He caught his name amongst those sounds, accompanied by strains of soft sad music. Everything is lost, 'Abla. He put his hand to his chest, and from beneath his shield, which was covered with the blood of heroes, he pulled out a photograph from the pocket of his shirt, and held it in the palm of his hand. It was a photograph of 'Abla, with a little smile on her face. Her cheekbones stood out at the edges of her fine dark face, and her curly hair sat upon her head like the lump that was clogging 'Antarah's chest.

He turned the photograph onto its other side, on which was written the words 'Remember me always.' There was a drawing of a heart pierced by a spear, with three drops sliding off it. In the middle, the very middle, the words 'Studio Dikran' had been stamped in blue ink, and the day and date were printed beneath them. He looked at it for a long time, then gently put it back inside his shirt.

'Antarah continued to lead his horse by the reins, walking around the tents until he drew near to his own tent. Before he arrived, he caught sight of his mother returning from the *souk*, carrying some things with her left hand, and leaning on her crutch with her right hand. Zabībah followed him into the tent, asking him why he had been absent. She put the things she had been carrying onto a large tray, brought a knife and began sorting them out, cutting up some of them, as she told 'Antarah about the exorbitant prices, about the shortage of foodstuffs and vegetable oil and about the power cuts. 'Antarah was covering his face with his right arm, and his thoughts were wandering far, far away, to where he could see 'Abla smiling at him, her teeth shining like the glint of swords.

He asked his mother to go to Shaddād, saying the name on its own without any titles, and to ask him to lend 'Antarah his horse because his own horse was too exhausted to travel. She did not get up, asking him to wait for a while until she had finished her tasks. He sprang up, snatched the tray on which the vegetables were placed, and flung it with all that was on it outside the tent. Then, he took her by the hand and led her outside the tent. He tied the tent's central pole to a rope and pulled it, and the tent collapsed before Zabībah's eyes. He said to her, 'Now, do you have peace of mind?' The old woman looked at him reproachfully and said, 'My son' and her mouth remained open. Then she took up her crutch and went down the road leading to the middle of the encampment. She returned a short time later and found ‘Antarah looking out towards the desert and chanting,

> ‘To the land of visitors she has departed, and has become unattainable to those who seek her, the daughter of Muḥzam’.

She let him finish, then said, ‘Shaddād does not give his horse to anyone.’

‘Antarah drew his sword and struck the water just at the edge of the tent. Water gushed out of it onto the sand, and ‘Antarah quickly went down the road along which Zabībah had returned. He spoke to no one, approached Shaddād's horse, untied him, mounted him and rode off to the amazement of everyone. Shaddād tried to stop him with gesticulations, but ‘Antarah was too quick for him. One of those standing next to Shaddād said, ‘He is your son, so let him be happy, if only for once.’ Shaddād paid no attention to the other members of the tribe, and continued to watch the warrior until he turned into a black speck in the glow of the setting sun.

That night, ‘Antarah did not sleep, and watched the stars in the sky, as he repeated the verses of ‘Umru-’ul-Qais about his condition and the stars in the sky that were tied with ropes to Mount Yathbul. Meanwhile, Zabībah laid herself down over a small rug, counting the angels' sheep, covering herself with her soft snoring.

As the first light of dawn cast itself over the desert sands, ‘Antarah was riding his horse, and the fighters were asking him to come to their rescue in battle. He struck at enemy lines, breaking them up and felling their heroes. Standing alone on the battlefield, he shouted at the top of his voice, ‘One warrior to one warrior, ten warriors to one, one hundred to one.’ They used him to shield themselves from the spears, complaining as they thronged around him. The voices of the fleeing fighters reached him from every nook and cranny, ‘Go on, ‘Antarah, get them!’

'Antarah went forward, and saw 'Abla's eyes beckoning to him, so he rode furiously through the sand until his body was wet with perspiration, and his spirit grew calmer, and his horse began to slow down. He saw her ahead of him looking out of her camel litter, signalling him to follow her. He went limp and followed her, flying over his horse, sitting with her inside the litter, kissing her hands and smelling her sleeves and lying on her knee, and the sedan chair swayed, so she asked him to leave. Then she reminded him to stop and mourn over the remains of an encampment. He looked at her wrist watch and asked her about the time, and she answered that it was a few minutes past ten. He caught sight of the remains of an encampment in the distance, and he urged his horse on towards them, then slipped off his back. He saw a desert lizard stretching itself on the walls of the crumbling remains. The gazelles had fled the glow of the burning heat, and rested in the ruins. He felt that water was boiling inside his head, and he stood there and chanted:

Have the poets not spared any ruins,
or have I recognized the house after mistaking it?

After finding that he was unable to complete the remainder of the verses because of the searing heat that had taken hold of his head, he cursed ruined encampments and poets, and rode on to search for 'Abla, whom he sought above all else.

He arrived in al-Hīrah as evening invaded it from every direction, sending the shades of the leaves of the departing sun through the palm trees. He was filled with the scent of the city, and he experienced a feeling of exultation as he watched the mass of buildings that crouched ahead of him. He grew slightly apprehensive as he watched the city walls, and the blackness that covered them. He stopped at a small building near the walls, handed over his horse to the boy standing at the door and entered.

The boy did not know what to do with the horse, so he set him free amongst the trees. 'Antarah said to the empty place, and to the man sitting behind the table, 'Good evening.' When no one responded, he sat down at one of the tables and ordered food and wine. He was hungry, so he ate, and he was tired, so his body relaxed after he had consumed three glasses. He finished the bottle and ordered another, and said, 'I don't care about a thing.' The place filled up with carousers and drinkers, and a band struck up a tune which transported 'Antarah. Then a singer, dripping with sweetness and tenderness, appeared. She picked up a microphone and sang, 'Has Love Seen Drunkards Such As Us?'*

'Antarah twirled his moustache, and cursed 'Abs, Shaddād, Zabībah and the desert encampments, and his head swelled, and his eyes bulged. Since he was on his own, he was not able to do much more than keep up with the other carousers by shaking his body right and left. He continued to do so until the Desert Dancer appeared. She, who was slender of waist and dark of eyes, had charmed all the cities and her name was well known amongst them all. 'Antarah caught sight of the young woman who had come out, showing more of her body than she hid. It was a body that was the colour of the desert sands when they reflected the moonlight. He saw, and he saw, and he had three more drinks, followed by three more, then three more. Before his eyes, her body twisted and shouted out to him, calling to him, but he was chained to his table and unable to break free. When she stretched her hands out to him, he tried to get up, and he stood, then swayed, staggered and fell lengthwise. No one paid him any attention, and the two boys standing near the door came up and tried to lift him, but failed because he was too heavy. They propped him up against the wall, leaving him as he was, and the other folk continued their conversation of the flesh.

'Antarah was eating sweetmeats with the angels. They fluttered around him with their short wings, each of them carrying a small plate made out of lower petals, holding a mouthful with three fingers and putting it into 'Antarah's mouth, as 'Antarah smiled quietly, opening his mouth slightly.

After the small angels had departed, 'Antarah rode his horse to the encampment of Banī 'Abs. When he approached their tents, he spurred his horse, who galloped ahead like a storm. He leaned towards the notice that announced the homeland of Banī 'Abs and hit it with his sword. He arrived at the pavilion of King Zuhayr, and hurriedly dismounted, and asked the King to gather the elders of the tribe, and the King did so. When they had arrived, he told them that the King of the Persians was after their land, and that he was on his way, after conquering Iraq and destroying it, bringing with him a huge army that was too large to count. 'Antarah said that he had seen it with his own two eyes, backed by navies, warships and planes.

'They are after your land, your money and your women,' he said.

'What is to be done?' they asked.

He said, 'We should dig trenches around our encampment, and station the spear throwers in them. The swordsmen shall hide amongst the trees behind them, and the archers shall sit in the trees.'

They decided that 'Antarah should command the campaign for the defence of the homeland, so he gathered the men and arranged them as he pleased. Then he chose some loafers to accompany him and assigned some of them to the rear lines so that they could bring him anyone who deserted his defensive position. After all this was put into effect, he appointed King Zuhair as his deputy, and sent him on a reconnaissance mission to inspect the frontlines. Then he sat upon his throne at the pavilion of King Zuhayr.

He clapped his hands, and the dancer appeared and began to

twist before him as she performed the 'cobra' dance. King 'Antarah sat upon the throne, wearing the crown of sovereignty on his head. His father, Shaddād, and his uncle, Mālik, stood behind him, each of them carrying a fan made of ostrich feathers with which they fanned the air around 'Antarah's head to relieve him of the desert heat. At his feet sat 'Abla and her sister Lamya, cutting and filing his toenails. Next to him, the Tunisian singer who had sung for love and drunkards, lay down, twisting onto his thigh. Meanwhile, Queen Zabībah, who was wearing jewels and precious stones, and a pearl- studded golden crown, stared into space, her hands spread over her knees.

'Antarah then ordered his chief clerk to issue a statement for the fighters on the front line urging them by means of strong resistance to foil the plans of the enemy and preserve the honour and dignity of the Arabs.

The women came, each one from a different country – from Samarkand, Love Abad, Damascus, Aleppo, and Baghdad, from India and Constantinople, from Rome, Denmark and Greece. Each of them performed her number, then lay down in her coloured flimsy scarves in front of 'Antarah until they formed a golden bracelet, completing the circle with 'Abla and Lamya. 'Antarah was enchanted by the women that lay before him. Then the singer whispered to him, and he kicked 'Abla and her sister Lamya and gestured to them to stand some distance away. Then he descended from his throne and lay down amongst the women, and they gathered around him and covered him with their bodies. He felt a great weight and a cold ecstasy eased his head and body. He opened his eyes and saw a boy holding an empty water bucket asking him to wake up. He got up and sat at his table, and found men he did not know sharing it with him. They asked him if he had any objections, and he gestured with his hands to indicate that he did not. Then he ordered some drinks for them, and chanted:

When I come round, my generosity fails not
for my character and open-handedness to you are known.'
One of the men asked him, 'Are you a poet, brother?'

'Antarah wanted to beg the question so that he would not have to recite more poetry and reveal his true identity, so he responded by saying that he did not write poetry, but that he knew many verses by heart. They insisted that he should recite some poetry to them, so he chanted:

'If the King his people does degrade
the lowness within ourselves we refuse to admit'

They signalled each other to subdue him, then pulled him out of his chair. Then ensued the following scene, which you watched at Cinema Cairo: ''Antarah shackled in irons, roaring in the face of his tormentors.' That was on the first day. On the fifth day, most of his bones had been broken, and his moustache had been plucked. The front of his mouth had been emptied of its contents, and his blood- covered shirt had been torn, revealing the marks of electric shocks and cigarette butts. And they continued to ask him about the name of the poet who had written that poem.

Because 'Antarah was chivalrous and loyal, he refused to sacrifice his friend, the poet, and he insisted that he did not know his name, and that he had met him one day at the Okaṭh Cafe and heard him recite the poem, of which he had memorised that one verse. Patrols went to the cafe and destroyed it completely. When they could find no one there who wrote poetry, they decided that everyone there should be further investigated. They returned to 'Antarah and found him talking to the Jinnies and shaking the walls, and his chains were falling back on to him, creating the feeling of coolness.

Years later, he was released, and took to the corners of walls, tying his head with a coloured band to protect it from the winter cold and the summer heat. In his hand, he held a piece of coloured chalk, and he entered the cafes to recite poetry about wisdom and people's morals, then going outside again, and scribbling everywhere ‘I am ‘Antarah .’

Glossary

Abu-Isma'īl The father of Isma'īl. This compound form of address is very popular in Arabic culture and it is used to address or call a person with Abu (or Umm for mother) of the eldest son, and sometimes, eldest daughter.

'Alqam Colocynth known for its bitter taste.

Alla una, alla due, alla tre Italian loan words used by local auctioneers with the intention of announcing the last bid to win.

Ember An Orkney sea-fowl.

'Aqīq Ravine worn out by a torrent; carnelian.

Caliph's honey and al-Bashīr's coffee The intention is not literal. The reference is ironic because it implies treachery. During the nineteenth century in Lebanon Prince Bashīr al-Shihābī used to offer his guests honey and coffee as a sign of hospitality and good will. Then his men would attack the guests, taking them by surprise and slaying them.

Cock of the Jinn A nickname for al-Kalbī, an Abbasīde poet (eighth-century) born in Hums, very close to Hamah in Syria. He killed his maid because she had an affair with his son. But he lived to regret his act.

Damūr Dress made of Damascene cloth.

Dimaqs Damascene silk.

Hajj The Moslem who makes the pilgrimage to Mecca, and the one who makes it seven times is supposed to be a good example for piety. The reference here is evidently ironical.

Has Love Seen Drunkard as us a poem sung by the Umm-Kulthūm, the most popular singer in the Arab world. In appreciation she is occasionally imitated by young amateurs.

Howdaj A shaded camel-born vehicle for women.

al-Iṣlāḥ al-Zirā'ī Agricultural reform introduced by the government following the Egyptian Revolution of 1952. It promised to redistribute agricultural land and abolish the feudal system.

Jawqa Something like a musical chorus which sings a refrain.

Kufiyyah Headcloth for men still worn in some rural areas.

Mish Cheese that is matured by prolonged immersion in yoghurt and salt in an earthenware urn.

Muzāyid A person who engages in counter-bidding in auction; opportunist.

Omar Ibn al-Khaṭṭāb used to go among his subjects The second Caliph to rule after Abu-Bakr (Prophet Mohammad's successor). He was known to mingle with his people in disguise at night to acquaint himself with their conditions so as to be able to do justice. The reference in the story is ironic.

Qintār An Arabic weight unit that is equivalent to 600 pounds.

Qunbāz An old popular Damascene costume for men still worn by some rural men with the traditional headcloth (Kufiyyah).

Ryal A currency unit used in Egypt during the era of Napoleon Bonaparte. It equals twenty Egyptian piasters. Although the ryal is no longer used in Egypt the word still signifies twenty piasters.

Taftīsh The word literally means inspection. It refers to a government controlled estate in Egypt, which is tended for the state by the *fallāh* in exchange for a meagre portion of the total produce.

Bibliography

'Aflaq, Michael, "The Death of Sindbad" in Ḍuqan Qarqut, *Michael 'Aflaq*, Beirut: al-Mu'assasah al-Arabiyyah Liddirasat wal-Nashre, 1993, pp. 27-31.

"Sindbad and his Mistress" in Ḍuqan Qarqut, *Michael 'Aflaq*, pp. 124-27.

Bergonzi, Bernard, *The Turn of the Century*, (London: Macmillan, 1973).

Duwwarāh, Fu'ād, "A Comment on 'Abu-Zayd Surrenders", *al-Majallah*, 10 (1966), p. 89.

Fahmī, 'Abd al-Rahman, "The Seven Voyages of Sindbad", *al-Ādāb* (August 1964), pp. 11-13, 71-6.

Frye, Northrop, *The Fables of Identity: Studies in Poetic Mythology* (New York: Harcourt, 1963).

Gerhardt, Mia, *The Art of Story Telling: A Literary Study of the Thousand and One Nights* (Leiden: E. J. Brill, 1963).

Habībī, Emīle, "The Blue Charm and the Return of Jubaynah", in *The Double Trilogy of the Six Days* (970; reprinted Beirut: Dā'irat al-'Ilām wal-Thaqāfah, 1980), pp. 36-41.

Hafez, Ṣabrī, "The Dilemma of Freedom in Modern Arabic Fiction", *Ḥiwār*, 10 (1964), pp. 52-62.

_____, "The Egyptian Novel in the Sixties", *Journal of Arabic Literature*, 7 (1976), pp. 84-8.

Haqqī, Yahya, "Editorial", *al-Majallah*, 10 (1966), p. 5.

Haniyyah, Akram, 'Shaṭir Ḥasan and the Season of Drought', in *The Defeat of Shaṭir Ḥasan* (1979; reprinted Jerusalem: Dar al-Kātib, 1980), pp. 7-13.

Hawī, Khalīl, "The Faces of Sindbad", *al-Ādāb* (January 1958), pp. 62-3.

_____, "Sindbad on his Eighth Voyage", *al-Ādāb* (June 1958), pp. 4-5.

The two poems were reprinted in book form in a collection titled

The Harp and the Wind (Beirut: Dār al-Ṭalī'ah, 1961).

Jabra, Ibrahīm Jabra, *The Eighth Voyage* (Beirut: al-Maktabah al-Aṣriyyah, 1967).

al-Jayyūsī, Salma, "Commitment in the Last Quarter of the Century", *al-Ādāb*, 25 (December 1977), p. 142.

Johnson-Davies, Denys, trans., *Modern Arabic Short Stories* (1967; reprinted London: Heinemann, 1976).

Kafka, Franz, *The Penal Colony, Stories and Short Pieces,* trans. Willa and Edwin Muir (New York: Schocken Books, 196).

Khartāsh, Faysal "'Antarah Ibn Zabībah" *al-Tarīq* (September - October, 1995), pp. 77-80.

al-Khatīb, Hussām, *Comparative Literature*, Vol. II (Damascus: al-Insha' Press, 1982).

Levi-Strauss, Claude, *Tristes Tropiques*, trans. J. and D. Weightman (New York: Atheneum, 1974).

Maḥfūz, Najīb, *Layālī Alf Layla* (Cairo: Maktabat Miṣre, 1979), translated by Denys Johnson-Davies as *Arabian Nights and Days*: Cairo: American University of Cairo, 1994.

Manzalāwī, Maḥmūd, *Arabic Writing Today, The Short Story* (Cairo: American Research Centre in Egypt, 1968).

Mardrus, J. C., *The Book of the Thousand Nights and One Night*, Vol. II, trans. Powys Mathers (London: Bibliophile Books, 1964).

al-Marzūqī, "Night 1002" *Narratives* (July 1967), pp. 139-42.

al-Masnāwī, Mustafa, "'Abd Allah Samsa in Wāqwāq Island", in *Tāriq Who Has not Conquered Andalus* (1978; reprinted Beirut: al-Mu'assasah al-Arabiyyah Liddirāsāt wal-Nashre, 1979), pp. 64-72.

Muḥassib, Ḥasan, "Abu-Zayd Surrenders", *al-Majallah* (August 1966), pp. 84-8.

al-Najjār, Mohammad, *The Tales of Shuṭṭar* in *Arabic Heritage* (Kuwait: 'Ālam al-Ma'rifah, 1981).

al-Nassāj, Sayyid Ḥāmid, *The Development of the Short Story in Egypt* (Cairo: Dār al-Kitāb al-'Arabī, 1968).

Ostle, R. C. ed., *Studies in Modern Arabic Literature* (Tedding House: Warminster, 1975).

Qandīl, Mohammad al-Mansī, "Sindbad", *from* "Old Sorrows: Five Tales from *The Arabian Nights*", *al-Talī'ah* (September 1972), p. 178.

Rushdī, Rashād, *Fann al-Qiṣṣah al-Qaṣirah* (Beirut: Dār-al-'Awadah, 1959).

al-Sayyāb, Badre, *Poetry*, Vol. I. (Beirut, Dar - al 'Awdah: 1971), pp. 463- 73.

Shaheen, Mohammad, "The Blue Charm and the Return of Jubaynah: Translation and Commentary", *Journal of Arabic Literature*, 15 (1984), pp. 114-20.

al-Shaṭṭī, Sulayman, *I am Myself the Other* (Kuwait: Dār al-Nahj al-Jadīd, 1994), pp. 83-100.

Shuqair, Maḥmūd, "The Orphans' Cow", in *Bread for Others and Other Stories* (1961; reprinted Jerusalem Saladdin Publications, 1975), pp. 37-46.

Shaw, Valerie, *The Short Story: A Critical Introduction* (London: Longman, 1983).

Surūr, Najīb, 'Sindbad the Porter', *al-Ādāb* (August, 1955), pp. 25-6.

Tāmir, Zakariyyā, "Spring in the Ashes", in *Spring in the Ashes* (Damascus: Maktabat Annūri, 1973), pp. 75-85.

Williams, Raymond, *The Long Revolution* (London: Chatto & Windus, 1961).

The following journals devoted special issues to the short story:

al-Majallah (August 1966)

al-Hilāl, 77 (1969)

al-Ādāb (April 1973)

Fusūl, 2 (1982)

Index